REMEMBERING

THE

HOLOCAUST

REMEMBERING
THE
HOLOCAUST
A Debate

JEFFREY C. ALEXANDER

With Commentaries by
Martin Jay
Bernhard Giesen
Michael Rothberg
Robert Manne
Nathan Glazer
Elihu Katz and Ruth Katz

OXFORD
UNIVERSITY PRESS
2009

OXFORD
UNIVERSITY PRESS

Oxford University Press, Inc., publishes works that further
Oxford University's objective of excellence
in research, scholarship, and education.

Oxford   New York
Auckland   Cape Town   Dar es Salaam   Hong Kong   Karachi
Kuala Lumpur   Madrid   Melbourne   Mexico City   Nairobi
New Delhi   Shanghai   Taipei   Toronto

With offices in
Argentina   Austria   Brazil   Chile   Czech Republic   France   Greece
Guatemala   Hungary   Italy   Japan   Poland   Portugal   Singapore
South Korea   Switzerland   Thailand   Turkey   Ukraine   Vietnam

Copyright © 2009 by Oxford University Press, Inc.

Published by Oxford University Press, Inc.
198 Madison Avenue, New York, New York 10016

www.oup.com

Oxford is a registered trademark of Oxford University Press.

Library of Congress Cataloging-in-Publication Data
Alexander, Jeffrey C., 1947–
Remembering the holocaust : a debate / Jeffrey C. Alexander
with commentaries by Martin Jay ... [et al.].
p. cm.
Includes bibliographical references and index.
ISBN 978-0-19-532622-2
1. Holocaust, Jewish (1939–1945)—History.
2. Holocaust, Jewish (1939–1945), in literature.
3. Holocaust, Jewish (1939–1945), in art.
4. Holocaust (Jewish theology).   I. Jay, Martin, 1944–
II. Title.
D804.3.A427 2009
940.53'18—dc22   2008042630

2 4 6 8 9 7 5 3 1

Printed in the United States of America
on acid-free paper

To all our children

Acknowledgments

Earlier versions of jeffrey c. alexander, "on the social construction of Moral Universals," were published in *The European Journal of Social Theory* 5 (1) 2002: 5–86; Alexander, *The Meanings of Social Life* (Oxford, 2003, pp. 27–84); Alexander et al., *Cultural Trauma and Collective Identity* (University of California Press, 2004, pp. 196–263); and, in redacted form, in R. Friedland and J. Mohr, eds., *Matters of Culture: Cultural Sociology in Practice* (Cambridge University Press, 2004, pp. 196–224).

The authors would like to express their appreciation to James Cook, our editor from Oxford University Press, for his direction in organizing this volume.

FOREWORD

ONE HEARS OVER AND AGAIN THAT WE ARE IN A POST-THEORY PHASE. Yet Jeffrey Alexander's already classic essay on the construction of moral universals, and the responses that accompany it like a planetary constellation, show how energetic that period was and still is. This is especially true for a cultural sociology that refuses to let the specter of relativism frighten it away from demonstrating the rich and complex way meanings are made, coded, changed, and consumed.

It would be melodramatic to talk of the "Death of Meaning" after full awareness of the nature and extent of the Holocaust had sunk in. The "postmodern" is sometimes seen in that light. But what is mainly apparent is a cultural analysis that is neither foundationalist nor nihilistic. It counters depersonalizing forces in modern society that contribute to what Zygmunt Bauman has called the "production of moral indifference"—hence the emphasis on meaning, in particular moral meaning, as it challenges us constantly. Meaning should not be left to the semioticians any more than to the politicians. Besieged by large historical events apparently beyond our control, as well as media chatter and 24/7 reporting, we get little respite from having to think about either national or international and humanitarian crises.

More than sixty years after the Holocaust discussions about it do not take place over an ideological corpse. We continue to be confronted by attempted genocides. Globalization has struck here, too. While ideologies are more suspect than ever (I will come back to this point), Alexander's type of sociology explores, as literary study does, how meaningfulness is constructed, but it includes as its object the changeable significance of macro-cultural events. Meanings drawn from the Holocaust have changed over time; narrative frameworks, culture-specific encodings, and other collective perspectives that surround a core phenomenon are discernible in the events being studied, becoming a part, as it were, of their temporal texture.

Alexander lays out persuasively what had been only partly recognized. Over time the Holocaust moves from being considered a horrific and criminal by-product of a savage war to being seen as a core event in itself: a "trauma-drama" and an "engorged" symbol of ultimate evil. Continuing to have an impact on the public memory in the West and Middle East, the catastrophe has not faded and is affecting even the consciousness of faraway countries. Yet as a murderous trauma-drama it blocks the ameliorative vision of a March of Time that culminates in a global civil society. Alexander sets out to retrieve something of what is often called the Enlightenment Project, an "ascending" or "progressive" historical narrative.

His well-armored argument remains in the realm of collective representations, their dissemination and influence. It makes the moral and political responses to the Holocaust intelligible in those terms and does not deal (except in perceptive pages of his postscript on Israel, the final chapter in this volume) with a profoundly disturbing element. I am alluding to a common post-Holocaust perplexity, a sense that a key humanistic dictum, "Nothing human is alien to me," was suddenly falsified. Once again, this time even more radically, we do not understand the behavior of our own species. A clear sign of this is *evil* being used to describe the perpetrators and *trauma* the effect of that evil on its innumerable victims.

What we do know clearly is that genocides are incited by a demagogic leader who lends credence to a scapegoating myth and enforces that "narrative." Yet because genocide is a massive, collective action, backed by mobs as well as supported by the complicity of many organizers, including the "writing-desk" murderer (or the radio whip, as in Rwanda), it reveals a darkness in human nature more generally. Once we realize that the Holocaust was coded as a good, sponsored by the leadership of a nation and often enthusiastically accepted by a large number of citizens, the impenetrability of evil confronts us in its starkest form.

Indeed, a symptom of post-Holocaust trauma is that normative assumptions about the human species are questioned more than ever. Can human nature still be trusted? The breach of civilized values was too great—and in a nation that had produced so many significant philosophers, scientists, scholars, and artists. The intellectual shock—a secondary trauma, as it were—is not only that it happened but also that it happened with only scattered pockets of resistance and even a degree of cooperation among the cultured classes.

That the Shoah has become widely recognized as *the* image of evil is, paradoxically, the one good coming from that evil. Thus Alexander rescues a universal-in-the-making from our shaken trust in any grand thesis about humanity's steady moral and political progress. Even this positive development, however, can be challenged. For several of the formal commentators in this volume, the universalism thesis comes up against national and geopolitical limits. A case is made—confronted by Alexander in his response to the commentators—that by the 1990s an "Americanization" of the Holocaust as well as its "Europeanization" had sanctified moral reactions to the event without an adequate self-critical reflection about the West's imperialistic and colonial policies. Thus the acknowledgment by these nations of a moral universal, necessary to prevent Holocausts, seems somewhat rhetorical. In Israel, moreover, with its right to exist being challenged, and the memory of the genocide still fresh in the collective memory, the political lessons from the Holocaust play a daily and much more complex role. Alexander therefore deepens and recasts the challenge to his universalization thesis as a question: "How can the movement from a [politically and morally] progressive to a tragic [nonprogressive] trauma narration create moral particularism alongside universalism?"

He is careful, that is, not to present his theory as the reworking of a triumphalist narrative. His findings retain a more-than-Hegelian respect for the local situation—for lasting memory scars in the individual culture or nation, whether the original wounding was all too real or a cultivated and partly imaginary grievance. The word *create*, moreover, in Alexander's reformulation of the issue maintains an emphasis on human agency within "social construction." In brief, moral particularism, too, like the moral universal, has to be recognized, articulated, achieved. Nation, state, tribe, and religious identity remain the carriers of that particularism.

There is a further, complicating issue. How far can we go in claiming that a new collective representation is in the process of becoming a moral universal? Is that universality, at least partly, a technological illusion, a media effect? (The meaning of advanced technology's impact, Alexander says elsewhere, is one of the portentous questions of our time.) A moral universal must surely be more than a collective representation. Even if it is a social construct expressing an ideal, what secular authority can assure its universal scope and moral efficacy?[1]

After the Holocaust, because of our darkened species-image, there is a decisive alteration in the way we may have to think of ourselves. Alexander, despite noting the contrast between the "tragic trauma" narration and a "progressive" one, shies away from seeing them as irreconcilable. His call for "a moral particularism alongside universalism," poignant as it is, is nevertheless an impasse evaded.

Am I simply less optimistic than Alexander? Or is his thesis a reinforcement of the international community's (initially indecisive) confrontation of genocidal events in the decade before 2001, when the essay was composed? The future, if not darker, has certainly become more opaque. The moral universal being constructed must embrace the reality that many groups, living in the aftermath of an attempted genocide, or fearing the repetition of a reversal of values that coded genocide as good, even as salvational, no longer trust the idea of a stable, basically uniform human character or the possibility of policing that instability.

We have also finally become aware that something is indeed wrong with most "grand narratives" or upward generalizations. Too much death and suffering accompany these comprehensive and often grandiose ideologies. No wonder that within the Holocaust trauma-drama there lodges a radical—and completely rational—suspicion concerning the demagogic abuse of collective superstitions often accompanying such schemes. There is, in particular, a bitter memory of the pernicious power of stereotypes.

J.-F. Lyotard thought modern political religions had permanently disqualified the *grand récit*. The pseudo-facts feeding fascist ideology were swept into the orbit of an unchecked megalomaniac and quasi-messianic distortion that incited hatred and legitimized murderousness on such a scale that regression and delusion pale as descriptive words. It seems incredible that the plan to exterminate all Jews and subjugate the Slavs and other ethnic groups designated as inferior was justified in the mind of the perpetrators by the narrative inflation of a cliché: *that it was necessary to do so for the defense of*

---

1. The year 2008 marked the sixtieth anniversary of the U.N.'s Genocide Convention. While the very finding of a name for the crime and establishing a legal mechanism for its recognition and prevention are a real advance, there has also been, it is well known, a reluctance to give that incriminating label to a specific perpetration precisely because that act would entail very serious obligations on the part of the international community.

culture. Propagandists elaborated a mythical Aryan culture and claimed it had to be saved from racial pollution.

Encouraged by Alexander's chapter in part I and this volume as a whole, I conclude with a hopeful reflection. Is it possible that a contemporary universal narrative might emerge—one that is not fatefully "grand"? The struggle, at least, for such an outcome could motivate works of imagination and intellect and inspire them to discern, like Alexander's version of cultural sociology, a movement toward moral universals.

It would be an additional "good from evil" if the Holocaust trauma-drama, or what the Cambridge anthropologists called a "dromenon" (a scene of mysterious wounding, killing, and the like), were to become a shared nucleus of art, like the House of Atreus theme central to the Oresteia tragedies that have come down to us. The difference in content is obvious. But it only intensifies the question of what role art plays in healing the wounds inflicted by internecine conflict, war, and genocide. Cultural trauma, in any case, has moved onto the agenda of sociology. Alexander notes in his response to the commentators: "We have become less optimistic about the creation of a global civil society, more sensitive to the continuing festering of local wounds. It is a time to explore a relationship between cultural trauma and collective identity."

The wound is in danger of becoming the identity. A damaging rather than a moral particularism then inflames the collective memory and is politically exploited. This is where ritual and symbolic inventions become relevant. They can be perverted, as in Nazi Germany, where *Kultur* is "purified" and national power is endowed with a monumental aesthetic aura. But the arts can also lead to an ideal catharsis of grief, melancholy, resentment, and even the passion for revenge.

There is a forgetfulness akin to repression, but there is also artistic sublimation. Art's refracted or slant modes of representation, competitive with religious remembrance, make the memory of suffering, and even of guilt, more tolerable. Greek tragedy achieved such a transmutation. Can a trauma, however, so close to our time as the Holocaust, so close that it still seems like a recent wound, attain a similar universality and rival the affective and reflective impact of those ancient works?

Since the search is on for moral universals, and the above example touches mainly on artistic universals (that a relation between the two exists is made abundantly clear by Alexander's own use of categories from rhetorical and poetic theory), we would have to review more resources than those of "high art." A new narrative genre, independent of art criteria, has recently sprung up: that of Holocaust testimonies. The testimony as a "little narrative" (Lyotard's *petit récit*) provides encouragement for bringing to notice and wide dissemination the personal story of victims of organized, state-sanctioned violence. Nor should we forget to look again at what is already popular and influential, embedded in the life of so many: the primal Christian scenario (its revolutionary mixture of humble and grand) and the Hebrew Bible's basic narrative, although the latter does not possess quite so central a "dromenon."

Let me suggest, then, in support of Alexander's attempts to preserve and define more cogently the "progressive narrative," that the Hebrew Bible is in good part an epic dealing with the birth pangs of nation building. A reading of that fact cannot be avoided—or remain free of controversy—in the context of a seemingly endless Middle Eastern conflict. Yet viewed as a story with significance for all nationalisms, the Bible's blend of sacred and secular history portrays the shaping of tribes into a unified people by means of covenanted moral universals. So that, even if the political birth I refer to is endangered by Philistine and Amalekite, as well as lapses on the part of the emerging nation itself, the hope is planted that a humane rather than destructive nationalism will prevail.

—*Geoffrey Hartman*

CONTENTS

PART III   RESPONSE TO COMMENTATORS

Contributors

Jeffrey C. Alexander is the Lillian Chavenson Saden Professor of Sociology and a Director of the Center for Cultural Sociology at Yale University.

Bernhard Giesen is Professor of Sociology at the University of Konstanz, Germany, and his recent books include *Intellectuals and the Nation: Collective Identity in a German Axial Age* (1998) and *Triumph and Trauma* (2004).

Nathan Glazer is Professor Emeritus of Sociology and Education at Harvard University. He was an editor of *The Public Interest*.

Martin Jay is the Sidney Hellman Ehrman Professor of History at the University of California, Berkeley.

Elihu Katz is Trustee Professor at the Annenberg School for Communication, University of Pennsylvania, Emeritus Professor of Sociology and Communication at the Hebrew University of Jerusalem and Scientific Director of The Guttman Institute of Applied Social Research.

Ruth Katz is the Emanuel Alexander Professor Emerita of Musicology at the Hebrew University, Jerusalem.

Robert Manne is Professor of Politics at La Trobe University, Melbourne, Australia.

Michael Rothberg is Associate Professor of English and Director of The Unit for Criticism and Interpretive Theory at the University of Illinois at Urbana-Champaign. His most recent book is *Multidirectional Memory: Remembering the Holocaust in the Age of Decolonization* (2009).

PART I

REMEMBERING THE HOLOCAUST

THE SOCIAL CONSTRUCTION
OF MORAL UNIVERSALS

Jeffrey C. Alexander

HOW DID A SPECIFIC AND SITUATED HISTORICAL EVENT, AN EVENT marked by ethnic and racial hatred, violence, and war, become transformed into a generalized symbol of human suffering and moral evil, a universalized symbol whose very existence has created historically unprecedented opportunities for ethnic, racial, and religious justice, for mutual recognition, and for global conflicts becoming regulated in a more civil way?[1] This cultural transformation has been achieved because the originating historical event, traumatic in the extreme for a delimited particular group, has come over the last fifty years to be redefined as a traumatic event for all of humankind.[2] Now free-floating rather than situated—universal rather than particular—this traumatic event vividly "lives" in the memories of contemporaries whose parents and grandparents never felt themselves even remotely related to it.

In what follows, I explore the social creation of a cultural fact and the effects of this cultural fact on social and moral life.

In the beginning, in April 1945, the Holocaust was not the "Holocaust." In the torrent of newspaper, radio, and magazine stories reporting the discovery by American infantrymen of the Nazi concentration camps, the empirical remains of what had transpired were typified as "atrocities." Their obvious awfulness, and indeed their strangeness, placed them for contemporary observers at the borderline of the category of behavior known as "man's inhumanity to man." Nonetheless, qua atrocity, the discoveries were placed side by side—metonymically and semantically—with a whole series of other brutalities that were considered to be the natural results of the ill wind of this second, very unnatural, and most inhuman world war.

The first American reports on "atrocities" during that Second World War had not, in fact, even referred to actions by German Nazis, let alone to their Jewish victims, but to the Japanese army's brutal treatment of American and other allied prisoners of war after the loss of Corregidor in 1943. On January 27, 1944, the United States released sworn statements by military officers who had escaped the so-called Bataan Death March. In the words of contemporary journals and magazines, these officers had related "atrocity stories" revealing "the inhuman treatment and murder of American and Filipino soldiers who were taken prisoner when Bataan and Corregidor fell." In response to these accounts, the U.S. State Department had lodged protests to the Japanese government about its failure to live up to the provisions of the Geneva Prisoners of War Convention (*Current History*, March 1944: 249). Atrocities, in other words, were a signifier specifically connected to war. They referred to war-generated events that transgressed the rules circumscribing how national killing could normally be carried out.[3] Responding to the same incident, *Newsweek*, in a section entitled "The Enemy" and under the headline "Nation Replies in Grim Fury to Jap Brutality to Prisoners," reported that "with the first impact of the news, people had shuddered at the story of savage *atrocity* upon Allied prisoners of war by the Japanese" (February 7, 1944: 19, italics added).[4]

It is hardly surprising, then, that it was this nationally specific and particular war-related term that was employed to represent the grisly Jewish mass murders discovered by American GIs when they liberated the Nazi camps.[5] Through April 1945, as one camp after another was discovered, this collective representation was applied time after time.[6] When, toward the end of that month, a well-known Protestant minister explored the moral implications of the discoveries, he declared that, no matter how horrifying and repulsive, "it is important that the full truth be made known so that a clear indication may be had of the nature of the enemy we have been dealing with, as well of as a realization *of the sheer brutalities that have become the accompaniment of war.*" The *New York Times* reported this sermon under the headline "Bonnell Denounces German Atrocities" (April 23, 1945: 23, italics added). When alarmed American Congressmen visited Buchenwald, the *Times* headlined that they had witnessed firsthand the "*War Camp Horror*" (April 26, 1945: 12, italics added). When a few days later the U.S. army released a report on the extent of the killings in Buchenwald, the *Times* headlined it an "Atrocity Report" (April 29, 1945: 20). A few days after that, under the headline "Enemy Atrocities in France Bared," the *Times* wrote that a just-released report had shown that "in

France, German brutality was not limited to the French underground or even to the thousands of hostages whom the Germans killed for disorders they had nothing to do with, but was practiced almost systematically against entirely innocent French people" (May 4, 1945: 6).

The Nazis' anti-Jewish mass murders had once been only putative atrocities. From the late thirties on, reports about them had been greeted with widespread public doubt about their authenticity. Analogous to the allegations about German atrocities during World War I that later had been thoroughly discredited, they were dismissed as a kind of Jewish moral panic. Only three months before the GIs' "discovery" of the camps, in introducing a firsthand report on Nazi mass murder from a Soviet-liberated camp in Poland, *Collier's* magazine acknowledged: "A lot of Americans simply do not believe the stories of Nazi mass executions of Jews and anti-Nazi Gentiles in eastern Europe by means of gas chambers, freight cars partly loaded with lime and other horrifying devices. These stories are so foreign to most Americans' experience of life in this country that they seem incredible. Then, too, some of the atrocity stories of World War I were later proved false" (January 6, 1945: 62).[7] From April 3, 1945, however, the date when the GIs first liberated the concentration camps, all such earlier reports were retrospectively accepted as facts, as the realistic signifiers of Peirce rather than the "arbitrary" symbols of Saussure. That systematic efforts at Jewish mass murder had occurred, and that the numerous victims and the few survivors had been severely traumatized, the American and worldwide audience now had little doubt.[8] Their particular and unique fate, however, even while it was widely recognized as representing the grossest of injustices, did not itself become a traumatic experience for the audience to which the mass media's collective representations were transmitted—that is, for those looking on, either from near or from far. Why this was not so defines my initial explanatory effort here.

For an audience to be traumatized by an experience that they themselves do not directly share, symbolic extension and psychological identification are required. This did not occur. For the American infantrymen who first made contact, for the general officers who supervised the rehabilitation, for the reporters who broadcast the descriptions, for the commissions of Congressmen and influentials who quickly traveled to Germany to conduct on-site investigations, the starving, depleted, often weird-looking and sometimes weird-acting Jewish camp survivors seemed like a foreign race. They could just as well have been from Mars, or from hell. The identities and characters of these Jewish survivors rarely were personalized through interviews or individualized through biographical sketches; rather, they were presented as a mass, and often as a mess, a petrified, degrading, and smelly one, not only by newspaper reporters but also by some of the most powerful general officers in the Allied High Command. This depersonalization made it more difficult for the survivors' trauma to generate compelling identification.

Possibilities for universalizing the trauma were blocked not only by the depersonalization of its victims but also by their historical and sociological specification. As I have indicated, the mass murders semantically were immediately linked to other "horrors" in the bloody history of the century's second great war and to the historically specific national and ethnic conflicts that underlay it. Above all, it was never forgotten that these victims were Jews. In retrospect, it is bitterly ironic, but it is also sociologically understandable, that the American audience's sympathy and feelings of identity flowed much more easily to the non-Jewish survivors, whether German or Polish, who had been kept in better conditions and looked more normal, more composed, more human. Jewish survivors were kept for weeks and sometimes even for months in the worst areas and under the worst conditions of what had become, temporarily, displaced persons camps. American and British administrators felt impatient with many Jewish survivors, even personal repugnance for them, sometimes resorting to threats and even to punishing them.[9] The depth of this initial failure of identification can be seen in the fact that when American citizens and their leaders expressed opinions and made decisions about national quotas for emergency postwar immigration, displaced German citizens ranked first, Jewish survivors last.

How could this have happened? Was it not obvious to any human observer that this mass murder was fundamentally different from the other traumatic and bloody events in a modern history already dripping in blood, that it represented not simply evil but "radical evil," in Kant's remarkable phrase (Kant, 1960),[10] that it was unique? To understand why none of this was obvious, to understand how and why each of these initial understandings and behaviors was radically changed, and how this transformation had vast repercussions for establishing not only new moral standards for social and political behavior but unprecedented, if still embryonic, regulatory controls, it is important to see the inadequacy of commonsense understandings of traumatic events.

There are two kinds of common-sense thinking about trauma, forms of thinking that comprise what I call "lay trauma theory."[11] These commonsensical forms of reasoning have deeply informed thinking about the effects of the Holocaust. They are expressed in the following strikingly different conceptualizations of what happened after the revelations of the mass killings of Jews.

- *The Enlightenment version.* The "horror" of onlookers provoked the postwar end of anti-Semitism in the United States. The commonsense assumption here is that because people have a fundamentally "moral" nature—as a result of their rootedness in Enlightenment and religious traditions—they will perceive atrocities for what they are and react to them by attacking the belief systems that provided legitimation.
- *The psychoanalytic version.* When faced with the horror, Jews and non-Jews alike reacted not with criticism and decisive action but with silence and bewilderment. Only after two or even three decades of repression and denial were people finally able to begin talking about what happened and to take actions in response to this knowledge.

Enlightenment and psychoanalytic forms of lay trauma thinking have permeated academic efforts at understanding what happened after the death-camp revelations. One or the other version has informed not only every major discussion of the Holocaust but also virtually every contemporary effort to investigate trauma more generally, efforts that are, in fact, largely inspired by Holocaust debates.[12]

What is wrong with this lay trauma theory is that it is "naturalistic," either in the naïvely moral or the less naïvely psychological sense. Lay trauma theory fails to see that there is an interpretive grid through which all "facts" about trauma are mediated, emotionally, cognitively, and morally. This grid has a supraindividual, cultural status; it is symbolically structured and sociologically determined. No trauma interprets itself: Before trauma can be experienced at the collective (not individual) level, there are essential questions that must be answered, and answers to these questions change over time.

The Cultural Construction of Trauma

Coding, Weighting, Narrating

Elie Wiesel, in a moving and influential statement in the late 1970s, asserted that the Holocaust represents an "ontological evil." From a sociological perspective, however, evil is epistemological, not ontological. For a traumatic event to have the status of evil is a matter of its *becoming* evil. It is a matter of how the trauma is known, how it is coded.[13] "At first glance it may appear a paradox," Diner has noted—and certainly it does—but, considered only in and of itself, "Auschwitz *has* no appropriate narrative, only a set of statistics" (Diner, 2000: 178). Becoming evil is a matter, first and foremost, of representation. Depending on the nature of representation, a traumatic event may be regarded as ontologically evil, or its badness, its "evilness," may be conceived as contingent and relative, as something that can be ameliorated and overcome. This distinction is theoretical, but it is also practical. In fact, decisions about the ontological versus contingent status of the Holocaust were of overriding importance in its changing representation.

If we can deconstruct this ontological assertion even further, I would like to suggest that the very existence of the category "evil" must be seen not as something that naturally exists but as an arbitrary construction, the product of cultural and sociological work. This contrived binary, which simplifies empirical complexity to two antagonistic forms and reduces every shade of gray between, has been an essential feature of all human societies but especially important in those Eisenstadt (1982) has called the Axial Age civilizations. This rigid opposition between the sacred and profane, which in Western philosophy has typically been constructed as a conflict between normativity and instrumentality, not only defines what people care about but also establishes vital safeguards around the shared normative "good." At the same time it places powerful, often aggressive barriers against anything that is construed as threatening the good, forces defined not merely as things to be avoided but as sources of horror and pollution that must be contained at all costs.

The Material "Base": Controlling the Means of Symbolic Production

Yet if this grid is a kind of functional necessity, how it is applied very much depends on who is telling the story, and how. This is first of all a matter of cultural power in the most mundane, materialist sense: Who controls the means of symbolic production?[14] It was certainly not incidental to the public understanding of the Nazis' policies of mass murder, for example, that for an extended period of time it was the Nazis themselves who were in control of the physical and cultural terrain of their enactment. This fact of brute power made it much more difficult to frame the mass killings in a distinctive way.

Nor is it incidental that, once the extermination of the Jews was physically interrupted by Allied armies in 1945, it was America's "imperial republic"—the perspective of the triumphant, forward-looking, militantly and militarily democratic New World warrior—that directed the organizational and cultural responses to the mass murders and their survivors. The contingency of this knowledge is so powerful that it might well be said that, if the Allies had not won the war, the "Holocaust" would never have been discovered.[15] Moreover, if it had been the Soviets and not the Allies who "liberated" most of the camps, and not just those in the Eastern sector, what was discovered in those camps might never have been portrayed in a remotely similar way.[16] It was, in other words, precisely and only because the means of symbolic production were not controlled by a victorious postwar Nazi regime, or even by a triumphant communist one, that the mass killings could be called the Holocaust and coded as evil.

Creating the Culture Structure

Still, even when the means of symbolic production came to be controlled by "our side," even when the association between evil and what would become known as the Holocaust trauma was assured, this was only the beginning, not the end. After a phenomenon is coded as evil, the question that immediately follows is: How evil is it? In theorizing evil, this refers to the problem not of coding but of weighting. For there are degrees of evil, and these degrees have great implications in terms of responsibility, punishment, remedial action, and future behavior. Normal evil and radical evil cannot be the same.

Finally, alongside these problems of coding and weighting, the meaning of a trauma cannot be defined unless we determine exactly what the "it" is. This is a question of narrative: What were the evil and traumatizing actions in question? Who was responsible? Who were the victims? What were the immediate and long-term results of the traumatizing actions? What can be done by way of remediation or prevention?

What these theoretical considerations suggest is that even after the physical force of the Allied triumph and the physical discovery of the Nazi concentration camps, the nature of what was seen and discovered had to be coded, weighted, and narrated. This complex cultural construction, moreover, had to be achieved immediately. History does not wait; it demands that representations be made, and they will be. Whether or not some newly reported event is startling, strange, terrible, or inexpressibly weird, it must be "typified," in the sense of Husserl and Schutz—that is, it must be explained as a typical and even anticipated example of some thing or category that was known about before.[17] Even the vastly unfamiliar must somehow be made familiar. To the cultural process of coding, weighting, and narrating, in other words, what comes before is all-important. Historical background is critical, both for the first "view" of the traumatic event and, as "history" changes, for later views as well. Once again, these shifting cultural constructions are fatefully affected by the power and identity of the agents in charge, by the competition for symbolic control, and by the structures of power and distribution of resources that condition it.

Background Constructions

Nazism as the Representation of Absolute Evil

What was the historical structure of "good and evil" within which, on April 3, 1945, the "news" of the Nazi concentration camps was first confirmed to the American audience? To answer this question, it is first necessary to describe what came before. In what follows I will venture some observations, which can hardly be considered definitive, about how social evil was coded, weighted, and narrated during the interwar period in Europe and the United States.

In the deeply disturbing wake of World War I, there was a pervasive sense of disillusionment and cynicism among mass and elite members of the Western "audience," a distancing from protagonists and antagonists that, as Paul Fussell has shown, made irony the master trope of that first postwar era.[18] This trope transformed "demonology"—the very act of coding and weighting evil—into what many intellectuals and lay persons alike considered to be an act of bad faith. Once the coding and weighting of evil were delegitimated, however, good and evil became less distinct from one another and relativism became the dominant motif of the time. In such conditions, coherent narration of contemporary events becomes difficult if not impossible. Thus it was that, not only for many intellectuals and artists of this period but for many ordinary people as well, the startling upheavals of these interwar years could not easily be sorted out in a conclusive and satisfying way.

It was in the context of this breakdown of representation that racism and revolution, whether fascist or communist, emerged as compelling frames, not only in Europe but also in the United States. Against a revolutionary narrative of dogmatic and authoritarian modernism on the Left, there arose the narrative of reactionary modernism, equally revolutionary but fervently opposed to rationality and cosmopolitanism.[19] In this context, many democrats in Western Europe and the United States withdrew from the field of representation itself, becoming confused and equivocating advocates of disarmament, nonviolence, and peace "at any price." This formed the cultural frame for isolationist political policy in both Britain and the United States.

Eventually the aggressive military ambition of Nazism made such equivocation impossible to sustain. While racialism, relativism, and narrative confusion continued in the United States and Britain until the very beginning of World War II, and even continued well into it, these constructions were countered by increasingly forceful and confident representations of good and evil that coded liberal democracy and universalism as unalloyed goods and Nazism, racism, and prejudice as deeply corrosive representations of the polluting and profane.

From the late 1930s on, there emerged a strong, and eventually dominant, antifascist narrative in Western societies. Nazism was coded, weighted, and narrated in apocalyptic, Old Testament terms as "the dominant evil of our time." Because this radical evil aligned itself with violence and massive death, it not merely justified but also compelled the risking of life in opposing it, a compulsion that motivated and justified massive human sacrifice in what came later to be known as the last "good war."[20] That Nazism was an absolute, unmitigated evil, a radical evil that threatened the very future of human civilization, formed the presupposition of America's four-year prosecution of the world war.[21]

The representation of Nazism as an absolute evil emphasized not only its association with sustained coercion and violence but also, and perhaps even especially, the way Nazism linked violence with ethnic, racial, and religious hatred. In this way, the most conspicuous example of the practice of Nazi evil—its policy of systematic discrimination, coercion, and, eventually, mass violence against the Jews—was initially interpreted as "simply" another horrifying example of the subhumanism of Nazi action.

Interpreting Kristallnacht: Nazi Evil as Anti-Semitism

The American public's reaction to *Kristallnacht* demonstrates how important the Nazis' anti-Jewish activities were in crystallizing the polluted status of Nazism in American eyes. It also provides a prototypical example of how such representations of the evils of anti-Semitism were folded into the broader and more encompassing symbolism of Nazism. *Kristallnacht* refers, of course, to the rhetorically virulent and physically violent expansion of the Nazi repression of Jews that unfolded throughout German towns and cities on November 9 and 10, 1938. These activities were widely recorded. "The morning editions of most American newspapers reported the *Kristallnacht* in banner headlines," according to one historian of that fateful event, "and the broadcasts of H. V. Kaltenborn and Raymond Gram Swing kept the radio public informed of Germany's latest adventure" (Diamond, 1969: 198). Exactly why these events assumed such critical importance in the American public's continuing effort to understand "what Hitlerism stood for" (201) goes beyond the simple fact that violent and repressive activities were, perhaps for the first time, openly, even brazenly, displayed in direct view of the world public sphere. Equally important was the altered cultural framework within which these activities were observed. For *Kristallnacht* occurred just six weeks after the now infamous Munich agreements, acts of appeasing Hitler's expansion that were understood, not only by isolationists but also by many opponents of Nazism, indeed by the vast majority of the American people, as possibly reasonable accessions to a possibly reasonable man (197). In other words, *Kristallnacht* initiated a process of understanding fueled by symbolic contrast, not simply observation.

What was interpretively constructed was the cultural difference between Germany's previously apparent cooperativeness and reasonableness— representations of the good in the discourse of American civil society—and its subsequent demonstration of violence and irrationality, which were taken to be representations of anticivil evil. Central to the ability to draw this contrast was the ethnic and religious hatred Germans demonstrated in their violence against Jews. If one examines the American public's reactions, it clearly is this anti-Jewish violence that is taken to represent the evil of Nazism. It was with reference to this violence that the news stories of the *New York Times* employed the rhetoric of pollution to further code and weight Nazi evil: "No foreign propagandist bent upon blackening the name of Germany before the world could outdo the tale of beating, of blackguardly assaults upon defenseless and innocent people, which degraded that country yesterday" (quoted in Diamond, 1969: 198). The *Times's* controversial columnist Anne O'Hare McCormick wrote that "the suffering [the Germans] inflict on others, now that they are on top, passes all understanding and mocks all sympathy," and she went on to label *Kristallnacht* "the darkest day Germany experienced in the whole post-war period" (quoted in Diamond, 1969: 199). The *Washington Post* identified the Nazi activities as "one of the worst setbacks for mankind since the Massacre of St. Bartholomew" (quoted in Diamond, 1969: 198–99).

This broadening identification of Nazism with evil, simultaneously triggered and reinforced by the anti-Jewish violence of *Kristallnacht*, stimulated influential political figures to make more definitive judgments about the antipathy between American democracy and German Nazism than they had up until that point. Speaking on NBC radio, Al Smith, the former New York governor and democratic presidential candidate, observed that the events confirmed that the German people were "incapable of living under a democratic government" (quoted in Diamond, 1969: 200). Following Smith on the same program, Thomas E. Dewey, soon to be New York governor and a future presidential candidate, expressed the opinion that "the civilized world stands revolted by the bloody pogrom against a defenseless people...by a nation run by madmen" (quoted in Diamond, 1969: 201). Having initially underplayed America's official reaction to the events, four days later President Franklin Roosevelt took advantage of the public outrage by emphasizing the purity of the American nation and its distance from this emerging representation of violence and ethnic hatred: "The news of the past few days from Germany deeply shocked public opinion in the United States....I myself could scarcely believe that such things could occur in a twentieth century civilization" (quoted in Diamond, 1969: 205).

Judging from these reactions to the Nazi violence of *Kristallnacht,* it seems only logical that, as one historian has put it, "most American newspapers or journals" could "no longer...view Hitler as a pliable and reasonable man, but as an aggressive and contemptible dictator [who] would have to be restrained" (Diamond, 1969: 207). What is equally striking, however, is that in almost none of the American public's statements of horror is there explicit reference to the identity of the victims of *Kristallnacht* as Jews. Instead they are referred to as a "defenseless and innocent people," as "others," and as a "defenseless people" (quoted in Diamond, 1969: 198, 199, 201). In fact, in the public statement just quoted, President Roosevelt goes well out of his way to separate his moral outrage from any link to a specific concern for the fate of the Jews. "Such news from *any part* of the world," the President insists, "would inevitably produce similar profound reaction among Americans in *any part* of the nation" (quoted in Diamond, 1969: 205, italics added).

In other words, despite the centrality of the Nazis' anti-Jewish violence to the emerging American symbolization of Nazism as evil, there existed—at that point in historical and cultural time—a reluctance for non-Jewish Americans to identify with Jewish people as such. Jews were highlighted as vital representations of the evils of Nazism: their fate would be understood only in relation to the German horror that threatened democratic civilization in America and Europe. This failure of identification would be reflected seven years later in the distantiation of the American soldiers and domestic audience from the traumatized Jewish camp survivors and their even less fortunate Jewish compatriots whom the Nazis had killed.

Anti–Anti-Semitism: Fighting Nazi Evil by Fighting for the Jews

It was also during the 1930s, in the context of the Nazi persecution of German Jews, that a historically unprecedented attack on anti-Semitism emerged in the United States. It was not that Christians suddenly felt genuine affection for, or identification with, those whom they had vilified for countless centuries as the killers of Christ.[22] It was that the logic of symbolic association had dramatically and fatefully changed. Nazism was increasingly viewed as the vile enemy of universalism, and the most hated enemies of Nazism were the Jews. The laws of symbolic antinomy and association thus were applied. If Nazism singled out the Jews, then the Jews must be singled out by democrats and anti-Nazis. Anti-Semitism, tolerated and condoned for centuries in every Western nation, and for the preceding fifty years embraced fervently by proponents of American "nativism," suddenly became distinctly unpopular in progressive circles throughout the United States (Gleason, 1981; Higham, 1984).[23]

What I will call "anti–anti-Semitism"[24] became particularly intense after the United States declared war on Nazi Germany. The nature of this concern is framed in a particularly clear manner by one leading historian of American Jewry: "The war saw the merging of Jewish and American fates. Nazi Germany was the greatest enemy of both Jewry and the United States" (Shapiro, 1992: 16). For the first time, overtly positive representations of Jewish people proliferated in popular and high culture alike. It was during this period that the phrase "Judeo-Christian tradition" was born. It appeared as Americans tried to fend off the Nazi enemy that threatened to destroy the sacred foundations of Western democratic life (Silk, 1984).

Mass Murder under the Progressive Narrative

Nazism marked a traumatic epoch in modern history. Yet, while coded as evil and weighted in the most fundamental, *weltgeschichte* (world-historical) terms, it was narrated inside a framework that offered the promise of salvation and triggered actions that generated confidence and hope.[25] What I will call the "progressive narrative" proclaimed that the trauma created by social evil would be overcome, that Nazism would be defeated and eliminated from the world, that it would eventually be relegated to a traumatic past whose darkness would be obliterated by a new and powerful social light. The progressivity of this narrative depended on keeping Nazism situated and historical, which prevented this representation of absolute evil from being universalized and its cultural power from being equated, in any way, shape, or form, with the power possessed by the good. In narrative terms, this asymmetry, this insistence on Nazism's anomalous historical status, assured its ultimate defeat. In popular consciousness and in dramas created by cultural specialists, the origins of Nazism were linked to specific events in the interwar period and to particular organizations and actors within it, to a political party, to a crazy and inhuman leader, to an anomalous nation that had demonstrated militaristic and violent tendencies over the previous one hundred years.

Yes, Nazism had initiated a trauma in modern history, but it was a liminal trauma presenting "time out of time," in Victor Turner's sense.[26] The trauma was dark and threatening, but it was, at the same time, anomalous and, in principle at least, temporary. As such, the trauma could and would be removed via a just war and a wise and forgiving peace.[27] The vast human sacrifices demanded by the winds of war were measured and judged in terms of this progressive narrative and the salvation it promised. The blood spilled in the war sanctified the future peace and obliterated the past. The sacrifice of millions could be redeemed and the social salvation of their sacred souls achieved, not by dwelling in a lachrymose manner on their deaths but by eliminating Nazism, the force that had caused their deaths, and by planning the future that would establish a world in which there could never be Nazism again.

Framing Revelations about the Jewish Mass Murder

While initially received with surprise, and always conceived with loathing, the gradual and halting but eventually definitive revelations of Nazi plans for displacing, and quite possibly murdering, the entirety of European Jewry actually confirmed the categorizing of evil already in place: the coding, weighting, and narrating of Nazism as an inhuman, absolutely evil force. What had been experienced as an extraordinary trauma by the Jewish victims was experienced by the audience of others as a kind of categorical vindication.[28] In this way, and for this reason, the democratic audience for the reports on the mass murders experienced distance from, rather than identification with, the trauma's victims. The revelations had the effect, in some perverse sense, of normalizing the abnormal.

The empirical existence of Nazi plans for the "Final Solution," as well as extensive documentation of their ongoing extermination activities, had been publicly documented by June 1942 (Dawidowicz, 1982; Laqueur, 1980; Norich, 1998–99). In July of that year more than twenty thousand persons rallied in Madison Square Garden to protest the Nazis' war against the Jews. Though he did not attend in person, President Franklin Roosevelt sent a special message that what he called "these crimes" would be redeemed by the "final accounting" following the Allied victory over Nazism. In March 1943 the American Jewish Congress announced that 2 million Jews had already been massacred and that millions more were slated for death. Its detailed descriptions of the "extermination" were widely reported in the American press.[29] Dawidowicz shows that, by March 1944, when the Germans occupied Hungary and their intention to liquidate its entire Jewish population became known, "Auschwitz was no longer an unfamiliar name" (Dawidowicz, 1982).

Yet it was this very familiarity that seemed to undermine the sense of astonishment that might have stimulated immediate action. For Auschwitz was typified in terms of the progressive narrative of war, a narrative that made it impossible to denormalize the mass killings, to make the Holocaust into the "Holocaust." As I indicated in my earlier reconstruction of the discourse about atrocity, what eventually came to be called the Holocaust was reported to contemporaries as a war story, nothing less but nothing more. In private conferences with the American president, Jewish leaders demanded that Allied forces make special efforts to target and destroy the death camps. In describing these failed efforts to trigger intervention, a leading historian explains that the leaders "couldn't convince a preoccupied American President and the American public of the significance of Auschwitz for their time in history" (Feingold, 1974: 250). In other words, while Auschwitz was coded as evil, it simply was not weighted in a sufficiently dire way.

In these symbolically mediated confrontations, attention was not focused on the mass killings in and of themselves. What was definitely not illuminated or asserted was the discovery of an evil unique in human history. The evil of that time had already been discovered, and it was Nazism, not the massive killing of European Jews. The trauma that this evil had created was a second world war. The trauma that the Jews experienced in the midst of their liquidation was represented as one among a series of effects of Nazi evil. When the *London Times* reported Adolph Hitler's death, on May 2, 1945—in the month following the death-camp revelations—its obituary described the German dictator as "the incarnation of absolute evil" and only briefly mentioned Hitler's "fanatical aversion to Jews" (quoted in Benn, 1995: 102). As one historian has put it, "the processed mass murders became merely another atrocity in a particularly cruel war" (quoted in Benn, 1995: 102).[30] The mass murders were explained, and they would be redeemed, within the framework of the progressive struggle against Nazism.

To fully understand the initial, frame-establishing encounter between Americans and the Jewish mass murder, it is vital to remember that narratives, no matter how progressive and future oriented, are composed of both antagonists and protagonists. The antagonists and their crimes were well established: The German Nazis had murdered the Jews in a gigantic, heinous atrocity of war. The protagonists were the American GIs, and their entrance into the concentration camps was portrayed not only as a discovery of such horrendous atrocities but also as another, culminating stage in a long and equally well-known sequence of "liberation," with all the ameliorating expectations that utopian term implies.

"When the press entered the camps of the western front," the cultural historian Barbie Zelizer writes, "it found that the most effective way to tell the atrocity story was as a chronicle of liberation" (1998: 63). In fact, Zelizer entitles her own detailed reconstruction of these journalist encounters "Chronicles of Liberation" (63–85). When readers of the *New York Times* and *Los Angeles Times* were confronted, on April 16, 1945, with the photo from Buchenwald of bunk beds stuffed to overflowing with haunted, pathetically undernourished male prisoners, they were informed that they were looking at "freed slave laborers" (183). On May 5, the *Picture Post* published a six-page spread of atrocity photos. Framing the heart-wrenching visual images, the theme of forward progress was palpable. One collective caption read: "These Were Inmates of Prison Camps Set Free in the Allied Advance: For Many We Came Too Late" (129). Photos of dead or tattered and starving victims were often juxtaposed with pictures of well-dressed, well-fed German citizens from the surrounding towns, pointedly linking the crime to the particular nature of the German people themselves. In a sidebar story entitled "The Problem That Makes All Europe Wonder," the *Picture Post* described "the horror that took place within the sight and sound of hundreds of thousands of seemingly normal, decent German people. How was it possible? What has happened to the minds of a whole nation that such things should have been tolerated for a day?" (quoted in Zelizer, 1998: 128). The same photos often included a representative GI standing guard, passing judgment looking on the scene. The text alongside another widely circulated photo in the *Picture Post* made the progressive answer to such questions perfectly plain. "It is not enough to be mad with rage. It is no help to shout about 'exterminating' Germany. Only one thing helps: the attempt to understand how men have sunk so far, and the firm resolve to face the trouble, the inconvenience and cost of seeing no nation gets the chance to befoul the world like this again" (quoted in Zelizer, 1998: 129). It was within this highly particularized progressive narrative that the first steps toward universalization actually took place. Because the Jewish mass killings came at the chronological conclusion of the war, and because they without doubt represented the most gruesome illustration of Nazi atrocities, they came very quickly to be viewed not merely as symptoms but also as emblems and iconic representations of the evil that the progressive narrative promised to leave behind. As the novelist and war correspondent Meyer Levin wrote of his visit to Ohrdruf, the first camp American soldiers liberated, "it was as though we had penetrated at last to the center of the black heart, to the very crawling inside of the vicious heart" (quoted in Abzug, 1985: 19). On the one hand, the trauma was localized and particularized—it occurred in this war, in this place, with these persons. On the other hand, the mass murder was universalized. Within months of the initial revelations, indeed, the murders frequently were framed by a new term, *genocide,* a crime defined as the effort to destroy an entire people, which, while introduced earlier, during the war period itself, came to be publicly available and widely employed only after the discovery of the Nazi atrocities.[31]

In response to this new representation, the scope of the Nuremberg War Crimes Tribunal was enlarged. Conceived as a principal vehicle for linking the postwar Allied cause to progressive redemption, the trials were now to go beyond prosecuting the Nazi leaders for crimes of war to considering their role in the mass murder of the Jewish people. Justice Robert Jackson, the chief American prosecutor, promised that the trial would not only prosecute those responsible for the war but also would present "undeniable proofs of incredible events"—the Nazi crimes (quoted in Benn, 1995: 102). The first three counts of the twenty-thousand-word indictment against the twenty-three high-ranking Nazi officials concerned the prosecution of the war itself. They charged conspiracy, conducting a war of aggression, and violating the rules of war. The fourth count, added only in the months immediately preceding the October trial in Nuremberg, accused the Nazi leaders of something new, namely of "crimes against humanity." This was the first step toward universalizing the public representation of the Jewish mass murder. From the perspective of the present day, however, it appears as a relatively limited one, for it functioned to confirm the innocent virtue and national ambitions of one particular side. In its first report on the indictments, for example, the *New York Times* linked the Jewish mass murder directly to the war itself and placed its punishment within the effort to prevent any future "war of aggression." Under the headline "The Coming War Trials," the paper noted that "the authority of this tribunal to inflict punishment is directly from victory in war" and that its goal was "to establish the principle that no nation shall ever again go to war, except when directly attacked or under the sanction of a world organization" (October 9, 1945: 20). The Nuremberg trials were not, in other words, perceived as preventing genocide or crimes against humanity as such. At that time the commission of such crimes could not be conceived apart from the Nazis and the recently concluded aggressive war.

The force of the progressive narrative meant that, while the 1945 revelations confirmed the Jewish mass murder, they did not create a trauma for the postwar audience. Victory and the Nuremburg war trials would put an end to Nazism and alleviate its evil effects. Postwar redemption depended on putting mass murder "behind us," moving on, and getting on with the construction of the new world.

> From the end of the war until the early 1960s, a "can-do," optimistic spirit pervaded America. Those who had returned from the war were concerned with building a family and a career, not with dwelling on the horrors of the past.... It did not seem to be an appropriate time to focus on a painful past, particularly a past which seemed to be of no direct concern to this country. This event had transpired on another continent. It had been committed by another country against "an-other" people. What relevance did it have for Americans? (Lipstadt, 1996: 195–214).

[As for] the terms in which Americans of the mid-1950s were pre-
pared to confront the Holocaust: a terrible event, yes, but ultimately
not tragic or depressing; an experience shadowed by the specter of a
cruel death, but at the same time not without the ability to inspire,
console, uplift. . . . Throughout the late 1940s and well into the 50s,
a prevalent attitude was to put all of "that" behind one and get on
with life. (Rosenfeld, 1995: 37–38)

After the War, American Jewry turned—with great energy and
generosity—to liquidating the legacy of the Holocaust by caring
for the survivors [who] were urged to put the ghastly past behind
them, to build new lives in their adopted homes. . . . When a proposal for a Holocaust memorial in New York City came before
representatives of the leading Jewish organizations in the late 1940s,
they unanimously rejected the idea: it would, they said, give currency to the image of Jews as "helpless victims," an idea they wished
to repudiate. (Novick, 1994: 160)

It was neither emotional repression nor good moral sense that created the
early responses to the mass murder of the Jews. It was, rather, a system of collective representations that focused its beam of narrative light on the triumphant expulsion of evil. Most Americans did not identify with the victims of
the Jewish trauma. Far from being implicated in it, Americans had defeated
those responsible for the mass murders and righteously engaged in restruc-
turing the social and political arrangements that had facilitated them. This
did not mean that the mass murder of Jews was viewed with relativism or
equanimity. According to the progressive narrative, it was America's solemn
task to redeem the sacrifice of this largest of all categories of Nazi victims. In
postwar America, the public redeemed the sacrifices of war by demanding
the thorough denazification not only of German but of American society.
As Sumner Welles eloquently framed the issue a month after the GIs had
entered the Nazi death camps,

The crimes committed by the Nazis and by their accomplices
against the Jewish people are indelible stains upon the whole of
our modern civilization. . . . They are stains which will shame our
generation in the eyes of generations still unborn. For we and our
governments, to which we have entrusted power during these years

between the Great Wars, cannot shake off the responsibility for having permitted the growth of world conditions which made such horrors possible. The democracies cannot lightly attempt to shirk their responsibility. No recompense can be offered the dead....But such measure of recompense as can be offered surely constitutes the moral obligation of the free peoples of the earth as soon as their victory is won. (Welles, 1945: 511)

Purifying America and Redeeming the Murder of the Jews

Propelled by the logic of this progressive understanding of redemption, in America's immediate postwar years the public legitimation of anti-Semitism was repeatedly attacked and some of its central institutional manifestations destroyed. The longstanding anti–anti-Semitism framing the progressive narrative, and crystallized during the interwar years by leading figures in the American intellectual and cultural elite, culminated in the immediate postwar period in a massive shift of American public opinion on the Jewish question (Stember, 1966). Only days after the hostilities ceased, in response to an appeal from the National Council of Christians and Jews, the three candidates for mayor of New York City pledged to "refrain from appeals to racial and religious divisiveness during the campaign." One of them made explicit the connection of this public anti–anti-Semitism to the effort to remain connected to, and enlarge on, the meaning of America's triumph in the anti-Nazi war.

> This election will be the first held in the City of New York since our victory over nazism and Japanese fascism. It will therefore be an occasion for a practical demonstration of democracy in action—a democracy in which all are equal citizens, in which there is not and never must be a second class citizenship and in which...the religion of a candidate must play no part in the campaign. (*New York Times*, October 1, 1945: 32)

In an influential article, Leonard Dinnerstein has documented the vastly heightened political activism of Jewish groups in the immediate postwar period from 1945 to 1948 (Dinnerstein, 1981–82). He records how these newly surfaced and often newly formed groups held conferences, wrote editorials, and issued specific proposals for legal and institutional changes.

By 1950, these activities had successfully exposed and often defeated anti-Jewish quotas and, more generally, created an extraordinary shift in the practical and cultural position of American Jews. During the same month that New York's mayoral candidates announced their anti–anti-Semitism, the *American Mercury* published an article, "Discrimination in Medical Colleges," replete with graphs and copious documentation, detailing the existence of anti-Jewish quotas in some of America's most prestigious professional institutions. While the specific focus was anti-Jewish discrimination, these facts were narrated in terms of the overarching promise of America and democracy. The story began with a vignette about "Leo, a bright and personable American lad" who "dreamed of becoming a great physician."

> [He] made an excellent scholastic record [but] upon graduation . . . his first application for admission to a medical school . . . was mysteriously turned down. He filed another and another—at eighty-seven schools—always with the same heartbreaking result . . . not one of the schools had the courage to inform Leo frankly that he was being excluded because he was a Jew. . . . The excuse for imposing a quota system usually advanced is that there ought to be some correlation between the number of physicians of any racial or religious strain and the proportion of that race or religion in the general population [but] the surface logic of this arithmetic collapses as soon as one subjects it to *democratic or sheerly human,* let alone scientific, tests. [It is] spurious and *un-American* arithmetic. (October, 1945: 391–99, italics added)[32]

Earlier that year, an "Independent Citizens Committee" had asked three hundred educators to speak out against restricting Jewish enrollment in the nation's schools. Ernest Hopkins, the president of Dartmouth College, refused, openly defending Dartmouth's Jewish quota on the grounds that German Nazism had been spurred because a large proportion of the German professions had become Jewish. A storm of public opprobrium followed Hopkins's remarks. The *New York Post* headlined, "Dartmouth Bars Jews 'To End Anti-Semitism,' Says Prexy." The next day, the rival tabloid, *PM,* placed Hopkins's picture side by side with the Nazi ideologue Alfred Rosenberg and accused the Dartmouth president of "spouting the Hitler-Rosenberg line" (quoted in "Sense or Nonsense?" *Time,* August 20, 1945: 92). In an article entitled "Anti-Semitism at Dartmouth," the *New Republic* brought a progressive perspective to the controversy by suggesting that it could bring "us a step nearer to amelioration of one of the outstanding blots on American civilization *today.*" Anti-Semitism belonged to the outmoded past that had been shattered by the anti-Nazi war: "We can *no longer* afford the luxury of these *obsolete* myths of racial differentiation, Mr. Hopkins; if you don't believe it, ask Hitler" (August 20, 1945: 208–9, italics added).

In the years that followed, the fight against quotas continued to be informed by similar themes. In 1946, an educational sociologist wrote in the *American Scholar* that such restrictions were "in contradistinction to the *growing* realization which has come as a result of the war." Quotas must be abolished if postwar progress were to be made.

> *Today,* our society as a whole sees the relationship between social welfare and prejudices which thwart the development of the capacities of individuals. This threat to the basic concepts of democracy is so plain that almost all of us, except the vested interests, have seen it. The question is whether or not the colleges and universities have seen it and are willing to bring their practices into line with *present day* insights, even though some of their most precious traditions be jeopardized. (Dodson, 1946: 268, italics added)

Similar connections between the anti-Nazi war, anti-quotas, and the progress of anti–anti-Semitism informed another popular magazine article the following year: "It is extremely regrettable that *in 1946*, the children of [parents] who are returning from all parts of the world where they have been engaged in mortal combat to preserve democracy, are confronted with the same closed doors that greeted their 'alien' fathers" (Hart, 1947: 61). In 1949, *Collier's* published an article describing the "scores of college men to whom fraternities" for "'fullblooded Aryans' are a little nauseating *in this day.*" Quoting the finding of an Amherst College alumni committee that exclusive fraternities gave young men "a false and undemocratic sense of superiority," the article claimed that "the anti-discrimination movement is hopping from campus to campus" (Whitman, 1949: 34–35).

While Jewish voluntary organizations had begun to organize in 1943–45, they entered the American public sphere as aggressive political advocates only after 1945, an intervention that marked the first time Jews had forcefully entered the civil sphere as advocates for their own rather than others' causes. In the prewar period, and even less in earlier times, such an explicit and aggressively Jewish public intervention would certainly have been repelled; in fact, it would only have made anti-Semitism worse. In the postwar period, however, despite their failure to identify with the Jewish victims of Nazism, the American non-Jewish audience was determined to redeem them. If, as Dinnerstein writes, Jewish groups intended to "mobilize public opinion against intolerance, and [thus to] utilize the courts and legislative bodies" (1981–1982: 137) in their anti-Semitic fight, they were able to carry on these political activities only because postwar public opinion had already been defined as committed to "tolerance."

Progress toward establishing civil relations between religious and ethnic groups was woven into the patriotic postwar narratives of the nation's mass-circulation magazines. *Better Homes and Gardens* ran such stories as "Do You Want Your Children to Be Tolerant?"

> The old indifference and local absorption cannot continue. If we relapse into our *before-the-war* attitudes and limitations, war will burst upon us as suddenly and as unexpectedly as the atomic bomb fell upon the people of Hiroshima—and we shall be as helpless. (Buck, 1947: 135, italics added)

In another piece in *Better Homes and Gardens* the same year, "How to Stop the Hate Mongers in Your Home Town," a writer observed: "I suspect that many a decent German burgher, hearing tales of Nazi gangs, likewise shrugged off the implications of uncurbed racial and religious persecution" (Carter, 1947: 180). The following year, the *Saturday Evening Post* profiled "the story of the Jewish family of Jacob Golomb." The lengthy article concluded with the by now widely expected forward-looking line:

> As a family, the Golombs are more than just nice folks who lead busy, fruitful, decent lives; a family whose sons have sprung, in time of national emergency, with promptness to the defense of their country. As members of a race with a long history of persecution, they have kept the faith, since Abraham Golomb's time, that the United States really was, or *would soon be*, the land of the genuinely free. They are still convinced. (Perry, 1948: 96, italics added)

Four years later, America's most popular photo magazine published "*Life* Goes to a Bar Mitzvah: A Boy Becomes a Man" (October 13, 1952: 170–76).

The anti–anti-Semitism theme also entered popular culture through the movies. In the 1945 box office hit *Pride of the Marines*, the Jewish protagonist Larry Diamond chided a friend for pessimism about the possibility of eliminating prejudice in the postwar years. He did so by connecting their present situation to the progressive ideals that had sustained their anti-Nazi war: "Ah, come on, climb out of your foxholes, what's a matter you guys, don't you think anybody learned anything since 1930? Think everybody's had their eyes shut and brains in cold storage?" (Short, 1981: 161). Diamond goes on to remark that, if and when prejudice and repression dare to show their ugly heads in the postwar United States, he will fight to defeat them, just as he has learned to fight in the war: "I fought for me, for the right to live in the USA. And when I get back into civilian life, if I don't like the way things are going, O.K. it's my country; I'll stand on my own two legs and holler! If there's enough of us hollering we'll go places—Check?" (161). The narrative of progress is forcefully extended from the anti-Nazi war into the post-Nazi peace. Diamond had been "the pride of the marines," and the war's progressive narrative is fundamentally tied to assertions about the utopian telos of the United States. As the movie's closing music turns into "America the Beautiful," Diamond wraps it up this way: "One happy afternoon when God was feeling good, he sat down and thought of a rich beautiful country and he named it the USA. All of it, Al, the hills, the rivers, the lands, the whole works. Don't tell me we can't make it work in peace like we do in war. Don't tell me we can't pull together. Don't you see it guys, can't you see it?" (161–62).

Two years later, a movie promoting anti–anti-Semitism, *Gentleman's Agreement,* won the Academy Award for best motion picture, and another, *Crossfire,* had been nominated as well. Both are conspicuously progressive, forward-looking narratives. In the final dialogue of *Gentlemen's Agreement,* the film's future-oriented, utopian theme could not be more clear. "Wouldn't it be wonderful," Mrs. Green asks Phil, "if it turned out to be everybody's century, when people all over the world, free people, found a way to live together? I'd like to be around to see some of that, even a beginning" (quoted in Short, 1981: 180).[33]

As they had immediately before and during the war, "Jews" held symbolic pride of place in these popular-culture narratives because their persecution had been preeminently associated with the Nazi evil. In fact, it was not tolerance as such that the progressive narrative demanded but tolerance of the Jews.[34] Thus, despite their feelings of solidarity with their foreign co-religionists, Jewish leaders carefully refrained from publicly endorsing the wholesale lifting of anti-immigration quotas after 1945. They realized that the idea of immigration remained so polluted by association with stigmatized others that it might have the power to counteract the ongoing purification of Jewishness. In the preceding half-century, anti-immigration and anti-Semitism had been closely linked, and Jews did not want to pollute "Jewishness" with this identity again. While demonstrating their support in private, Jewish leaders resolutely refused to make any public pronouncements about lifting the immigration quotas (Dinnerstein, 1981–82: 140).

What Dinnerstein has called the "turnabout in anti-Semitic feelings" represented the triumph over Nazism, not recognition of the Holocaust trauma. News about the mass murder, and any ruminations about it, disappeared from newspapers and magazines rather quickly after the initial reports about the camps' liberation, and the Nazis' Jewish victims came to be represented as displaced persons, potential immigrants, and potential settlers in Palestine, where a majority of Americans wanted to see a new, and redemptive, Jewish state. This interpretation suggests that it was by no means simply Realpolitik that led President Truman to champion, against his former French and British allies, the postwar creation of Israel, the new Jewish state. The progressive narrative demanded a future-oriented renewal. Zionists argued that the Jewish trauma could be redeemed, that Jews could both sanctify the victims and put the trauma behind them, only if they returned to Jerusalem. According to the Zionist worldview, if Israel were allowed to exist, it would create a new race of confident and powerful Jewish farmer-warriors who would redeem the anti-Jewish atrocities by developing such an imposing military power that the massive murdering of the Jews would never, anywhere in the world, be allowed to happen again. In important respects, it was this convergence of progressive narratives in relation to the war and the Jewish mass killings that led the postwar paths of the United States and the state of Israel to become so fundamentally intertwined. Israel would have to prosper and survive for the redemptive telos of America's progressive narrative to be maintained.

These cultural-sociological considerations do not suggest that the postwar American fight against anti-Semitism was in any way morally inauthentic. It was triggered by grassroots feelings as deep as those that had motivated the earlier anti-Nazi fight. When one looks at these powerful new arguments against anti-Semitism, it is only retrospectively surprising to realize that the "atrocities" revealed in 1945—the events and experiences that defined the trauma for European Jews—figure hardly at all. This absence is explained by the powerful symbolic logic of the progressive narrative, which already had been established in the prewar period. With the victory in 1945, the United

States got down to the work of establishing the new world order. In creating a Nazi-free future, Jewishness came for the first time to be analogically connected with core American symbols of "democracy" and "nation."

In the course of this postwar transformation, American Jews also became identified with democracy in a more primordial and less universalistic way, namely as newly minted, patriotic representations of the nation. "After 1945," a leading historian of that period remarks, "other Americans no longer viewed the Jews as merely another of the many exotic groups within America's ethnic and religious mosaic. Instead, they were now seen as comprising one of the country's three major religions" (Shapiro, 1992: 28). This patriotic-national definition was expressed by the Jewish theologian Will Herberg's insistence on the "Judeo-Christian" rather than "Christian" identity of the religious heritage of the United States (quoted in Shapiro, 1992: 53).[35] As I have indicated, what motivated this intense identification of anti–anti-Semitism with the American nation was neither simple emotional revulsion for the horrors of the Jewish mass killings nor commonsense morality. It was, rather, the progressive narrative frame. To end anti-Semitism, in President Truman's words, was to place America alongside "the moral forces of the world" (quoted in Shapiro, 1992: 143). It was to redeem those who had sacrificed themselves for the American nation, and according to the teleology of the progressive narrative, this emphatically included the masses of murdered European Jews.

The critical point is this: What was a trauma for the victims was not a trauma for the audience.[36] In documenting this for the American case, I have examined the principal carrier group for the progressive narrative, the nation that in the immediate postwar world most conspicuously took the lead in "building the new world upon the ashes of the old." I have shown that the social agents, both Jewish and non-Jewish Americans, who took the lead in reconstructing a new moral order dedicated themselves to redeeming those who had been sacrificed to the anti-Nazi struggle, and most especially to the Jewish victims, by putting an end to anti-Semitism in the United States. The goal was focused not on the Holocaust but on the need to purge postwar society of Nazi-like pollution.

Jewish Mass Murder under the Tragic Narrative

I will now show how a different kind of narrative developed in relation to the Nazis' mass murder of the Jews, one that gave the evil it represented significantly greater symbolic weight. I will treat this new culture structure both as cause and as effect. After reconstructing its internal contours, I will examine the kind of "symbolic action" it caused and how these new meanings compelled the trauma of the mass murders to be seen in a radically different way, with significant consequences for social and political action that continue to ramify to the present day.[37] After completing this analytic reconstruction of the new cultural configuration, I will proceed to a concrete examination of how it was constructed in real historical time, looking at changes in carrier groups, moral contexts, and social structural forces. Finally, I will examine some of the long-term ramifications of the highly general, decontextualized, and universal status that the trauma of the Holocaust came to assume.

The New Culture Structure

Ever since Dilthey defined the method specific to the *Geisteswissenschaften*—literally "sciences of the spirit" but typically translated as "human sciences"—it has been clear that what distinguishes the hermeneutic from the natural scientific method is the challenge of penetrating beyond the external form to inner meaning of actions, events, and institutions. Yet to enter into this thicket of subjectivity is not to embrace impressionism and relativism. As Dilthey emphasized, meanings are governed by structures just as surely as are economic and political processes; they are just governed in different ways. Every effort at interpretive social science must begin with the reconstruction of this culture structure.[38]

DEEPENING EVIL

In the formation of this new culture structure, the coding of the Jewish mass killings as evil remained, but its weighting substantially changed. It became burdened with extraordinary gravitas. The symbolization of the Jewish mass killings became generalized and reified, and in the process the evil done to the Jews became separated from the profanation of Nazism per se. Rather than seeming to "typify" Nazism, or even the nefarious machinations of any particular social movement, political formation, or historical time, the mass killings came to be seen as not being typical of anything at all. They came to be understood as a unique, historically unprecedented event, as evil on a scale that had never occurred before.[39] The mass killings entered into universal history, becoming a "world-historical" event in Hegel's original sense, an event whose emergence onto the world stage threatened, or prom-ised, to change the fundamental course of the world.[40] In the introduction to an English collection of his essays on Nazi history and the Holocaust, the German-Israeli historian Dan Diner observes that "well into the 1970s, wide-ranging portraits of the epoch would grant the Holocaust a modest (if any) mention."[41] By contrast, "it now tends to fill the entire picture.... The growing centrality of the Holocaust has altered the entire warp and woof of our sense of the passing century.... The incriminated event has thus become the epoch's marker, its final and inescapable wellspring" (Diner, 2000: 1).

The Jewish mass killings became what we might identify, in Durkheimian terms, as a sacred-evil, an evil that recalled a trauma of such enormity and horror that it had to be radically set apart from the world and all of its other traumatizing events. It became inexplicable in ordinary, rational terms. As part of the Nazi scheme of world domination, the Jewish mass killing was heinous, but at least it had been understandable. As a sacred-evil, set apart from ordinary evil things, it had become mysterious and inexplicable. One of the first to comment on, and thus to characterize, this postprogressive inex-plicability was the Marxist historian Isaac Deutscher. This great biographer of Trotsky, who had already faced the consequences of Stalinism for the myth of communist progress, was no doubt preconditioned to see the tragic dimen-sions of the Holocaust. In 1968, in "The Jewish Tragedy and the Historian," Deutscher suggested that comprehending the Holocaust "will not be just a matter of time." What he meant was that there would not be progress.

> I doubt whether even in a thousand years people will understand Hitler, Auschwitz, Majdanek, and Treblinka better than we do now. Will they have a better historical perspective? On the contrary, posterity may even understand it all even less than we do. Who can analyze the motives and the interests behind the enormities of Auschwitz.... We are confronted here by a huge and ominous mystery of the generation of the human character that will forever baffle and terrify mankind. (Deutscher, 1968: 163)

For Deutscher, such a huge and mysterious evil, so resistant to the normal progress of human rationality, suggested tragedy and art, not scientific fact gathering. "Perhaps a modern Aeschylus and Sophocles could cope with this theme," he suggested, "but they would do so on a level different from that of historical interpretation and explanation" (1968: 164). Geoffrey Hartman, the literary theorist who has directed Yale University's Video Archive for the Holocaust since 1981 and has been a major participant in postsixties discussions of the trauma, points to the enigma that, while no historical event has ever "been so thoroughly documented and studied," social and moral "understanding comes and goes; it has not been progressive." By way of explaining this lack of progress, Hartman suggests that

> The scholars most deeply involved often admit an "excess" that remains dark and frightful....Something in the...Shoah remains dark at the heart of the event....A comparison with the French Revolution is useful. The sequence *French Revolution: Enlightenment* cannot be matched by *Holocaust: Enlightenment.* What should be placed after the colon? "Eclipse of Enlightenment" or "Eclipse of God"? (Hartman, 1996: 3–4)

To this day the Holocaust is almost never referred to without asserting its inexplicability. In the spring of 1999, a *New York Times* theater reviewer began his remarks on *The Gathering*, a newly opened drama, by asserting that "the profound, agonizing mystery of the Holocaust echoes through the generations and across international borders," presenting "an awesome human and theological enigma as an old century prepares to give way to a new millennium" (van Gelder, 1999: 1).

This separateness of sacred-evil demanded that the trauma be renamed, for the concept of "mass murder" and even the notion of "genocide" now appeared unacceptably to normalize the trauma, to place it too closely in proximity to the banal and mundane. In contrast, despite the fact that the word *holocaust* did have a formally established English meaning—according to the *Oxford English Dictionary*, "something wholly burnt up" (Garber and Zuckerman, 1989: 199)—it no longer performed this sign function in everyday speech. Rather, the term entered into ordinary English usage in the early 1960s as a proper rather than a common noun.[42] Only several years after the Nazis' mass murder did Israelis begin to employ the Hebrew word *shoah*, the term by which the Torah evoked the kind of extraordinary sufferings God had periodically consigned to the Jews. In the official English translation of the phrase "Nazi *shoah*" in the preamble to the 1948 Israeli Declaration of Independence, one can already find the reference to "Nazi holocaust"(Novick, 1999: 132). With the decline of the progressive narrative, in other words, as *Holocaust* became the dominant representation for the trauma, it implied the sacral mystery, the "awe-fullness," of the transcendental tradition. *Holocaust* became part of contemporary language as an English symbol that stood for that thing that could not be named.[43] As David Roskies once wrote, "it was precisely the nonreferential quality of 'Holocaust' that made it so appealing" (quoted in Garber and Zuckerman, 1989: 201).

This new linguistic identity allowed the mass killings of the Jews to become what might be called a bridge metaphor: It provided the symbolic extension so necessary if the trauma of the Jewish people were to become a trauma for all humankind. The other necessary ingredient, psychological identification, was not far behind. It depended on configuring this newly weighted symbolization of evil in a different narrative frame.

SUFFERING, CATHARSIS, AND IDENTIFICATION

The darkness of this new postwar symbolization of evil cast a shadow over the progressive story that had thus far narrated its course. The story of redeeming Nazism's victims by creating a progressive and democratic world order could be called an ascending narrative, for it pointed to the future and suggested confidence that things would be better over time. Insofar as the mass killings were defined as a Holocaust, and insofar as it was the very emergence of this sacred-evil, not its eventual defeat, that threatened to become emblematic of "our time,"[44] the progressive narrative was blocked, and in some manner overwhelmed, by a sense of historical descent, by a falling away from the good. Recent Holocaust commentators have drawn this conclusion time and again. According to the progressive narrative, the Nazis' mass murder of the Jews would provide a lesson for all humankind, a decisive learning process on the way to a better world. Reflecting on the continuing fact of genocidal mass murders in the post-Holocaust world, however, Hartman revealingly suggests that "these developments raise questions about our species, our preconceptions that we are the human, the 'family of man.' Or less dramatically, we wonder about the veneer of progress, culture, and educability."

In dramaturgical terms, the issue concerns the position occupied by evil in the historical narrative. When Aristotle first defined tragedy in the *Poetics,* he linked what I have here called the weight of the representation of suffering to temporal location of an event in plot:

Tragedy is the representation of a complete, i.e., whole action *which has some magnitude* (for there can be a whole action without magnitude). A whole is that which has a beginning, a middle and a conclusion. A beginning is that which itself does not of necessity follow something else, but after which there naturally is, or comes into being, something else. A conclusion, conversely, is that which itself naturally follows something else, either of necessity or for the most part, but has nothing else after it. A middle is that which itself naturally follows something else, and has something else after it. Well-constructed plots, then, should neither begin from a random point nor conclude at a random point, but should use the elements we have mentioned. (Aristotle, 1987: 3.2.1, italics added)

In the progressive narrative frame, the Jewish mass killings were not an end but a beginning. They were part of the massive trauma of World War II, but in the postwar period they and related incidents of Nazi horror were regarded as a birth trauma, a crossroads in a chronology that would eventually be set right. By contrast, the newly emerging world-historical status of the mass murders suggested that they represented an end point, not a new beginning, a death trauma rather than a trauma of birth, a cause for despair, not the beginning of hope. In place of the progressive story, then, there began to emerge the narrative of tragedy. The end point of a narrative defines its telos. In the new tragic understanding of the Jewish mass murder, suffering, not progress, became the telos toward which the narrative was aimed.

In this tragic narrative of sacred-evil, the Jewish mass killings become not an event in history but an archetype, an event out of time. As archetype, the evil evoked an experience of trauma greater than anything that could be defined by religion, race, class, region—indeed, by any conceivable sociological configuration or historical conjuncture. This transcendental status, this separation from the specifics of any particular time or space, provided the basis for psychological identification on an unprecedented scale. The contemporary audience cares little about the second and third installments of Sophocles' archetypal story of Oedipus, the tragic hero. What we are obsessed with is Oedipus' awful, unrecognized, and irredeemable mistake, how he finally comes to recognize his responsibility for it, and how he blinds himself from guilt when he understands its full meaning. Tragic narratives focus attention not on some future effort at reversal or amelioration—"progress," in the terms I have employed here—but on the nature of the crime, its immediate aftermath, and on the motives and relationships that led up to it.

A tragic narrative offers no redemption in the traditionally religious, Judeo-Christian sense.[45] There is no happy ending, no sense that something else could have been done, and no belief that the future could, or can, necessarily be changed. Indeed, protagonists are tragic precisely because they have failed to exert control over events. They are in the grip of forces larger than themselves—impersonal, even inhuman forces that often are not only beyond control but, during the tragic action itself, beyond comprehension. This sense of being overwhelmed by unjust force or fate explains the abjection and helplessness that permeates the genre of tragedy and the experience of pity it arouses.

Instead of redemption through progress, the tragic narrative offers what Nietzsche called the drama of the eternal return. As it now came to be understood, there was no "getting beyond" the story of the Holocaust. There was only the possibility of returning to it: not transcendence but catharsis. Hartman resists "the call for closure" on just these grounds. "Wherever we look, the events of 1933–1945 cannot be relegated to the past. They are not over; anyone who comes in contact with them is gripped, and finds detachment difficult." Quoting from Lawrence Langer's *Admitting the Holocaust*, Hartman suggests that "those who study it must 'reverse history and progress and find a way of restoring to the imagination of coming generations the depth of the catastrophe'" (Hartman, 1996: 2, 5).

As Aristotle explained, catharsis clarifies feeling and emotion. It does so not by allowing the audience to separate itself from the story's characters, a separation, according to Frye, that defines the very essence of comedy (Frye, 1971 [1957]). Rather, catharsis clarifies feeling and emotion by forcing the audience to identify with the story's characters, compelling them to experience their suffering with them, and to learn, as often they did not, the true causes of their death. That we survive and they do not, that we can get up and leave the theater while they remain forever prostrate—this allows the possibility of catharsis, that strange combination of cleansing and relief, that humbling feeling of having been exposed to the dark and sinister forces that lie just beneath the surface of human life and of having survived.[46] We seek catharsis because our identification with the tragic narrative compels us to experience dark and sinister forces that are also inside of ourselves, not only inside others. We "redeem" tragedy by experiencing it, but despite this redemption, we do not get over it. Rather, to achieve redemption we are compelled to dramatize and redramatize, experience and reexperience the archetypal trauma. We pity the victims of the trauma, identifying and sympathizing with their horrible fate.

Aristotle argued that the tragic genre could be utilized only for the "sorts of occurrence [that] arouse dread, or compassion in us" (Aristotle, 1987: 4.1.2). The blackness of tragedy can be achieved only if, "first and foremost, the [suffering] characters should be good," for "the plot should be constructed in such a way that, even without seeing it, someone who hears about the incidents will shudder and feel pity at the outcome, as someone may feel upon hearing the plot of the Oedipus" (4.2.1, 4.1.1.3). It is not only the fact of identification, however, but its complexity that makes the experience of trauma as tragedy so central to the assumption of moral responsibility, for we identify not only with the victims but with the perpetrators as well. The creation of this cultural form allows the psychological activity of internalization rather than projection, acceptance rather than displacement.[47]

THE TRAUMA–DRAMA OF ETERNAL RETURN

In the tragic narration of the Holocaust, the primal event became a "trauma-drama" that the "audience" returned to time and time again. This became, paradoxically, the only way to ensure that such an event would happen "never again." This quality of compulsively returning to the trauma-drama gave the story of the Holocaust a mythical status that transformed it into the archetypical sacred-evil of our time. Insofar as it achieved this status as a dominant myth, the tragedy of the Holocaust challenged the ethical self-identification, the self-esteem, of modernity—indeed, the very self-confidence that such a thing as "modern progress" could continue to exist. For to return to the trauma-drama of the Holocaust, to identify over and over again with the suffering and helplessness of its victims, was in some sense to give that confidence-shattering event a continuing existence in contemporary life. It was, in effect, to acknowledge that it *could* happen again.

In this way, the tragic framing of the Holocaust fundamentally contributed to postmodern relativism and disquiet. Because the tragic replaced the progressive narrative of the Nazi mass murder, the ethical standards protecting good from evil seemed not nearly as powerful as modernity's confident pronouncements had promised they would be. When the progressive narrative had organized understanding, the Nazi crimes had been temporalized as "medieval," in order to contrast them with the supposedly civilizing standards of modernity. With the emergence of the more tragic perspective, the barbarism was lodged within the essential nature of modernity itself.[48]

Rather than maintaining and perfecting modernity, as the postwar progressive narrative would have it, the path to a more just and peaceful society seemed now to lead to postmodern life (Bauman, 1989).[49]

It would be wrong, however, to imagine that because a trauma-drama lies at the center of the Holocaust's tragic narration, with all the ambition of exciting pity and emotional catharsis that this implies, that this lachrymose narrative and symbol actually became disconnected from the ethical and the good.[50] While it is undeniable that the Jewish mass killings came to assume a dramaturgical form, their significance hardly became aestheticized—that is, turned into a free-floating, amoral symbol whose function was to entertain rather than to instruct.[51] The events of the Holocaust were not dramatized for the sake of drama itself but, rather, to provide what Martha Nussbaum once described as "the social benefits of pity" (Nussbaum, 1992).[52] The project of renaming, dramatizing, reifying, and ritualizing the Holocaust contributed to a moral remaking of the (post)modern (Western) world. The Holocaust story has been told and retold in response not only to emotional need but also to moral ambition. Its characters, its plot, and its pitiable denouement have been transformed into a less nationally bound, less temporally specific, and more universal drama. This dramatic universalization has deepened contemporary sensitivity to social evil. The trauma-drama's message, like that of every tragedy, is that evil is inside all of us and in every society. If we are all the victims and all the perpetrators, then there is no audience that can legitimately distance itself from collective suffering, either from its victims or from its perpetrators.

This psychological identification with the Jewish mass killings and the symbolic extension of its moral implications beyond the immediate parties involved has stimulated an unprecedented universalization of political and moral responsibility. To have created this symbol of sacred-evil in contemporary time, then, is to have so enlarged the human imagination that it is capable, for the first time in human history, of identifying, understanding, and judging the kinds of genocidal mass killings in which national, ethnic, and ideological groupings continue to engage today.[53] This enlargement has made it possible to comprehend that heinous prejudice with the intent to commit mass murder is not something from an earlier, more "primitive" time or a different, "foreign" place, committed by people with values we do not share. The implication of the tragic narrative is not that progress has become impossible. It has had the salutary effect, rather, of demonstrating that progress is much more difficult to achieve than moderns once believed. If progress is to be made, morality must be universalized beyond any particular time and place.[54]

The New Social Processes

Most Western people today would readily agree with the proposition that the Holocaust was a tragic, devastating event in human history. Surely it was, and is. One implication of my discussion, however, is that this perception of its moral status is not a natural reflection of the event itself. The Jewish mass killings first had to be dramatized—as a tragedy. Some of the most eloquent and influential Holocaust survivors and interpreters have disagreed sharply, and moralistically, with this perspective, insisting that fictional representations must not be allowed to influence the perception of historical reality. In 1978, Elie Wiesel excoriated NBC for producing the *Holocaust* miniseries, complaining that "it transforms an ontological event into soap-opera" and that "it is all make-believe." Because "the Holocaust transcends history," Wiesel argued, "it cannot be explained nor can it be visualized" (Wiesel, 1978: 1). In response to *Schindler's List*, Claude Lanzman said much the same thing. Writing that the Holocaust "is above all unique in that it erects a ring of fire around itself," he claimed that "fiction is a transgression" and that "there are some things that cannot and should not be represented" (quoted in Hartman, 1996: 84).[55]

I take a very different perspective here. Thus far I have reconstructed the internal patterning of the culture structure that allowed the new, tragic dramatization to take place. I would like now to turn to the historically specific social processes, both symbolic and social structural, that made this new patterning attractive and, eventually, compelling. While my reference here is primarily to the United States, I believe some version of this analysis also applies to those other Western societies that attempted to reconstruct liberal democracies after World War II.[56]

I have earlier shown how the struggle against anti-Semitism became one of the primary vehicles by which the progressive narrative redeemed those who had been sacrificed in the war against Nazi evil. Fighting anti-Semitism was not the only path to redemption, of course; for America and its victorious allies, there was a whole new world to make. At the same time, the struggle against anti-Semitism had a special importance. The understanding of Nazism as an absolute evil stemmed not only from its general commitment to anti-civil domination but also from its effort to legitimate such violence according to the principles of prejudice and primordiality. Because the Jewish people were by far the most conspicuous primordial target, symbolic logic dictated that to be anti-Nazi was to be anti–anti-Semitic.[57]

As I have also suggested, the rhetoric and policies of this anti–anti-Semitism did not require that non-Jewish Americans positively identify with Jews, any more than the role that the Holocaust played in the postwar progressive narrative depended on a sense of identification with the weary and bedraggled survivors in the concentration camps themselves. To narrate the Holocaust in a tragic manner, however, did depend on just such an identification being made. This identification was a long time in coming, and it depended on a number of factors unrelated to public opinion and cultural change.[58] Nonetheless, it certainly depended, in addition to such social structural factors, on the fact that the cultural idiom and the organizational apparatus of anti-Semitism had, indeed, been attacked and destroyed in the early "progressive" postwar years, and that, for the first time in American history, Jews seemed, to a majority of Christian Americans, not that much different from anybody else. As the tragic narrative crystallized, the Holocaust drama became, for an increasing number of Americans, and for significant proportions of Europeans as well, the most widely understood and emotionally compelling trauma of the twentieth century. These bathetic events, once experienced as traumatic only by Jewish victims, became generalized and universalized. Their representation no longer referred to events that took place at a particular time and place but to a trauma that had became emblematic, and iconic, of human suffering as such. The horrific trauma of the Jews became the trauma of all humankind.[59]

The Production of New Social Dramas

How was this more generalized and universalized status achieved? Social narratives are not composed by some hidden hand of history. Nor do they appear all at once. The new trauma-drama emerged in bits and pieces. It was a matter of this story and that, this scene and that scene from this movie and that book, this television episode, and that theater performance, this photographic capturing of a moment of torture and suffering. Each of these glimpses into what Meyer Levin had called, in April 1945, "the very crawling inside of the vicious heart" contributed some element to the construction of this new sensibility, which highlighted suffering, helplessness, and dark inevitability and which, taken together and over time, reformulated the mass killing of the Jews as the most tragic event in Western history. It is not the purpose of the following to provide anything approaching a thick description of this process of symbolic reconstruction but only to identify the signposts along this new route and the changing "countryside" that surrounded it.

PERSONALIZING THE TRAUMA AND ITS VICTIMS

In the course of constructing and broadcasting the tragic narrative of the Holocaust, there were a handful of actual dramatizations—in books, movies, plays, and television shows—that played critically important roles. Initially formulated for an American audience, they were distributed worldwide, seen by tens and possibly hundreds of millions of persons, and talked incessantly about by high-, middle-, and lowbrow audiences alike. In the present context, what seems most important about these dramas is that they achieved their effect by personalizing the trauma and its characters. This personalization brought the trauma drama "back home." Rather than depicting the events on a vast historical scale, rather than focusing on larger-than-life leaders, mass movements, organizations, crowds, and ideologies, these dramas portrayed the events in terms of small groups, families and friends, parents and children, brothers and sisters. In this way, the victims of trauma became everyman and everywoman, every child and every parent.

The prototype of this personalizing genre was Anne Frank's famous *Diary*. First published in Holland in 1947,[60] the edited journals appeared in English in 1952. They became the basis for a Pulitzer Prize–winning Broadway play in 1955 and in 1959 a highly acclaimed and equally popular but immensely more widely influential Hollywood movie. This collective representation began in Europe as the journal recorded by a young Dutch girl in hiding from the Nazis and evolved, via a phase of Americanization, into a universal symbol of suffering and transcendence. This transmogrification was possible, in the first place, precisely because Anne's daily jottings focused less on the external events of war and Holocaust—from which she was very much shut off—than on her inner psychological turmoil and the human relationships of those who shared her confinement. Anne's father, Otto Frank, the only family member surviving the camps, supervised the publications and dramatizations of his daughter's journals, and he perceived very clearly the relation between Anne's personal focus and the *Diary*'s potentially universalizing appeal. Writing to Meyer Levin, a potential dramatist who insisted, by contrast, on the specifically Jewish quality of the reminiscence, Otto Frank replied that

> as to the Jewish side you are right that I do not feel the same you do....I always said that Anne's book is not a war book. War is the background. It is not a Jewish book either, though [a] Jewish sphere, sentiment and surrounding is the background....It is read

and understood more by gentiles than in Jewish circles. So do not make a Jewish play out of it." (quoted in Doneson, 1987: 152)[61]

When dramatists for the *Diary* were finally chosen—Francis Goodrich and Albert Hackett—Frank criticized their initial drafts on similar grounds.

> Having read thousands of reviews and hundreds of personal letters about Anne's book from different countries in the world, I know what creates the impression of it on people and their impressions ought to be conveyed by the play to the public. Young people identify themselves very frequently with Anne in their struggle during puberty and the problems of the relations [between] mother-daughter are existing all over the world. These and the love affair with Peter attract young people, whereas parents, teachers, and psychologists learn about the inner feelings of the young generation. When I talked to Mrs. [Eleanor] Roosevelt about the book, she urged me to give permission for [the] play and film as only then we could reach the masses and influence them by the mission of the book which she saw in Anne's wish to work for mankind, to achieve something valuable still after her death, her horror against war and discrimination. (quoted in Doneson, 1987: 153)

This impulse to facilitate identification and moral extension prompted the dramatists to translate into English the *Diary*'s pivotal Hanukkah song, which was sung, and printed, in the original Hebrew in the earlier book version. They explained their reasoning in a letter to Frank. To have left the song in its original Hebrew, they wrote,

> would set the characters in the play apart from the people watching them...for the majority of our audience is not Jewish. And the thing that we have striven for, toiled for, fought for throughout the whole play is to make the audience understand and identify themselves...to make them one with them...that will make them feel "that, but for the grace of God, might have been I." (quoted in Doneson, 1987: 154)

Frank agreed, affirming that it "was my point of view to try to bring Anne's message to as many people as possible even if there are some who think it a sacrilege" from a religious point of view (quoted in Doneson, 1987: 154). Years later, after the unprecedented success of both the theatre and screen plays, the dramatists continued to justify their decision to abandon Hebrew in the dramaturgic terms of facilitating psychological identification and symbolic extension.

> What we all of us hoped, and prayed for, and what we are devoutly thankful to have achieved, is an identification of the audience with the people in hiding. They are seen, not as some strange people, but persons like themselves, thrown into this horrible situation. With them they suffer the deprivations, the terrors, the moments of tenderness, of exaltation and courage beyond belief. (quoted in Doneson, 1987: 155)

In the course of the 1960s, Anne Frank's tragic story laid the basis for psychological identification and symbolic extension on a mass scale. In 1995, the director of Jewish Studies at Indiana University reported that

> The Diary of a Young Girl is... widely read in American schools, and American youngsters regularly see the stage and film versions as well. Their teachers encourage them to identify with Anne Frank and to write stories, essays, and poems about her. Some even see her as a kind of saint and pray to her. During their early adolescent years, many American girls view her story as their story, her fate as somehow bound up with their fate. (Rosenfeld, 1995: 37)

The symbolic transformation effected by Anne Frank's Diary established the dramatic parameters and the stage for the rush of books, television shows, and movies that in the decades following crystallized the mass murder of the Jews as the central episode in a tragic rather than progressive social narrative. As this new genre became institutionalized, representation of Nazism and World War II focused less and less on the historical actors who had once been considered central. In 1953 the acclaimed Billy Wilder movie Stalag 17 had portrayed the grueling plight of U.S. soldiers in a German prisoner-of-war camp. It never mentioned the Jews (Shapiro, 1992: 4). In the early 1960s, a widely popular evening television show, Hogan's Heroes, also portrayed American soldiers in a Nazi prison. It didn't mention "Jews," either. Indeed, the prison camp functioned as a site for comedy, lampooning the misadventures arising from the casual intermixing of Americans with Nazi camp guards and often portraying the latter as bemusing, well-intended buffoons. By the late 1960s, neither comedy nor romance was a genre that audiences felt comfortable applying to that earlier historical time. Nor was it possible to leave out of any dramatization what by then was acknowledged to be the period's central historical actor, the concentration-camp Jews.[62]

This transition was solidified in Western popular culture by the miniseries *Holocaust*, the stark family drama that unfolded over successive evenings to a massive American audience in April 1978. This four-part, nine-and-a-half-hour drama, watched by nearly 100 million Americans, personalized the grisly and famous landmarks of the Third Reich, following ten years in the lives of two fictional families, one of assimilated Jews and the other of a high-ranking SS official.

This extraordinary public attention was repeated, to even greater cathartic effect, when the bathetic drama was later broadcast to record-breaking television audiences in Germany.[63] German critics, commentators, and large sections of the public at large were transfixed by what German commentators described as "the most controversial series of all times" and as "the series that moved the world." During and after this German broadcast, which was preceded by careful public preparation and accompanied by extensive private and public discussion, German social scientists conducted polls and interviews to trace its remarkable effects. They discovered that the resulting shift in public opinion had put a stop to a burgeoning "Hitler revival" and quelled longstanding partisan demands for "balance" in the presentation of the Jewish mass murder. In the wake of the drama, neutralizing terms like "the Final Solution" gave way in German popular and academic discussion to the English term *Holocaust*, and the German Reichstag removed the statute of limitations on Nazis who had participated in what were now defined not as war crimes but as crimes against humanity. The trauma-drama thus continued to work its universalizing effects.[64]

ENLARGING tHE CIRCLE OF pERPETRATORS

Corresponding to the personalization that expanded identification with the victims of the tragedy, a new understanding developed of the perpetrators of the Holocaust that removed them from their historically specific particularities and made them into universal figures with whom members of widely diverse groups felt capable not of sympathizing but of identifying.

The critical event initiating this reconsideration was undoubtedly the 1961 trial of Adolph Eichmann in Jerusalem. Here was a personal and singular representation of the Nazis' murders brought back into the present from the abstract mists of historical time, compelled to "face the music" after being captured by Israeli security forces in a daring extralegal mission right out of a spy novel or science fiction book. The trial received extraordinary press coverage in the United States. That summer, Gallup conducted a series of in-depth interviews with five hundred randomly selected residents of Oakland, California, and found that 84 percent of those sampled met the minimum criterion for awareness of this faraway event, a striking statistic, given American indifference to foreign affairs (Lipstadt, 1996: 212, n. 54). At least seven books were published about Eichmann and his trial in the following year (196).

The first legal confrontation with the Holocaust since Nuremburg, the trial was staged by Israel not to generalize away from the originating events but to get back to them. As Prime Minister Ben-Gurion put it, the trial would give "the generation that was born and educated after the Holocaust in Israel...an opportunity to get acquainted with the details of this tragedy about which they knew so little" (Braun, 1994: 183). The lessons were to be drawn from, and directed to, particular places and particular peoples, to Germany, the Nazis, Israel, and the Jews—in Ben-Gurion's words, to "the dimensions of the tragedy which *our people* experienced" (Lipstadt, 1996: 213, italics added). By the time it was over, however, the Eichmann trial paradoxically had initiated a massive universalization of Nazi evil, best captured by Hannah Arendt's enormously controversial insistence that the trial compelled recognition of the "banality of evil." This framing of Nazi guilt became highly influential, even as it was sharply and bitterly disputed by Jews and non-Jews alike. For as a banally evil person, Eichmann could be "everyman." Arendt herself had always wanted to make just such a point. In her earliest reaction to the Nazi murders, the philosopher had expressed horror and astonishment at the Nazis' absolute inhumanity. For this she was rebuked by her mentor and friend Karl Jaspers, who cautioned against making the Nazis into "monsters" and "supermen." To do so, Jaspers warned, would merely confirm the Nazis in their grandiose Nietzschean fantasies and relieve others of responsibility as well.[65] Because of Arendt's singular influence, the antagonists in the trauma began to seem not so different from anybody else.[66] The trial and its aftermath eventually became framed in a manner that narrowed the once great distance between postwar democratic audience and evil Nazis, connecting them rather than isolating them from one another. This connection between audience and antagonist intensified the trauma's tragic dramaturgy.

During this same period, other forces also had the effect of widening the circle of "perpetrators." Most spectacularly, there was Stanley Milgram's experiment demonstrating that ordinary, well-educated college students would "just follow the orders" of professional authority, even to the point of gravely endangering the lives of innocent people. These findings raised profoundly troubling questions about the "good nature" of all human beings and the democratic capacity of any human society. Milgram appeared on the cover of *Time* magazine, and "the Milgram experiment" became part of the folklore of the 1960s. It generalized the capacity for radical evil, first demonstrated by the Nazis, to the American population at large, synergistically interacting with the symbolic reconstruction of perpetrators that Arendt on Eichmann had begun. In one interview Milgram conducted with a volunteer after he had revealed to him the true nature of the experiment, the volunteer remarked: "As my wife said: 'You can call yourself Eichmann'" (quoted in Novick, 1999: 137).[67]

In the decades that followed, other powerful cultural reconstructions of the perpetrators followed in this wake. In 1992, Christopher Browning published a widely discussed historical ethnography called *Ordinary Men: Reserve Police Battalion 101 and the Final Solution in Poland* (Browning, 1992), which focused on the everyday actions and motives of Germans who were neither members of the professional military nor particularly ideological but who nonetheless carried out systematic and murderous cleansings of the Jews. When four years later Daniel Goldhagen published *Hitler's Willing Executioners: Ordinary Germans and the Holocaust* (1996), his aim was to shift blame back to what he described as the unprecedented and particular kind of anti-Semitism, what he called "eliminationist," of the Germans themselves. Browning's critical response to Goldhagen was based on historical evidence, but it also decried the moral particularity that Goldhagen's argument seemed to entail. Indeed, Browning connected his empirical findings about the "ordinariness" of perpetrators to the necessity for universalizing the moral implications of Nazi crimes, and in doing so he pointed all the way back to Milgram's earlier findings.

What allowed the Nazis to mobilize and harness the rest of society to the mass murder of European Jewry? Here I think that we historians need to turn to the insights of social psychology—the study of psychological reactions to social situations. . . . We must ask, what really is a human being? We must give up the comforting and distancing notions that the perpetrators of the Holocaust were fundamentally a different kind of people because they were products of a radically different culture. (Browning, 1996: A72)[68]

In the realm of popular culture, Steven Spielberg's blockbuster movie *Schindler's List* must also be considered in this light. In a subtle but unmistakable manner, the movie departicularizes the perpetrators by showing the possibilities that "even Germans" could be good.[69]

Losing Control of the Means of Symbolic Production

It was in this context of tragic transformation—as personalization of the drama increased identification beyond the Jewish victims themselves, and as the sense of moral culpability became fundamentally widened beyond the Nazis themselves—that the United States government, and the nation's authoritative interlocutors, lost control over the telling of the Holocaust story. When the American government and its allies defeated Nazi Germany in 1945 and seized control of strategic evidence from the death camps, they had taken control of the representation process away from the Nazis and assured that the Jewish mass murder would be presented an anti-Nazi way. In this telling of the story, naturally enough, the former Allies—America most powerfully but Britain and France as well—presented themselves as the moral protagonists, purifying themselves as heroic carriers of the good. As the 1960s unfolded, the Western democracies were forced to concede this dominant narrative position. This time around, however, control over the means of symbolic production changed hands as much for cultural reasons as by the force of arms.[70]

In the "critical years" from the mid-1960s to the end of the 1970s, the United States experienced a sharp decline in its political, military, and moral prestige. It was during this period that, in the eyes of tens of millions of Americans and others, the domestic and international opposition to America's prosecution of the Vietnam War transformed the nation, and especially its government and armed forces, into a symbol not of salvationary good but of apocalyptic evil. This transformation was intensified by other outcroppings of "the sixties," particularly the revolutionary impulses that emerged out of the student and black power movements inside the United States and guerilla movements outside it. These "real-world" problems allowed the United States to be identified in terms that had, up until that time, been reserved exclusively for the Nazi perpetrators of the Holocaust. According to the progressive narrative, it could only be the Allies' World War II enemy who represented radical evil. As America became "Amerika," however, napalm bombs were analogized with gas pellets and the flaming jungles of Vietnam with the gas chambers. The powerful American army that claimed to be prosecuting a "good war" against Vietnamese communists—in analogy with the lessons that Western democracies had learned in their earlier struggle against Nazism—came to be identified, by influential intellectuals and a wide swath of the educated Western public, as perpetrating genocide against the helpless and pathetic inhabits of Vietnam. Bertrand Russell and Jean-Paul Sartre established a kind of counter–"War Crimes Tribunal" to apply the logic of Nuremberg to the United States. Indefensible incidents of civilian killings, like the My Lai massacre of 1968, were represented, not as anomalous incidents, but as typifications of this new American-made tragedy.[71]

This process of material deconstruction and symbolic inversion further contributed to the universalization of the Holocaust: It allowed the moral criteria generated by its earlier interpretation to be applied in a less nationally specific and thus less particularistic way. This inversion undermined still further the progressive narrative under which the mass killings of the Jews had earlier been framed. For the ability to leave the trauma drama behind, and to press ahead toward the future, depended on the material and symbolic existence of an unsullied protagonist who could provide salvation for survivors by leading them into the promised land. "Vietnam" and "the sixties" undercut the main agent of this progressive narrative. The result was a dramatic decline in the confidence that a new world order could be constructed in opposition to violence and coercion; if the United States itself committed war crimes, what chance could there be for modern and democratic societies ever to leave mass murder safely behind?

As a result of these material and symbolic events, the contemporary representatives of the historic enemies of Nazism lost control over the means of symbolic production. The power to present itself as the purified protagonist in the worldwide struggle against evil slipped out of the hands of the American government and patriotic representatives more generally, even as the framing of the drama's triggering trauma shifted from progress to tragedy. The ability to cast and produce the trauma-drama, to compel identification and channel catharsis, spread to other nations and to antigovernment groups, and even to historic enemies of the Jewish people. The archetypical trauma-drama of the twentieth century became ever more generalized and more accessible, and the criteria for moral responsibility in social relations, once closely tied to American perspectives and interests, came to be defined in a more evenhanded, more egalitarian, more self-critical—in short, a more universalistic—way.

Perhaps the most visible and paradoxical effect of this loss of the American government's control over the means of symbolic production control was that the morality of American leadership in World War II came to be questioned in a manner that established polluting analogies with Nazism.[72] One issue that now became "troubling," for example, was the justification for the Allied firebombings of Dresden and Tokyo. The growing climate of relativism and reconfiguration threatened to undermine the coding, weighting, and narrating that once had provided a compelling rationale for those earlier events that were in themselves so massively destructive of civilian life. In a similar manner, but with much more significant repercussions, the symbolic implications of the atomic bombings of Hiroshima and Nagasaki began to be fundamentally reconfigured.

From being conceived as stages in the unfolding of the progressive narrative, influential groups of Westerners came to understand the atomic bombings as vast human tragedies. Younger generations of Americans, in fact, were increasingly responsive to the view of these events that had once been promoted exclusively by Japan, the fascist Axis power against which their elders had waged war. The interpretation of the suffering caused by the atomic bombings became separated from the historical specifics of time and place. With this generalization, the very events that had once appeared as high points of the progressive narrative came to be constructed as unjustifiable, as human tragedies, as slaughters of hundreds of thousands of innocent and pathetic human beings—in short, as typifications of a "Holocaust."[73]

Perhaps the most pointed example of what could happen after America lost control over the Holocaust story was the way in which its redemptive role in the narrative was challenged. Rather than being portrayed as the chief prosecutor of Nazi perpetrators—as chief prosecutor, the narrative's protagonist along with the victims themselves—the American and the British wartime governments were accused of having at least indirect responsibility for allowing the Nazis to carry out their brutal work. A steady stream of revisionist historical scholarship emerged, beginning in the 1970s, suggesting that the anti-Semitism of Roosevelt and Churchill and of American and British citizens had prevented them from acting to block the mass killings; for they had received authenticated information about German plans and activities as early as June 1942.[74]

This analogical linkage between the Allies and the perpetrators quickly became widely accepted as historical fact. On September 27, 1979, when the President's Commission on the Victims of the Holocaust issued a report recommending the American establishment of a Holocaust Museum, it listed as one of its primary justifications that such a public construction would give the American nation an opportunity to compensate for its early, "disastrous" indifference to the plight of the Jews (quoted in Linenthal, 1995: 37). When the museum itself was eventually constructed, it enshrined this inversion of the progressive narrative in the exhibitions themselves. The third floor of the museum is filled with powerfully negative images of the death camps, and is attached by an internal bridge to a tower whose rooms display actual artifacts from the camps. As visitors approach this bridge, in the midst of the iconic representations of evil, they confront a photomural of an U.S. Air Force intelligence photograph of Auschwitz-Birkenau, taken on May 31, 1944. The text attached to the mural informs visitors: "Two freight trains with Hungarian Jews arrived in Birkenau that day; the large-scale gassing of these Jews was beginning. The four Birkenau crematoria are visible at the top of the photograph" (quoted in Linenthal, 1995: 217). Placed next to the photomural is what the principal ethnographer of the museum project, Edward Linenthal, has called "an artifactual indictment of American indifference." It is a letter, dated August 14, 1944, from John J. McCloy, assistant secretary of war. According to the text, McCloy "rejected a request by the World Jewish Congress to bomb the Auschwitz concentration camp." This rejection is framed in the context not of physical impossibility, or in terms of the vicissitudes of a world war, but as the result of moral diminution. Visitors are informed that the U.S. Air Force "could have bombed Auschwitz as early as May 1944," since U.S. bombers had "struck Buna, a synthetic-rubber works relying on slave labor, located less than five miles east of Auschwitz-Birkenau." But despite this physical possibility, the text goes on to note, the death camp "remained untouched." The effective alignment of Allied armies with Nazi perpetrators is more than implicit: "Although bombing Auschwitz would have killed many prisoners, it would also have halted the operation of the gas chambers and, ultimately, saved the lives of many more" (quoted in Linenthal, 1995: 217–18). This authoritative reconstruction, it is important to emphasize, is not a brute empirical fact, any more than the framework that had previous sway. In fact, within the discipline of American history, the issue of Allied indifference remains subject to intensive debate (Linenthal, 1995: 219–24).[75] At every point in the construction of a public discourse, factual chronicles must be encased in symbolically coded and narrated frames.

Eventually, this revision of the progressive narrative about exclusively Nazi perpetrators extended, with perhaps even more profound consequences, to other Allied powers and to the neutrals in that earlier conflict as well. As the charismatic symbol of French resistance to German occupation, Charles de Gaulle had woven a narrative, during and after the war, that purified his nation by describing it as first the victim and later the courageous opponent of Nazi domination and the "foreign" collaborators in Vichy.[76] By the late 1970s and 1980s, however, a younger generation of French and non-French historians challenged this definition, seriously polluting the earlier Republican government, and even some of its postwar socialist successors, by documenting massive French collaboration with the antidemocratic, anti-Semitic regime.[77]

In the wake of these reversals, it seemed only a matter of time until the nations who had been "neutral" during the earlier conflict would also be forced to relinquish symbolic control over how their own stories were told, at least in the theatre of Western opinion, if not on their own national stage. Austria, for example, had long depicted itself as a helpless victim of Nazi Germany. When Kurt Waldheim ascended to the position of secretary-general of the United Nations, however, his hidden association with the Hitler regime was revealed, and the symbolic status of the Austrian nation, which rallied behind their ex-president, began to be publicly polluted as a result.[78] Less than a decade later, Switzerland became subject to similar inversion of its symbolic fortunes. The tiny republic had prided itself on its long history of decentralized canton democracy and the benevolent, universalizing neutrality of its Red Cross. In the mid-nineties, journalists and historians documented that the wartime Swiss government had "purified" Nazi gold. In return for gold that had been plundered from the bodies of condemned and already dead Jews, Swiss bankers gave to Nazi authorities acceptable, unmarked currency that could much more readily be used to finance the war.

This discussion of how the non-Jewish agents of the progressive narrative were undercut by "real-world" developments would be incomplete without some mention of how the Israeli government, which represented the other principal agent of the early, progressive Holocaust story, also came to be threatened with symbolic reconfiguration. The rise of Palestinian liberation movements inverted the Jewish nation's progressive myth of origin, for it suggested, at least to more liberally inclined groups, an equation between Nazi and Israeli treatment of subordinate ethnic and religious groups. The battle for cultural position was not, of course, given up without a fight. When Helmut Schmidt, chancellor of West Germany, spoke of Palestinian rights, Menachem Begin, prime minister of Israel, retorted that Schmidt, a Wehrmacht officer in World War II, had "remained faithful to Hitler until the last moment," insisting that the Palestine Liberation Organization was a "neo-Nazi organization" (quoted in Novick, 1994: 161). This symbolic inversion vis-à-vis the newly generalized and reconfigured Holocaust symbol was deepened by the not-unrelated complicity of Israel in the massacres that followed the Lebanon invasion and by the documented reports of Palestinian torture and occasional death in Israeli prisons.

The Holocaust as Bridging Metaphor

Each of the cultural transformations and social processes I have described has had the effect of universalizing the moral questions provoked by the mass killings of the Jews, of detaching the issues surrounding the systematic exercise of violence against ethnic groups from any particular ethnicity, religion, nationality, time, or place. These processes of detachment and deepening emotional identification are thoroughly intertwined. If the Holocaust were not conceived as a tragedy, it would not attract such continuous, even obsessive attention; this attention would not be rewarded, in turn, if the Holocaust were not understood in a detached and universalizing way. Symbolic extension and emotional identification both are necessary if the audience for a trauma, and its social relevance, are to be dramatically enlarged. I will call the effects of this enlargement the "engorgement of evil."

Norms provide standards for moral judgment. What is defined as evil in any historical period provides the most transcendental content for such judgments. What Kant called radical evil, and what I have called here, drawing on Durkheim, sacred-evil, refers to something considered absolutely essential to defining the good "in our time." Insofar as the "Holocaust" came to define inhumanity in our time, then, it served a fundamental moral function. "Post-Holocaust morality"[79] could perform this role, however, only in a sociological way: it became a bridging metaphor that social groups of uneven power and legitimacy applied to parse ongoing events as good and evil in real historical time. What the "Holocaust" named as the most fundamental evil was the intentional, systematic, and organized employment of violence against members of a stigmatized collective group, whether defined in a primordial or an ideological way. Not only did this representation identify as radical evil the perpetrators and their actions but it polluted bystanders as well. According to the standards of post-Holocaust morality, one became normatively required to make an effort to intervene against any holocaust, regardless of personal consequences and cost. For as a crime against humanity, a "holocaust" is taken to be a threat to the continuing existence of humanity itself. It is impossible, in this sense, to imagine a sacrifice that would be too great when humanity itself is at stake.[80]

Despite the moral content of the Holocaust symbol, then, the primary, first-order effects of this sacred-evil do not work in a ratiocinative way. Radical evil is a philosophical term, and it suggests that evil's moral content can be defined and discussed rationally. Sacred-evil, by contrast, is a sociological term, and it suggests that defining radical evil, and applying it, involves motives and relationships, and institutions, that work more like those associated with religious institutions than with ethical doctrine. In order for a prohibited social action to be powerfully moralized, the symbol of this evil must become engorged. An engorged evil overflows with badness. Evil becomes labile and liquid; it drips and seeps, ruining everything it touches. Under the sign of the tragic narrative, the Holocaust did become engorged, and its seepage polluted everything with which it came into contact.

Metonymy

This contact pollution established the basis for what might be called metonymic guilt. Under the progressive narrative, guilt for the genocidal mass killings depended on being directly and narrowly responsible in the legal sense worked out and applied at the Nuremberg trials. It was not a matter simply of being "associated" with mass murders. In this legal framework, any notion of collective responsibility, the guilt of the Nazi party, the German government, much less the German nation, was ruled as unfair, as out of bounds. But as the Holocaust became engorged with evil, and as post-Holocaust morality developed, guilt could no longer be so narrowly confined. Guilt now came from simple propinquity, in semiotic terms from metonymic association.

To be guilty of sacred-evil did not mean, anymore, that one had committed a legal crime. It was about the imputation of a moral one. One cannot defend oneself against an imputed moral crime by pointing to exculpating circumstances or lack of direct involvement. The issue is one of pollution, guilt by actual association. The solution is not the rational demonstration of innocence but ritual cleansing: purification. In the face of metonymic association with evil, one must engage in performative actions, not only in ratiocinative, cognitive arguments. As the "moral conscience of Germany," the philosopher Jürgen Habermas, put it during the now famous *Historichstreich* among German historians during the 1980s, the point is to "attempt to expel shame," not to engage in "empty phrases" (quoted in Kampe, 1987: 63). One must *do* justice and *be* righteousness. This performative purification is achieved by returning to the past, entering symbolically into the tragedy, and developing a new relation to the archetypal characters and crimes. Habermas wrote that it was "only after and through Auschwitz" that postwar Germany could once again attach itself "to the political culture of the West" (quoted in Kampe, 1987: 63). Retrospection is an effective path toward purification because it provides for catharsis, although of course it doesn't guarantee it. The evidence for having achieved catharsis is confession. If there is neither the acknowledgment of guilt nor sincere apology, punishment in the legal sense may be prevented, but the symbolic and moral taint will always remain.

Once the trauma had been dramatized as a tragic event in human history, the engorgement of evil compelled contemporaries to return to the originating trauma-drama and to rejudge every individual or collective entity who was, or might have been, even remotely involved. Many individual reputations became sullied in this way. The list of once admired figures who were "outed" as apologists for, or participants in, the anti-Jewish mass murders stretched from such philosophers as Martin Heidegger to such literary figures as Paul de Man and such political leaders as Kurt Waldheim. In the defenses mounted by these tarnished figures or their supporters, the suggestion was never advanced that the Holocaust does not incarnate evil—an inhibition that implicitly reveals the trauma's engorged, sacred quality. The only possible defense was that the accused had, in fact, never been associated with the trauma in any way.

More than two decades ago, the U.S. Justice Department established the Office of Special Investigation, the sole purpose of which was to track down and expel not only major but also minor figures who had been associated in some manner with Holocaust crimes. Since then, the bitter denunciations of deportation hearings have echoed throughout virtually every Western country. In such proceedings, the emotional-cum-normative imperative is to assert the moral requirements for humanity. Media stories revolve around questions of the "normal," as in how could somebody who seems like a human being, who since World War II has been an upstanding member of the (French, American, Argentinian) community, have ever been involved in what now is universally regarded as an antihuman event? Issues of legality are often overlooked, for the issue is purification of the community through expulsion of a polluted object.[81] Frequently, those who are so polluted give up without a fight. In the spate of recent disclosures about Jewish art appropriated by Nazis and currently belonging to Western museums, directors have responded simply by asking for time to catalogue the marked holdings to make them available to be retrieved.

Analogy

The direct, metonymic association with Nazi crimes is the most overt effect of the way evil seeps from the engorged Holocaust symbol, but it is not the cultural process most often employed. The bridging metaphor works much more typically, and profoundly, through the device of analogy. In the 1960s and 1970s, such analogical bridging powerfully contributed to a fundamental revision in moral understandings of the historical treatment of minorities inside the United States. Critics of earlier American policy, and representatives of minority groups themselves, began to suggest analogies between various minority "victims" of white American expansion and the Jewish victims of the Holocaust. This was particularly true of Native Americans, who argued that genocide had been committed against them, an idea that gained wide currency and that eventually generated massive efforts at legal repair and monetary payments.[82] Another striking example of this domestic inversion was the dramatic reconfiguration, in the 1970s and 1980s, of the American government's internment of Japanese-American citizens during World War II. Parallels between this action and Nazi prejudice and exclusion became widespread, and the internment camps became reconfigured as concentration camps. What followed from this symbolic transformation were not only formal governmental "apologies" to the Japanese-American people but also actual monetary "reparations."

In the 1980s, the engorged, free-floating Holocaust symbol became analogically associated with the movement against nuclear power and nuclear testing and, more generally, with the ecological movements that emerged during that time. Politicians and intellectuals gained influence in their campaigns against the testing and deployment of nuclear weapons by telling stories about the "nuclear holocaust" that would be unleashed if their own, democratic governments continued their nuclear policies. By invoking this Holocaust-inspired narrative, they were imagining a disaster that would have such generalized, supranational effects that the historical particularities of ideological rightness and wrongness, winners and losers, would no longer matter. In a similar manner, the activists' evocative depictions of the "nuclear winter" that would result from the nuclear holocaust gained striking support from the images of "Auschwitz," the iconic representations of which were rapidly becoming a universal medium for expressing demented violence, abject human suffering, and "meaningless" death. In the environmental movement, claims were advanced that the industrial societies were committing "ecological genocide" against species of plant and animal life and that there was a danger that Earth itself would be exterminated.

In the 1990s, the evil that seeped from the engorged metaphor provided the most compelling analogical framework for framing the Balkan events. While there certainly was dispute over which historical signifier of violence would provide the "correct" analogical reference—dictatorial purge, ethnic rampage, civil war, ethnic cleansing, or genocide—it was the engorged Holocaust symbol that propelled first American diplomatic and then American-European military intervention against Serbian ethnic violence.[83] The part played by this symbolic analogy was demonstrated during the early U.S. Senate debate in 1992. Citing "atrocities" attributed to Serbian forces, Senator Joseph Lieberman told reporters that "we hear echoes of conflicts in Europe little more than fifty years ago." During the same period, the Democratic presidential nominee, Bill Clinton, asserted that "history has shown us that you can't allow the mass extermination of people and just sit by and watch it happen." The candidate promised, if elected, to "begin with air power against the Serbs to try to restore the basic conditions of humanity," employing antipathy to distance himself from the polluting passivity that had retrospectively been attributed to the Allies during the initial trauma-drama itself (quoted in *Congressional Quarterly*, August 8, 1992: 2374). While President Clinton initially proved more reluctant than candidate Clinton to put this metaphorical linkage into material form—with the resulting deaths of tens of thousands of innocents—it was the threat of just such military deployment that eventually forced Serbia to sign the Dayton Accords and to stop what were widely represented, in the American and European media, as its genocidal activities in Bosnia and Herzogovina.

When the Serbians threatened to enter Kosovo, the allied bombing campaign was initiated and justified by evoking the same symbolic analogies and antipathies. The military attacks were represented as responding to the widely experienced horror that the trauma-drama of the Holocaust was being reenacted "before our very eyes." Speaking to a veterans' group at the height of the bombing campaign, President Clinton engaged in analogical bridging to explain why the current Balkan confrontation should not be understood, and thus tolerated, as "the inevitable result…of centuries-old animosities." He insisted that these murderous events were unprecedented because they were a "systematic slaughter," carried out by "people with organized, political and military power," under the exclusive control of a ruthless dictator, Slobodan Milosevic. "You think the Germans would have perpetrated the Holocaust on their own without Hitler? Was there something in the history of the German race that made them do this? No. We've got to get straight about this. This is something political leaders do" (*New York Times,* May 14, 1999: A 12).

The same day in Germany, Joschka Fischer, foreign minister in the coalition "Red-Green" government, appeared before a special congress of his Green Party to defend the allied air campaign. He, too, insisted that the uniqueness of Serbian evil made it possible to draw analogies with the Holocaust. Fischer's deputy foreign minister and party ally, Ludger Volmer, drew rousing applause when, in describing President Milosevic's systematic cleansing policy, he declared: "My friends, there is only one word for this, and that word is Fascism." A leading opponent of the military intervention tried to block the bridging process by symbolic antipathy. "We are against drawing comparisons between the murderous Milosevic regime and the Holocaust," he proclaimed, because "doing so would mean an unacceptable diminishment of the horror of Nazi Fascism and the genocide against European Jews." Arguing that the Kosovars were not the Jews and Milosevic not Hitler protected the sacred-evil of the Holocaust, but the attempted antipathy was ultimately unconvincing. About 60 percent of the Green Party delegates believed the analogies were valid and voted to support Fischer's position.[84]

Two weeks later, when the allied bombing campaign had not yet succeeded in bringing Milosevic to heel, President Clinton asked Elie Wiesel to make a three-day tour of the Kosovar Albanians' refugee camps. A spokesperson for the U.S. embassy in Macedonia explained that "people have lost focus on why we are doing what we are doing" in the bombing campaign.

The proper analogy, in other words, was not being consistently made. The solution was to create direct, metonymic association. "You need a person like Wiesel," the spokesperson continued, "to keep your moral philosophy on track." In the lead sentence of its report on the tour, the *New York Times* described Wiesel as "the Holocaust survivor and Nobel Peace Prize winner." Despite Wiesel's own assertion that "I don't believe in drawing analogies," after visiting the camps analogizing was precisely the rhetoric in which he engaged. Wiesel declared that "I've learned something from my experiences as a contemporary of so many events." What he had learned was to apply the post-Holocaust morality derived from the originating trauma-drama: "When evil shows its face, you don't wait, you don't let it gain strength. You must intervene" (Rohde, 1999: 1).

During that tour of a camp in Macedonia, Elie Wiesel had insisted that "the world had changed fifty years after the Holocaust" and that "Washington's response in Kosovo was far better than the ambivalence it showed during the Holocaust." When, two weeks later, the air war, and the growing threat of a ground invasion, finally succeeded in expelling the Serbian forces from Kosovo, the *New York Times* "Week in Review" section reiterated the famous survivor's confidence that the Holocaust trauma had not been in vain, that the drama erected on its ashes had fundamentally changed the world, or at least the West. The Kosovo war had demonstrated that analogies were valid and that the lessons of post-Holocaust morality could be carried out in the most utterly practical way.

> It was a signal week for the West, no doubt about it. Fifty-four years after the Holocaust revelations, America and Europe had finally said "enough," and struck a blow against a revival of genocide. Serbian ethnic cleansers were now routed; ethnic Albanians would be spared further murders and rapes. Germany was exorcising a few of its Nazi ghosts. Human rights had been elevated to a military priority and a pre-eminent Western value. (Wines, 1999: 1)

Twenty-two months later, after Western support has facilitated the electoral defeat of Milosevic and the accession to the Yugoslav presidency of the reformer Vojilslav Kostunica, the former Serbian president and accused war criminal was arrested and forcably taken to jail. While President Kostunica did not personally subscribe to the authority of the war crimes tribunal in The

Hague, there was little doubt that he had authorized Milosevic's imprisonment under intensive American pressure. Though initiated by the Congress rather than the U.S. president, George W. Bush responded to the arrest by Holocaust typification. He spoke of the "chilling images of terrified women and children herded into trains, emaciated prisoners interned behind barbed wire and mass graves unearthed by United Nations investigators," all traceable to Milosevic's "brutal dicatorship" (quoted in Perlez, 2001: 6). Even among those Serbian intellectuals, like Aleksa Djilas, who criticized the Hague tribunal as essentially a political and thus particularistic court, there was recognition that the events took place within a symbolic framework that would inevitably universalize them and contribute to the possibility of a new moral order on a less particularist scale. "There will be a blessing in disguise through his trial," Djilas told a reporter on the day after Milosevic's arrest. "Some kind of new international order is being constructed, intentionally or not.... Something will crystallize: what kinds of nationalism are justified or not, what kinds of intervention are justified or not, how much are great powers entitled to respond, and how. It will not be a sterile exercise" (Erlanger, 2001: 8).

In the 1940s, the mass murder of the Jews had been viewed as a typification of the Nazi war machine, an identification that had limited its moral implications. Fifty years later, the Holocaust itself had displaced its historical context. It had itself become the master symbol of evil in relation to which new instances of grievous mass injury would be typified.[85]

Legality

As the rhetoric of this triumphant declaration indicates, the generalization of the Holocaust trauma-drama has found expression in the new vocabulary of "universal human rights." In some part, this trope has simply degendered the Enlightenment commitment to "the universal rights of man" first formulated in the French Revolution. In some other part, it blurs the issue of genocide with social demands for health and basic economic subsistence. Yet from the beginning of its systematic employment in the postwar period, the phrase has also referred specifically to a new legal standard for international behavior that would simultaneously generalize and make more precise and binding what came to be regarded as the "lessons" of the Holocaust events. Representatives of various organizations, both governmental and nongovernmental, have made sporadic but persistent efforts to formulate specific, morally binding codes, and eventually international laws, to institutionalize the moral judgments triggered by metonymic and analogic association with the engorged symbol of evil. This possibility has inspired the noted legal theorist Martha Minow to suggest an unorthodox answer to the familiar question: "Will the twentieth century be most remembered for its mass atrocities?"

> A century marked by human slaughter and torture, sadly, is not a unique century in human history. Perhaps more unusual than the facts of genocides and regimes of torture marking this era is the invention of new and distinctive legal forms of response. (Minow, 1998: 1)

This generalizing process began at Nuremberg in 1945, when the long-planned trial of Nazi war leaders was expanded to include the moral principle that certain heinous acts are "crimes against humanity" and must be recognized as such by everyone (Drinan, 1987: 334). In its first report on those indictments, the *New York Times* insisted that while "the authority of this tribunal to inflict punishment is directly derived from victory in war," it derived "indirectly from an intangible but nevertheless very real factor which might be called the dawn of a world conscience" (October 9, 1945: 20). This universalizing process continued the following year, when the United Nations General Assembly adopted Resolution 95, committing the international body to "the principles of international law recognized by the charter of the Nuremberg Tribunal and the judgment of the Tribunal" (quoted in Drinan, 1987: 334).[86] Two years later, the United Nations issued the Universal Declaration of Human Rights, whose opening preamble evoked the memory of "barbarous acts which have outraged the conscience of mankind."[87] In 1950, the International Law Commission of the United Nations adopted a statement spelling out the principles that the Declaration implied. "The core of these principles states that leaders and nations can be punished for their violations of international law and for their crimes against humanity. In addition, it is not a defense for a person to state that he or she was required to do what was done because of an order from a military or civilian superior" (quoted in Drinan, 1987: 334).

In the years since, despite President Truman's recommendation that the United States draft a code of international criminal law around these principles, despite the "human rights" foreign policy of a later Democratic president, Jimmy Carter, and despite the nineteen UN treaties and covenants condemning genocide and exalting the new mandate for human rights, new international legal codes were never drafted (Drinan, 1987: 334). Still, over the same period, an increasingly thick body of "customary law" was developed that militated *against* nonintervention in the affairs of sovereign states when they engage in systematic human rights violations.

> The long-term historical significance of the rights revolution of the last fifty years is that it has begun to erode the sanctity of state sovereignty and to justify effective political and military intervention. Would there have been American intervention in Bosnia without nearly fifty years of accumulated international opinion to the effect that there are crimes against humanity and violations of human rights which must be punished wherever they arise? Would there be a safe haven for the Kurds in northern Iraq? Would we be in Kosovo? (Ignatieff, 1999: 62)[88]

When the former Chilean dictator Augusto Pinochet was arrested in Britain and detained for more than a year in response to an extradition request by a judge in Spain, the reach of this customary law and its possible enforcement by national police first became crystallized in the global public sphere. It was at about the same time that the first internationally sanctioned War Crimes Tribunal since Nuremberg began meeting in The Hague to prosecute those who had violated human rights on any and all sides of the decade's Balkan wars.

The Dilemma of Uniqueness

As the engorged symbol bridging the distance between radical evil and what at some earlier point was considered normal or normally criminal behavior, the reconstructed Holocaust trauma became enmeshed in what might be called the dilemma of uniqueness. The trauma-drama could not function as a metaphor of archetypal tragedy unless it were regarded as radically different from any other evil act in modern times. Yet it was this very status—as a unique event—that eventually compelled it to become generalized and departicularized. For as a metaphor for radical evil, the Holocaust provided a standard of evaluation for judging the evility of other threatening acts. By providing such a standard for comparative judgment, the Holocaust became a norm, initiating a succession of metonymic, analogic, and legal evaluations that deprived it of "uniqueness" by establishing its degrees of likeness or unlikeness to other possible manifestations of evility.

In this regard, it is certainly ironic that this bridging process, so central to universalizing critical moral judgment in the post-Holocaust world, has time after time been attacked as depriving the Holocaust of its significance. Yet these very attacks have often revealed, despite themselves, the trauma-drama's new centrality in ordinary thought and action. One historically oriented critic, for example, mocked the new "Holocaust consciousness" in the United States, citing the fact that the Holocaust "is invoked as reference point in discussions of everything from AIDS to abortion" (Novick, 1994: 159). A literature professor complained about the fact that "the language of 'Holocaust'" is now "regularly invoked by people who want to draw public attention to human-rights abuses, social inequalities suffered by racial and ethnic minorities and women, environmental disasters, AIDS, and a whole host of other things" (Rosenfeld, 1995: 35). Another scholar decried the fact that "any evil that befalls anyone anywhere becomes a Holocaust" (quoted in Rosenfeld, 1995: 35).[89]

While no doubt well-intentioned in a moral sense, such complaints miss the sociological complexities that underlie the kind of cultural-moral process I am exploring here. Evoking the Holocaust to measure the evil of a non-Holocaust event is nothing more, and nothing less, than to employ a powerful bridging metaphor to make sense of social life. The effort to qualify as the referent of this metaphor is bound to entail sharp social conflict, and in this sense social relativization, for successful metaphorical embodiment brings legitimacy and resources. The premise of these relativizing social conflicts is that the Holocaust provides an absolute and nonrelative measure of evil. But the effects of the conflict are to relativize the application of this standard to any particular social event. The Holocaust is unique and not unique at the same time. This insoluble dilemma marks the life history of the Holocaust, once it had become a tragic archetype and a central component of moral judgment in our time.[90] Inga Clendinnen has described this dilemma in a particularly acute way, and her observations exemplify the metaphorical bridging process I have tried to describe here.

> There have been too many recent horrors, in Rwanda, in Burundi, in one-time Yugoslavia, with victims equally innocent, killers and torturers equally devoted, to ascribe uniqueness to any one set of atrocities on the grounds of their exemplary cruelty. I find the near-random terror practiced by the Argentinean military, especially

their penchant for torturing children before their parents, to be as horrible, as "unimaginable," as the horrible and unimaginable things done by Germans to their Jewish compatriots. Certainly the scale is different—but how much does scale matter to the individual perpetrator or the individual victim?

Again, the willful obliteration of long-enduring communities is surely a vast offence, but for three years we watched the carpet-bombings of Cambodia, when the bombs fell on villagers who could not have had the least understanding of the nature of their offence. *When we think of innocence afflicted, we see those unforgettable children of the Holocaust staring wide-eyed into the camera of their killers, but we also see the image of the little Vietnamese girl, naked, screaming, running down a dusty road, her back aflame with American napalm.* If we grant that "holocaust," the total consumption of offerings by fire, is sinisterly appropriate for the murder of those millions who found their only graves in the air, it is equally appropriate for the victims of Hiroshima, Nagasaki and Dresden [and for] Picasso's horses and humans screaming [in *Guernica*] under attack from untouchable murderers in the sky. (Clendinnen, 1999: 14, italics added)

Forgetting or Remembering?

Routinization and Institutionalizaton

As the sense that the Holocaust was a unique event in human history crystallized and its moral implications became paradoxically generalized, the tragic trauma-drama became increasingly subject to memorialization. Special research centers were funded to investigate its most minute details and to sponsor debates about its wider applications. College courses were devoted to it, and everything, from university chairs to streets and parks, was named for it. Monuments were constructed to honor the tragedy's victims. Major urban centers in the United States, and many outside it as well, constructed vastly expensive, and vastly expansive, museums to make permanent its moral lessons. The U.S. military distributed instructions for conducting "Days of Remembrance," and commemorative ceremonies were held annually in the Capitol Rotunda.

Because of the dilemma of uniqueness, all of these generalizing processes were controversial; they suggested to many observers that the Holocaust was being instrumentalized and commodified, that its morality and affect were being displaced by specialists in profit-making on the one hand and by specialists in merely cognitive expertise on the other. In recent years, indeed, the idea has grown that the charisma of the original trauma-drama is being routinized in a regrettably, but predictably, Weberian way.[91]

The moral learning process that I have described in the preceding pages does not necessarily deny the possibility that instrumentalization develops *after* a trauma-drama has been created and *after* its moral lessons have been externalized and internalized. In American history, for example, even the most sacred of the founding national traumas, the Revolution and the Civil War, have faded as objects of communal affect and collective remembering, and the dramas associated with them have become commodified as well. Still, the implications of what I have presented here suggest that such routinization, even when it takes a monetized and commodity form, does not necessarily indicate meaninglessness. Metaphorical bridging shifts symbolic significance, and audience attention, from the originating trauma to the traumas that follow in a sequence of analogical associations. But it does not, for that, inevitably erase or invert the meanings associated with the trauma that was first in the associational line. Nor does the effort to concretize the cultural meanings of the trauma in monumental forms have this effect. The American Revolution and the Civil War both remain resources for triumphant and tragic narration, in popular and high culture venues. It is only very infrequently, and very controversially, that these trauma-dramas are subjected to the kind of comic framing that would invert their still sacred place in American collective identity. As I have mentioned earlier, it is not commodification, but "comedization"—a change in the cultural framing, not a change in economic status—that indicates trivialization and forgetting.

Memorials and Museums: Crystallizing Collective Sentiment

A less Weberian, more Durkheimian understanding of routinization is needed. When they are first created, sacred-good and sacred-evil are labile and liquid. Objectification can point to the sturdier embodiment of these moral values, and even of the experiences they imply. Currently, the intensifying momentum to memorialize the Holocaust indicates a deepening institutionalization of its moral lessons and the continued recalling of its dramatic experiences rather than their routinization and forgetting. When, after years of conflict, the German parliament approved a plan for erecting a vast memorial of two thousand stone pillars to the victims of the Holocaust in the heart of Berlin, a leading politician proclaimed: "We are not building this monument solely for the Jews. We are building it for ourselves. It will help us confront a chapter in our history" (Cohen, 1999: 3).

In the Holocaust museums that are sprouting up throughout the Western world, the design is not to distance the viewer from the object in a dry, deracinated, or "purely factual" way. To the contrary, as a European researcher into this phenomenon has remarked, "Holocaust museums favor strategies designed to arouse strong emotions and particular immersion of the visitor into the past" (Baer, 1999).[92] The informational brochure to the Simon Wiesenthal Museum of Tolerance in Los Angeles, which houses the West Coast's largest Holocaust exhibition, promotes itself as a "high tech, hands-on experiential museum that focuses on...themes through interactive exhibits" (Baer, 1999).

From its very inception in 1979, the Holocaust Museum in Washington, D.C., was metonymically connected to the engorged symbolism of evil. According to the official report submitted to President Jimmy Carter by the President's Commission on the Victims of the Holocaust, the purpose of the museum was to "protect against future evil" (quoted in Linenthal, 1995: 37). The goal was to create a building through which visitors would reexperience the original tragedy, to find "a means," as some central staff members had once put it, "to convey both dramatically and soberly the enormity of the human tragedy in the death camps" (quoted in Linenthal, 1995: 212).[93] Rather than instrumentalizing or commodifying, in other words, the construction was conceived as a critical means for deepening psychological identification and broadening symbolic extension. According to the ethnographer of the fifteen-year planning and construction process, the design team insisted that the museum's interior mood should be so "visceral" that museum visitors "would gain no respite from the narrative."

> The feel and rhythm of space and the setting of mood were important. [The designers] identified different qualities of space that helped to mediate the narrative: constructive space on the third floor, for example, where as visitors enter the world of the death camps, the space becomes tight and mean, with a feeling of heavy

darkness. Indeed, walls were not painted, pipes were left exposed, and, except for fire exits and hidden elevators on the fourth and third floors for people who, for one reason or another, had to leave, there is no escape (Linenthal, 1995: 169–70)

According to the Museum's head designer, the exhibition was intended to take visitors on a journey:

> We followed those people under all that pressure as they moved from their normal lives into ghettos, out of ghettos onto trains, from trains to camps, within the pathways of the camps, until finally to the end.... If visitors could take that same journey, they would understand the story because they will have experienced the story. (quoted in Linenthal, 1995: 170)[94]

The dramatization of the tragic journey is in many respects quite literal, and this fosters identification. The visitor receives a photo passport/identity card representing a victim of the Holocaust, and the museum's permanent exhibition is divided into chronological sections. The fourth floor is "The Assault: 1933–39," the third floor "The Holocaust: 1940–44," and the second floor "Bearing Witness: 1945." At the end of each floor, visitors are asked to insert their passports to find out what happened to their identity-card "alter egos" during that particular phase of the Holocaust tragedy. By the time visitors have passed through the entire exhibit, they will know whether or not the person with whom they have been symbolically identified survived the horror or perished.

The identification process is deepened by the dramatic technique of personalization. The key, in the words of the project director, was connecting museum visitors to the "real faces of real people" (Linenthal, 1995: 181).[95]

> Faces of Holocaust victims in the exhibition are shattering in their power.... Polish school teachers, moments before their execution, look at visitors in agony, sullen anger, and despair.... Two brothers, dressed alike in matching coats and caps, fear etched on their faces, gaze at the camera, into the eyes of the visitors.... The faces... assault, challenge, accuse, and profoundly sadden visitors throughout the exhibition. (Linenthal, 1995: 174)[96]

At every point, design decisions about dramatization were made with the narrative of tragedy firmly in mind. Exhibit designers carefully avoided displaying any of the camp prisoners' "passive resistance," for fear it would trigger progressive narratives of heroism and romance. As a historian associated with such decisions remarked, the fear was that such displays might contribute to an "epic" Holocaust narrative in which resistance would gain "equal time" with the narrative of destruction (in Linenthal, 1995: 192). This dark dramatization, however, could not descend into a mere series of grossly displayed horrors, for this would undermine the identification on which the very communication of the tragic lessons of the Holocaust would depend.

> The design team faced a difficult decision regarding the presentation of horror. Why put so much effort into constructing an exhibition that was so horrible that people would not visit? They worried about word-of-mouth evaluation after opening, and feared that the first visitors would tell family and friends, "Don't go, it's too horrible."... The museum's mission was to teach people about the Holocaust and bring about civic transformation; yet... the public had to *desire* to visit. (198, italics in original)

It seems evident that such memorializations aim to create structures that dramatize the tragedy of the Holocaust and provide opportunities for contemporaries, now so far removed from the original scene, powerfully to reexperience it. In these efforts, personalization remains an immensely important dramatic vehicle, and it continues to provide the opportunity for identification so crucial to the project of universalization. In each Holocaust museum, the fate of the Jews functions as a metaphorical bridge to the treatment of other ethnic, religious, and racial minorities.[97] The aim is manifestly not to "promote" the Holocaust as an important event in earlier historical time, but to contribute to the possibilities of pluralism and justice in the world of today.

From Liberators to Survivors: Witness Testimonies

Routinization of charisma is certainly an inevitable fact of social life, and memorialization a much-preferred way to understand that it can institutionalize, and not only undermine, the labile collective sentiments that once circulated in a liquid form. It is important also not to view the outcome of such processes in a naturalistic, noncultural way. It is not "meaning" that is crystallized but particular meanings. In terms of Holocaust memorialization and routinization, it is the objectification of a narrative about tragedy that has been memorialized, not a narrative about progress.

The postwar memorials to World War II were, and are, about heroism and liberation. They centered on American GIs and the victims they helped. If the Holocaust had continued to be narrated within the progressive framework of the anti-Nazi war, it would no doubt have been memorialized in much the same way. Of course, the very effect of the progressive narrative was to make the Holocaust less visible and central, with the result that, as long as representations of contemporary history remained within the progressive framework, few efforts to memorialize the Holocaust were made. For that very reason, the few that were attempted are highly revealing. In Liberty State Park, in New Jersey, within visual sight of the proud and patriotic Statue of Liberty, there stands a statue called *Liberation*. The metal sculpture portrays two figures. The larger, a solemn American GI, walks deliberately forward, his eyes on the ground. He cradles a smaller figure, a concentration camp victim, whose skeletal chest, shredded prison garb, outstretched arms, and vacantly staring eyes exemplify his helplessness (Young, 1993: 320–32). Commissioned not only by the State of New Jersey but also by a coalition of American Legion and other veterans' organizations, the monument was dedicated only in 1985. During the ceremony, the state's governor made a speech seeking to reconnect the progressive narrative still embodied by the "last good war" to the growing centrality of the Holocaust narrative, whose symbolic and moral importance had by then already begun far to outstrip it. The defensive and patriotic tone of the speech indicates that, via this symbolic linkage, the state official sought to resist the skepticism about America's place in the world, the very critical attitude that had helped frame the Holocaust in a narrative of tragedy.

> To me, this monument is an affirmation of my American heritage. It causes me to feel deep pride in my American values. The monument says that we, as a collective people, stand for freedom. We, as Americans, are not oppressors, and we, as Americans, do not engage in military conflict for the purpose of conquest. Our role in the world is to preserve and promote that precious, precious thing that we consider to be a free democracy. Today we will remember those who gave their lives for freedom. (321)

The *Liberation* monument, and the particularist and progressive sentiments it crystallized, could not be further removed from the memorial processes that have crystallized in the years since. Propelled by the tragic transformation of the Jewish mass murder, in these memorials the actions and beliefs of Americans are often implicitly analogized with those of the perpetrators, and the U.S. army's liberation of the camps plays only a minimal role, if any. In these more universalized settings, the focus is on the broader, world-historical causes and moral implications of the tragic event, on creating symbolic extension by providing opportunities for contemporaries to experience emotional identification with the suffering of the victims.

It was in the context of this transformation that there emerged a new genre of Holocaust writing and memorializing, one that focuses on a new kind of historical evidence, direct "testimony," and a new kind of historical actor, the "survivor." Defined as persons who lived through the camp experiences, survivors provide a tactile link with the tragic event. As their social and personal role was defined, they began to write books, give speeches to local and national communities, and record their memories of camp experiences on tape and video. These testimonies have become sacralized repositories of the core tragic experience, with all the moral implications that this suffering has come to entail. They have been the object of two amply funded recording enterprises. One, organized by the Yale University Video Archive of the Holocaust, was already begun in 1981. The other, the Shoah Visual History Foundation, was organized by the film director Steven Spielberg in 1994, in the wake of the worldwide effects of his movie *Schindler's List*.

Despite the publicity these enterprises have aroused and the celebrity that has accrued to the new survivor identity, it is important to see that this new genre of memorialization has inverted the language of liberation that was so fundamental to the earlier, progressive form. It has created not heroes but antiheroes. Indeed, those who have created and shaped this new genre are decidedly critical of what they see as the "style of revisionism that crept into Holocaust writing after the liberation of the camps." They describe this style as a "natural but misguided impulse to romanticize staying alive and to interpret painful endurance as a form of defiance or resistance" (Langer, 2000: xiv). Arguing that survivor testimony reveals tragedy, not triumph, they suggest that it demands the rejection of any progressive frame.

No one speaks of having survived through bravery or courage. These are hard assessments for us to accept. We want to believe

66

in a universe that rewards good character and exemplary behavior. We want to believe in the power of the human spirit to overcome adversity. It is difficult to live with the thought that human nature may not be noble or heroic and that under extreme conditions we, too, might turn brutal, selfish, "too inhuman." (Greene and Kumar, 2000: xxv–xxvi)

In reacting against the heroic, progressive frame some of these commentators go so far as to insist on the inherent "meaninglessness" of the Holocaust, suggesting that the testimonies reveal "uncompensated and unredeemable suffering" (Langer, 2000: xv). Yet it seems clear that the very effort to create survivor testimony is an effort to maintain the vitality of the experience by objectifying and, in effect, depersonalizing it. As such, it helps to sustain the tragic trauma-drama, which allows an ever-wider audience redemption through suffering. It does so by suggesting the survival not of a few scattered and particular victims but of humanity as such.

> The power of testimony is that it requires little commentary, for witnesses are the experts and they tell their own stories in their own words. The perpetrators work diligently to silence their victims by taking away their names, homes, families, friends, possessions, and lives. The intent was to deny their victims any sense of humanness, to erase their individuality and rob them of all personal voice. Testimony reestablishes the individuality of the victims who survived—and in some instances of those who were killed—and demonstrates the power of their voices. (Greene and Kumar, 2000: xxiv)

Those involved directly in this memorializing process see their own work in exactly the same way. Geoffrey Hartman, the director of the Yale Video Archive, speaks about a new "narrative that emerges through the alliance of witness and interviewer" (Hartman, 1996: 153), a narrative based on the reconstruction of a human community.

> However many times the interviewer may have heard similar accounts, they are received as though for the first time. This is possible because, while the facts are known, while historians have labored—and are still laboring—to establish every detail, each of

these histories is animated by something in addition to historical knowledge: there is a quest to recover or reconstruct a recipient, an "affective community"...and [thus] the renewal of compassionate feelings. (153–54)

However "grim its contents," Hartman insists, testimony does not represent an "impersonal historical digest" but, rather, "that most natural and flexible of human communications, a story—a story, moreover, that, even if it describes a universe of death, is communicated by a living person who answers, recalls, thinks, cries, carries on" (Hartman, 1996: 154). The president of the Survivors of the Shoah Visual History Foundation, Michael Berenbaum, suggesting that the goal of the Spielberg group is "to catalogue and to disseminate the testimonies to as many remote sites as technology and budget will permit, [all] in the service of education," ties the contemporary moral meaning of the historical events to the opportunity for immediate emotional identification that testimonies provide: "In classrooms throughout the world, the encounter between survivors and children [has] become electrifying, the transmission of memory, a discussion of values, a warning against prejudice, antisemitism, racism, and indifference" (Berenbaum, 1998: xi).

Is the Holocaust Western?

While the rhetoric of Holocaust generalization refers to its *weltgeschichte* relevance—its world-historical relevance—throughout this essay I have tried to be careful in noting that this universalization has primarily been confined to the West. Universalization, as I have described it, depends on symbolically generated, emotionally vicarious participation in the trauma-drama of the mass murder of the Jews. The degree to which this participation is differentially distributed throughout the West is itself a question that further research will have to pursue. This "remembering" is much more pronounced in Western Europe and North America than in Latin America. Mexicans, pre-occupied with their national traumas dating back to the European conquest, are much less attached to the "Holocaust" than their northern neighbors— against whose very mythologies Mexicans often define themselves. The result may be that Mexican political culture is informed to a significantly lesser degree by "post-Holocaust morality." On the other hand, it is also possible that Mexicans translate certain aspects of post-Holocaust morality into local terms—for example, into the willingness to limit claims to national sovereignty in the face of demands by indigenous groups legitimating themselves in terms of broadly human rights.

Such variation is that much more intense when we expand our assessment to non-Western areas. What are the degrees of attachment to, vicarious participation in, and lessons drawn from the "Holocaust" trauma in non-Western civilizations? In Hindu, Buddhist, Confucian, Islamic, African, and still-communist regions and regimes, reference to the Holocaust, when made at all, is by literary and intellectual elites with markedly atypical levels of participation in the global discourse dominated by the United States and Western Europe. Of course, non-Western regions and nations have their own identity-defining trauma-dramas (Alexander and Gao, 2007). What is unclear is the degree to which the cultural work that constructs these traumas, and responds to them, reaches beyond issues of national identity and sovereignty to the universalizing, supranational ethical imperatives increasingly associated with the "lessons of post-Holocaust morality" in the West.

The authorized spokespersons for Japan, for example, have never acknowledged the empirical reality of the horrific mass murder their soldiers inflicted on native Chinese in Nanking, China, during the runup to World War II—the "Rape of Nanking." Much less have they apologized for it, or made any effort to share in the suffering of the Chinese people in a manner that would point to a universalizing ethic by which members of different Asian national and ethnic groupings could be commonly judged. Instead, the atomic bombings of Hiroshima have become an originating trauma for postwar Japanese identity. While producing an extraordinary commitment to pacificism, the dramatization of this trauma, which was inflicted on Japan by its wartime enemy, the United States, has had the effect of confirming rather than dislodging Japan in its role as narrative agent. The trauma has functioned, in other words, to block any effort to widen the circle of perpetrators, making it less likely that the national history of Japan will be submitted to some kind of supranational standard of judgment.

Such submission is very difficult, of course, in any strongly national context, in the West as well as in the East. Nonetheless, the analysis presented here compels us to ask this question: Can countries or civilizations that do not acknowledge the Holocaust develop universalistic political moralities? Obviously, non-Western nations cannot "remember" the Holocaust, but in the context of cultural globalization they certainly have become gradually aware of its symbolic meaning and social significance. It might also be the case that non-Western nations can develop trauma-dramas that are functional equivalents to the Holocaust (Alexander, forthcoming). It has been the thesis of this essay that moral universalism rests on social processes that construct and channel cultural trauma. If this is indeed the case, then globalization will have to involve a very different kind of social process than the ones that students of this supranational development have talked about so far: East and West, North and South must learn to share the experiences of one another's traumas and to take vicarious responsibility for the other's afflictions.

Geoffrey Hartman has recently likened the pervasive status of the Holocaust in contemporary society to a barely articulated but nonetheless powerful and pervasive legend. "In Greek tragedy... with its moments of highly condensed dialogue, the framing legend is so well known that it does not have to be emphasized. A powerful abstraction, or simplification, takes over. In this sense, and in this sense only, the Holocaust is on the way to becoming a legendary event" (Hartman, 2000: 16).

Human beings are story-telling animals. We tell stories about our triumphs. We tell stories about tragedies. We like to believe in the verisimilitude of our accounts, but it is the moral frameworks themselves that are real and constant, not the factual material that we employ them to describe. In the history of human societies, it has often been the case that narrative accounts of the same event compete with one another, and that they eventually displace one another over historical time. In the case of the Nazis' mass murder of the Jews, what was once described as a prelude and incitement to moral and social progress has come to be reconstructed as a decisive demonstration that not even the most "modern" improvements in the condition of humanity can ensure advancement in anything other than a purely technical sense. It is paradoxical that a decided increase in moral and social justice may eventually be the unintended result.

NOTES

1. In the inaugural conference of the United States Holocaust Research Institute, the Israeli historian Yehuda Bauer made a critical observation and posted a fundamental question to the opening session.

> About two decades ago, Professor Robert Alter of California published a piece in *Commentary* that argued that we had had enough of the Holocaust, that a concentration of Jewish intellectual and emotional efforts around

it was counterproductive, that the Holocaust should always be remembered, but that there were new agendas that had to be confronted.... Elie Wiesel has expressed the view that with the passing on of the generation of Holocaust survivors, the Holocaust may be forgotten.... But the memory is not going away; on the contrary, the Holocaust has become a cultural code, a symbol of evil in Western civilization. Why should this be so? There are other genocides: Hutu and Tutsi in Rwanda, possibly Ibos in Nigeria, Biharis in Bangladesh, Cambodia, and of course the dozens of millions of victims of the Maoist purges in China, the Gulag, and so forth. Yet it is the murder of the Jews that brings forth a growing avalanche of films, plays, fiction, poetry, TV series, sculpture, paintings, and historical, sociological, psychological and other research. (quoted in Berenbaum and Peck, 1998: 12)

The same opening session was also addressed by Raul Hilberg. As the editors of the conference book suggest, Hilberg's "magisterial work, *The Destruction of the European Jews*," which had been "written in virtual isolation and in opposition to the academic establishment nearly four decades earlier," had since "come to define the field" of Holocaust studies (Berenbaum and Peck, 1998: 1). Hilberg began his address as follows:

When the question is posed about where, as academic researchers of the Holocaust, we stand today, the simple answer is: in the limelight. Never before has so much public attention been lavished on our subject, be it in North America or in Western Europe.... Interest in our topic is manifest in college courses, which are developed in one institution or another virtually every semester; or conferences, which take place almost every month; or new titles of books, which appear practically every week. The demand for output is seemingly inexhaustible. The media celebrate our discoveries, and when an event in some part of the world reminds someone of the Holocaust, our researchers are often asked to explain or supply a connection instantaneously. (quoted in Berenbaum and Peck, 1998: 5)

This essay may be viewed as an effort to explain where the "limelight" to which Hilberg refers has come from and to answer Bauer's question "Why should this be so?"

2. As we will show, to be defined as a traumatic event for all humankind does not mean that the event is literally experienced or even represented as such by all humankind. As I suggest in the conclusion of this essay, indeed, only one part of contemporary humankind has even the normative aspiration of experiencing the originating event as a trauma—the "Western" versus the "Eastern" part of humankind—and this cultural-geographical difference itself may have fateful consequences for international relations, definitions of legal-moral responsibility, and the project of global understanding today.

3. Once an "atrocity" had involved murderous actions against civilians, but this definition was wiped out during the course of World War II.

4. The report continued in a manner that reveals the relation between such particularistic, war-and-nation-related definitions of atrocity and justifications for nationalistic military escalation of brutality in response: "Even though the truth of Japan's tribal viciousness had been spattered over the pages of history down through the centuries and repeated in the modern slaughters of Nanking and Hong Kong, word of this new crime had been a shock ... Secretary of State Cordell Hull speaking with bitter self-restraint [sic] excoriated the 'demons' and 'fiendishness' of Japan. Senator Alben W. Barkley exclaimed: 'Retribution [must] be meted out to these heathens—brutes and beasts in the form of man.' Lister Hill of Alabama was practically monosyllabic: 'Gut the heart of Japan with fire!'" The connection of such attributions of war atrocity to pledges of future military revenge illuminates the lack of indignation that later greeted the atomic bombing of Hiroshima and Nagasaki. This kind of particularistic framing of mass civilian murder would be lifted only decades later—after the Jewish mass murder had itself become generalized as a crime that went beyond national and war-related justifications. I discuss this later.

5. For a detailed "thick description" of these first encounters, see Robert Abzug, *Inside the Vicious Heart* (1985).

6. During April, under the entry "German Camps," the *New York Times Index* (1945: 1184) employed the noun eight times.

7. For a broad discussion of the role played by such analogies with alleged German World War I atrocities in creating initial unbelief, see Laqueur (1980). The notion of moral panic suggests, of course, a fantasized and distorted object or belief (Thompson, 1997). In this sense, trauma is different from panic. (See Alexander, 2003).

8. This is not to say that the fact of the Nazis' anti-Jewish atrocities was accepted all at once but that the Allies' discovery of the concentration camps, relayed by reporters and photographers, soon did put an end to the doubts, which had not been nearly as thoroughly erased by revelations about the Majdanek death camp liberated by Soviets months earlier. For a detailed discussion of this changing relationship between acceptance and doubt, see Zelizer (1998: 49–140).

9. In early October 1945, General George Patton, the much-heralded chief of the U.S. Third Army, became embroiled in controversy over what were taken to be anti-Semitic representations of the Jewish survivors in the camps Patton administered. The general had contrasted them pejoratively with the German and other non-German camp prisoners and given them markedly worse treatment. In light of the argument I will make hereafter, it is revealing that what was represented as intolerable about this conspicuous mistreatment of Jewish survivors was its implied equation of American and Nazi relations to Jews. The *New Republic* headlined its account of the affair "The Same as the Nazis."

Only on the last day of September did the nation learn that on the last day of August, President Truman had sent a sharp letter to General Eisenhower regarding the treatment of Jews in Germany. The President told the General bluntly that according to a report made by his special investigator, Earl Harrison, "we appear to be treating the Jews as the Nazi treated them, except that we do not exterminate them." Thousands of displaced Jews are still crowded in badly run concentration camps, improperly fed, clothed and housed, while comfortable homes nearby are occupied by former Nazis or Nazi sympathizers. These Jews are still not permitted to leave the camps except with passes, which are doled out to them on the absolutely incomprehensible policy that they should be treated as prisoners.... Americans will be profoundly disturbed to learn that anti-Semitism is rife in the American occupation forces just as is tenderness to Nazis. (October 8, 1945: 453)

Time reported the event in the same way:

Plain G.I.s had their problems, too. Ever since they had come to Germany, the soldiers had fraternized—not only with *Fraulein* but with a philosophy. Many now began to say that the Germans were really O.K., that they had been forced into the war, that the atrocity stories were fakes. Familiarity with the eager German women, the free-faced German young, bred forgetfulness of Belsen and Buchenwald and Oswieczim. (October 8, 1945: 31–32)

In a story headlined "The Case of General Patton," the *New York Times* wrote that Patton's transfer from his Bavarian post "can have and should have just one meaning," which was that the U.S. government "will not tolerate in high positions . . . any officers, however brave, however honest, who are inclined to be easy on known Nazis and indifferent or hard to the surviving victims of the Nazi terror" (October 3, 1945: 18). For more details on Patton's treatment of the Jewish camp survivors, see Abzug (1985).

10. In "Radical Evil: Kant at War with Himself" (Bernstein, 2001), Richard Bernstein has provided an illuminating discussion of Kant's use of this term. While Kant intended the term to indicate an unusual, and almost unhuman, desire not to fulfill the imperatives of moral behavior, Bernstein demonstrates that Kant contributed little to the possibility of providing standards of evaluation for what, according to post-Holocaust morality, is called radical evil today. Nonetheless, the term itself was an important addition to moral philosophy. I want to emphasize here that I am speaking about social representations of the Holocaust, not its actual nature. I do not intend, in other words, either here or elsewhere in this essay, to enter into the debate about the uniqueness of the Holocaust in Western history. As Norman Naimark (2001) and many others have usefully pointed out, there have been other

terrible ethnically inspired bloodlettings that arguably can be compared with it—for example, the Armenian massacre by the Turks; the killing fields in Cambodia, which claimed 3 million of a 7 million-person population; the Rwanda massacre. My point here is not to make claims about the objective reality of what would later come to be called the Holocaust but about the sociological processes that *allowed estimations* of its reality to shift over time. For an analysis of the discourse about uniqueness, see the section below on "The Dilemma of Uniqueness."

11. Alexander, 2003; Alexander, et al., 2004; Alexander and Gao, 2007; Alexander, forthcoming; Eyerman, 2008; and Goodman, 2009.

12. This commonsense link is repeated time and again, exemplifying not empirical reality but the semantic exigencies of what I will call the progressive narrative of the Holocaust. For example, in his influential account of the postwar attack on anti-Semitism, Leonard Dinnerstein (1981–82, p.149) suggests that "perhaps the sinking in of the knowledge that six million Jews perished in the Holocaust" was a critical factor in creating the identification with American Jews. A similarly rationalist approach is exhibited by Edward Shapiro (1992) in his book-length study of the changing position of Jews in postwar America. Shapiro observes that "after the Holocaust, anti-Semitism meant not merely the exclusion of Jews from clubs [etc.] but mass murder" (Shapiro, 1992: 16). The issue here is what "meant" means. It is not obvious and rational but highly contextual, and that context is culturally established. The distinguished historian of American history John Higham represents this Enlightenment version of lay trauma theory when he points to the reaction to the Holocaust as explaining the lessening of prejudice in the United States between the mid-1930s and the mid-1950s, which he calls "the broadest, most powerful movement for ethnic democracy in American history." Higham suggests that "in the 30s and 40s, the Holocaust in Germany threw a blazing light on every sort of bigotry," thus explaining the "traumatic impact of Hitlerism on the consciousness of the Western world" (Higham, 1984: 154). Movements for ethnic and religious tolerance in the United States, Higham adds, came only later, "only as the war drew to a close and the full horrors of the Nazi concentration camp spilled out to an aghast world" (171). Such Enlightenment versions of lay trauma theory seem eminently reasonable, but they simply do not capture the contingent, sociologically freighted nature of the trauma process. As I try to demonstrate hereafter, complex symbolic processes of coding, weighting, and narrating were decisive in the unpredicted postwar effort to stamp out anti-Semitism in the United States.

13. See the observation by the sociological theorist Gerard Delanty (2001: 43): "What I am drawing attention to is the need to address basic questions concerning cultural values, since violence is not always an empirical objective reality, but a matter of cultural construction in the context of publicly shaped discourses and is generally defined by reference to an issue."

14. Access to the "means of symbolic production," is one of the key elements in allowing successful social performances (Alexander, 2006a).

15. To think of what might have been, it is necessary to engage in a counterfactual thought experiment. The most successful effort to do so has occurred in a best-selling piece of middlebrow fiction called *Fatherland,* by Robert Harris (1992), a reporter for the London *Times.* The narrative takes place in 1967, in Berlin, during the celebrations of Adolph Hitler's seventieth birthday. The former Soviet Union and the United Kingdom were both conquered in the early 1940s, primarily because Hitler's general staff had overruled his decision to launch the Russian invasion before he had completed his effort to subjugate Great Britain. The story's plot revolves around the protagonists' efforts to reveal the hidden events of the Holocaust. Rumors had circulated of the mass killings, but no objective truth had ever been available. As for the other contention of this paragraph—that Soviet control over the camps' discoveries would also have made it impossible for the story to be told—one may merely consult the Soviets' presentation of the Auschwitz death camp outside Krakow, Poland. While Jewish deaths are not denied, the focus is on class warfare, Polish national resistance, and communist and Polish deaths. It is well known, for example, that the East Germans, under the Soviet regime, never took responsibility for their anti-Semitic past and its central role in the mass killing of Jews, focusing instead on the Nazis as nonnational, class-based, reactionary social forces.

16. In her detailed reconstruction of the shifting balance between doubt and belief among Western publics, Zelizer demonstrates that the Soviets' discovery of the Majdanek death camp in 1944 failed to quell disbelief because of broad skepticism about Russian reporters, particularly a dislike for the Russian literary newswriting style and tendency to exaggerate: "Skepticism made the Western press regard the liberation of the eastern camps as a story in need of additional confirmation. Its dismissive attitude was exacerbated by the fact that the U.S. and British forces by and large had been denied access to the camps of the eastern front [which made it] easier to regard the information trickling out as Russian propaganda" (Zelizer, 1998: 51).

17. In modern sociology, the great empirical student of typification is Harold Garfinkel, who, drawing up Husserl and Schutz, developed a series of supple operationalizations such as *ad-hocing, indexicality,* and the "etc. clause" to describe how typification is carried out empirically.

18. See Brooks (1995) for a literary approach to social transformation that is apposite Fussell's both in terms of method and history. Brooks describes the connection between the literary genre of melodrama and more general cultural romanticism in key literary works of the nineteenth century. Fussell observes how this romantic faith was shattered by the First World War, and how the ironic genre deeply affected literary and popular work that followed.

19. See Herf (1984) and also Philip Smith's (1998) investigations of the coding of Nazism and communism as variations on the modernist discourse of civil society.

20. For how the coding of an adversary as radical evil has compelled the sacrifice of life in modern war, see Alexander (1998) and Smith (2006).

21. The earlier failure of such nations as France to vigorously prepare for war against Germans had reflected an internal disagreement about the evility of Nazism, a disagreement fuelled by the longstanding anti-Semitism and anti-Republicanism triggered by the Dreyfus affair. For a discussion of this, see William Shirer's classic, *The Collapse of the Third Republic* (1969).

22. Statements and programs supporting better treatment of Jews were often, in fact, wittingly or unwittingly accompanied by anti-Semitic stereotypes. In the months before America entered the war against Germany, *Time* reported: "A states-manlike program to get a better deal for the Jews after the war was launched last week by the American Jewish Congress and the World Jewish Congress, of which the not invariably statesmanlike, emotional, and politics dabbling Rabbi Steven S. Wise is respectively president and chairman" (July 7, 1941: 44). Indeed, in his statisti-cal compilation of shifting poll data on the personal attitudes of Americans during this period, Stember (1966) shows that the percentage of Americans expressing anti-Semitic attitudes actually increased immediately before and during the early years of the anti-Nazi war, though it remained a minority. For a helpful discussion of anti-Semitism in the early twentieth century, see Hollinger (1996).

23. Higham (1984) shows how left-leaning intellectuals, artists, academics, and journalists set out to oppose the nativism of the 1920s and viewed the rise of Nazism in this context. While they focused particularly on the Jewish problem, they also discussed issues of race.

24. From the phrase of Clifford Geertz (1984): "anti–anti-relativism," which he traced to the phrase from the McCarthy era, "anti–anti-communism." Geertz writes that his point was not to embrace relativism but to reject anti-relativism, just as anti-McCarthyites had not wanted to embrace communism but to reject anti-commu-nism. Just so, progressive Americans of that time did not wish to identify with Jews but to reject anti-Semitism because, I am contending, of its association with Nazism.

25. The premise of the following argument is that "salvation" can continue to be a massive social concern even in a secular age. I have made this theoretical argument in relation to a reconsideration of the routinization thesis in Max Weber's sociology of religion (Alexander, 1983) and employed this perspective in empirical studies of secular culture (Alexander, 2003).

26. See Turner's introduction of "liminality" via his reconstruction of Van Gennep's ritual process (Turner, 1969).

27. In regard to the eventual peace treaty that would allow progress, the refer-ence was, of course, to the disastrous Versailles Treaty of 1919, which was viewed in the interwar period as having thwarted the progressive narrative that had motivated the Allied side during World War I. President Woodrow Wilson had presented the progressive narrative of that earlier struggle by promising that this "war to end all wars" would "make the world safe for democracy."

28. I should add by the Jewish *and non-Jewish* victims as well, for millions of persons were victims of Nazi mass murder in addition to the Jews—Poles, gypsies,

homosexuals, handicapped persons, and political opponents of all types. That virtually all of these non-Jewish victims were filtered out of the emerging collective representation of the Holocaust underlines the arbitrary quality of trauma representations. By *arbitrary*, I mean to refer to Saussure's foundational argument, in his *Course in General Linguistics*, that the relation between signifier and signified is not based on some intrinsically truthful or accurate relationship. The definition of the signifier—what we normally mean by the symbol or representation—comes not from its actual or "real" social referent per se but from its position within the field of other signifiers, which is itself structured by the broader sign system, or language, already in place. This is essentially the same sense of arbitrariness that is invoked by Wittgenstein's argument against Augustine's language theory in the opening pages of *Philosophical Investigations*. This notion of arbitrariness does not mean, of course, that representation is unaffected by noncultural developments, hence the extensive effort here to contextualize this analysis in historical terms.

29. In February, 1943, the widely read popular magazine *American Mercury* published a lengthy story by Ben Hecht, called "The Extermination of the Jews" (February 1943: 194–203), that described in accurate detail the events that had already unfolded and would occur in the future. The following report also appeared in *Time:*

> In a report drawn from German broadcasts and newspapers, Nazi statements, smuggled accounts and the stories of survivors who have reached the free world, the [World Jewish] Congress told what was happening in Poland, slaughterhouse of Europe's Jews. By late 1942, the Congress reported, 2,000,000 had been massacred. *Vernichtungskolonnen* (extermination squads) rounded them up and killed them with machine guns, lethal gas, high-voltage electricity, and hunger. Almost all were stripped before they died; their clothes were needed by the Nazis. ("Total Murder," March 8, 1943: 29)

Two months later, *Newsweek* reported the Nazi destruction of the Warsaw Ghetto: "When [the] Gestapo men and Elite Guard were through with the job, Warsaw, once the home of 450,000 Jews, was 'judenrein' (free of Jews). By last week all had been killed or deported" (May 24, 1943: 54). In October 1944 the widely popular journalist Edgar Snow published details about the "Nazi murder factory" in the Soviet-liberated town of Maidanek, Poland, in the *Saturday Evening Post* (October 28, 1944: 18–19).

Abzug (1985: 17) agrees that "the more sordid facts of mass slaughter, labor and death campus, Nazi policies of enslavement of peoples deemed inferior and extermination of Europe's Jews" were facts that were "known through news sources and widely publicized since 1942." In the manner of Enlightenment lay trauma theory—which would suggest that knowledge leads to redemptive action—Abzug qualifies his assertion of this popular knowledge by insisting that the American soldiers who opened up the camps and the American audience alike suffered from a failure of "imagination" in regard to the Nazi terror (17). According to the theory of cultural trauma that informs our analysis, however, this was less a failure of imagination than a matter of collective imagination being narrated in a certain way. It points not to an absence of perception but to the presence of the contemporary, progressive narrative framework, a framework that was brought into disrepute by later developments, which made it appear insensitive and even inhumane.

30. Another historian, Peter Novick, makes the same point:

> For most Gentiles, and a great many Jews as well, [the Holocaust] was seen as simply one among many dimensions of the horrors of Nazism. Looking at World War II retrospectively, we are inclined to stress what was distinctive in the murderous zeal with which European Jewry was destroyed. Things often appeared differently to contemporaries.... Jews did not stand out as the Nazis' prime victims until near the end of the Third Reich. Until 1938 there were hardly any Jews, qua Jews, in concentration camps, which were populated largely by Socialists, Communists, trade unionists, dissident intellectuals, and the like. Even when news of mass killings of Jews during the war reached the West, their murder was framed as one atrocity, albeit the largest, in a long list of crimes, such as the massacre of Czechs at Lidice, the French at Oradour, and American prisoners of war at Malmedy. (Novick, 1994: 160)

31. The term was introduced in 1944 by Polish-American author Ralph Lemkin, in his book *Axis Rule in Occupied Europe* (1944). As Lemkin defined it, genocide applied to efforts to destroy the foundations of national and ethnic groups and referred to a wide range of antagonistic activities, including attacks on political and social institutions, culture, language, national feelings, religion, economic existence, and personal security and dignity. It was intended to cover all of the antinational activities carried out by the Nazis against the occupied nations inside Hitler's Reich. In other words, when first coined, the term definitely did not focus on the element of mass murder that after the discovery of the death camps came to be attributed to it.

32. The author, Frank Kingdon, was a former Methodist minister.

33. In an article on the success of *Gentleman's Agreement*, in the *Saturday Review of Literature* (December 13, 1947: 20), the author asserted that "the Jewish people are the world symbol of [the] evil that is tearing civilization apart" and suggested that the book and movie's success "may mean that the conscience of America is awakening and that something at least will be done about it."

34. Short makes this Jewish exceptionalism clear when he writes that "with war raging in the Pacific, in Europe and in the shipping lanes of the Atlantic, Hollywood made a conscious effort to create a sense of solidarity amongst the nation's racial and ethnic groups (*excepting* the Japanese-Americans and the blacks)" (Short, 1981: 157, italics added).

35. See also Higham (1984) and Silk (1984).

36. It remains an empirical question whether American Jews were themselves traumatized by contemporary revelations about the Nazi concentration camps. Susan Sontag's remembered reactions as a California teenager to the revelatory photographs of the Belsen and Dachau death camps are often pointed to as typical of American Jewish reaction more generally: "I felt irrevocably grieved, wounded, but a part of my feelings started to tighten; something went dead; something still is crying" (quoted in Shapiro, 1992: 3, and in Abzug, 1985: vii). Yet that this and other oft-quoted retrospective reactions were shared by the wider Jewish public in the United States has been more of a working assumption by scholars of this period, particularly but by no means exclusively Jewish ones. Not yet subject to empirical demonstration, the assumption that American Jews were immediately traumatized by the revelations reflects Enlightenment lay trauma theory. It might also represent an effort at post hoc exculpation vis-à-vis possible guilt feelings that many American and British Jews later experienced about their lack of effort or even their inability to draw attention to the mass murders.

37. *Symbolic action* is a term developed by Kenneth Burke to indicate that understanding is also a form of human activity, relating action to expressive form and to the goal of parsing meaning. The term became popularized and elaborated in the two now classical essays published by Clifford Geertz in the early 1960s, "Religion as a Cultural System" and "Ideology as a Cultural System" (1973). Reference to "culture structure" refers to my effort to treat culture as a structure in itself. Only by analytically differentiating culture from social structure—treating it as a structure in its own right—does it move from being a dependent to an independent variable (Alexander, 2003). For related discussions of "culture structure," see Alexander and Smith, 2003; Kane (1998); Rambo and Chan (1990); and Magnuson (2008). This discussion of historical transformations in the symbolization of Jewish mass murder is also informed by my work in social performance, which conceptualizes a clear separation between symbolic action, on the one hand, and audience reception, on the other, and suggests a number of relatively independent cultural and institutional mediations that lay in between—such as social and hermeneutic power, means of symbolic production, and mise-en-scène. (Alexander, 2006a; Alexander, Giesen and Mast, 2006).

38. See Wilhelm Dilthey, "The Construction of the Historical World in the Human Sciences" (1976).

39. By the early 1990s, knowledge of the Holocaust among American citizens greatly exceeded knowledge about World War II. According to public opinion polls, while 97 percent of Americans knew about the Holocaust, far fewer could identity "Pearl Harbor" or the fact that the United States had unleashed an atomic bomb on Japan. Only 49 percent of those polled realized that the Soviets had fought with Americans during that war. In fact, the detachment of the Jewish mass killings from particular historical events had proceeded to the point that, according to an even more recent survey, more than one-third of Americans either didn't know that

the Holocaust took place during World War II or insisted that they "knew" it did not (Novick, 1999: 232).

40. Yehuda Bauer, in his editor's introduction to the first issue of *Holocaust and Genocide Studies*, suggested this new, *weltgeschichte* (world-historical) sensibility:

> There is not much point in dealing with one aspect of the Holocaust, because that traumatic event encompasses all of our attention; therefore, no concentration on one discipline only would meet the needs...We arrived at the conclusion that we would aim at a number of readers' constituencies: students, survivors, high school and college teachers, academics generally, and that *very large number of people who feel that the Holocaust is something that has changed our century, perhaps all centuries*, and needs to be investigated. (1986: 1, italics added)

This journal not only embodied the newly emerging generalization and universalization I am describing here but also can be viewed as an institutional carrier that aimed to promote its continuation. Thus, two years later, in an issue of the journal dedicated to papers from a conference entitled, "Remembering for the Future," held at Oxford University in July 1988, Bauer pointedly observed that "one half of the authors of the papers *are not Jewish*, bearing witness to the fact that among academics, at least, there exists a growing realization of the importance of the event to our civilization, a *realization that is becoming more widespread among those whose families and peoples were not affected by the Holocaust*" (1986: 255, italics added).

41. The historian Peter Gay, who coedited the *Columbia History of the World* in 1972, was reportedly embarrassed to find later that the enormous volume contained no mention of Auschwitz or of the murder of 6 million Jews, an embarrassment exacerbated by the fact that he himself was a Jewish refugee from Germany (Zelizer, 1998: 164–65).

42. As noted by Gerd Korman:

> In 1949, there was no "Holocaust" in the English language in the sense that word is used today. Scholars and writers have used "permanent pogrom"...or "recent catastrophe," or "disaster," or "the disaster." Sometimes writers spoke about annihilation and destruction without use of any of these terms. In 1953, the state of Israel formally injected itself into the study of the destruction of European Jewry, and so became involved in the transformation [by] establish[ing] Yad Vashem as a "Martyrs" and "Heroes' Remembrance Authority"...Two years later Yad Vashem translated *shoah* into "Disaster"....But then the change occurred quickly. When catastrophe had lived side by side with disaster the word holocaust had appeared now and then....Between 1957 and 1959, however, "Holocaust" took on...a specific meaning. It was used at the Second World Congress

of Jewish Studies held in Jerusalem, and when Yad Vashem published its third yearbook, one of the articles dealt with "Problems Relating to a Questionnaire on the Holocaust." Afterwards Yad Vashem switched from "Disaster" to "Holocaust"... Within the Jewish world the word became commonplace, in part because Elie Wiesel and other gifted writers and speakers, in public meetings or in articles...made it coin of the realm. (Korman, 1972: 259–61)

43. On *shoah*, see Ofer (1996). In telling the story of linguistic transformation inside the Hebrew language, Ofer shows that inside of Israel there was a similar narrative shift from a more progressive to a more tragic narrative frame and that this shift was reflected in the adoption of the word *shoah*, which had strong biblical connotations related to apocalyptic events in Jewish history, such as the flood and Job's sufferings: *shoah* was conspicuously not applied to such "everyday" disasters as pogroms and other repeated forms of anti-Semitic oppression. On the relative newness of the American use of the term *Holocaust*—its emergence only in the postprogressive narrative period—see John Higham's acute observation that "the word does not appear in the index to Richard H. Pells, *The Liberal Mind in a Conservative Age: American Intellectuals in the 1940s and 1950s*—in spite of the attention he gives to European influence and Jewish intellectuals" (Higham, personal communication). According to Garber and Zuckerman (1989: 202), the English term was introduced by Elie Wiesel, in the *New York Times Book Review* of October 27, 1963, in relation to the Jewish mass murder, but there is some debate about the originality of Wiesel's usage. Novick (1999: 133), for example, relates that the American journalist Paul Jacobs employed the term in an article on the Eichmann trial, in 1961, that he filed from Jerusalem for the American liberal magazine *New Leader*. Significantly, Jacobs wrote of "the Holocaust, as the Nazi annihilation of European Jewry is called in Israel." Whatever its precise origins—and Wiesel's 1963 usage may well have marked the beginning of a common usage—the symbolically freighted semantic transition, which first occurred in Israel and then in America, had wide ramifications for the universalization of meaning vis-à-vis the Jewish mass killing. Until the late 1970s, for example, Germans still used bureaucratic euphemisms to describe the events, such as the "Final Solution." After the German showing of the American television miniseries Holocaust, however, Holocaust replaced these terms, passing into common German usage. One German scholar, Jean Paul Bier, described Holocaust as an "American word" (1986: 203); another testified that, after the television series, the term "'Holocaust' became a metaphor for unhumanity" (Zielinski, 1986: 273).

44. For the central role of "our time" in the tropes of contemporary historical narratives, see Alexander, 2003.

45. This is not to say, however, that Christological themes of redemption through suffering played no part in the tragic dramatization. As anti-Semitic agitation increased in the late nineteenth century, Jesus frequently was portrayed by Jewish

artists as a Jew and his persecution presented as emblematic not only of Jewish suffering but also of the Christian community's hypocrisy in relation to it. During this same period, important Christian artists like Goya and Grosz began to develop "a new approach to Christ, using the Passion scenes outside their usual Biblical context as archetypical of the sufferings of modern man, especially in times of war" (Amishai-Maisels, 1988: 457). As the Nazi persecution intensified before and during World War II, this theme emerged with increasing frequency—for example in the despairing paintings of Marc Chagall. Again, the aim was to provide a mythically powerful icon of Jewish martyrdom and, at the same time, "to reproach the Christian world for their deeds" (464). With the liberation of the camps, there emerged a far more powerful way to establish this icon—through the images of emaciated, tortured bodies of the victims themselves. Immediately after the war, artists such as Corrado Cagli and Hans Grundig stressed the similarity between the camp corpses and Holbein's "Dead Christ," and Grundig even set the corpses on a gold background, emphasizing their similarity to medieval representations of martyrs. The most telling similarity between Christ and the corpses was not, however, invented by artists but was found in news photographs of those corpses whose arms were spread out in a cruciform pose. One such photograph, published under the title "Ecce Homo-Bergen Belsen," is said to have had an immediate and lasting effect on the artistic representation of the Holocaust (467). It was undoubtedly the case that, for many religious Christians, the transition of Jews from killers of Christ to persecuted victims of evil was facilitated by such iconographic analogies. Nonetheless, even here, in the pictorial equation of Jesus with the Nazi victims, the theme was tragedy but not redemption in the eschatological sense of Christianity. The symbolization held the pathos but not the promise of the crucifixion, and it was employed more as a criticism of the promises of Christianity than as an identification with its theodicy of hope. It should also be mentioned, of course, that the religious mythology and ritual surrounding the death of Christ draw heavily from the classical aesthetic genre of tragedy.

46. "Pity involves both distance and proximity. If the sufferer is too close to ourselves, his impending misfortune evokes horror and terror. If he is too distant, his fate does not affect us.... The ethical and political questions are: whom should we pity?... The tragic hero? Ourselves? Humanity? All three, and three in one" (Rorty, 1992: 12–13). Against Adorno's claim that the Holocaust must not be aestheticized in any way, Hartman (1996) insists that "art creates an unreality effect in a way that is not alienating or desensitizing. At best, it also provides something of a sage-house for emotion and empathy. The tears we shed, like those of Aeneas when he sees the destruction of Troy depicted on the walls of Carthage, are an acknowledgment and not an exploitation of the past" (157).

47. In these psychological terms, a progressive narrative inclines the audience toward projection and scapegoating, defense mechanisms that allow the actor to experience no responsibility for the crime. This distinction also points to the

difference between the genres of melodrama and tragedy, which otherwise have much in common. By breaking the world completely into black and white, and by providing assurance of the victory of the good, melodrama encourages the same kind of projection and scapegoating as progressive narratives; in fact, melodramatic narratives often drive progressive ones. For the significance of melodramatic narratives in the nineteenth century and their connection to stories, both fictional and realistic, of ethical triumph, see Brooks (1995). In practice, however, dramatizations of the Holocaust trauma, like virtually every other dramatization of tragedy in modern and postmodern society, often overlap with the melodramatic.

48. By the early 1940s, the Polish Ministry of Information, independent journalists, and underground groups released photos of corpses tumbled into graves or stacked onto carts. One such depiction, which appeared in the *Illustrated London News* in March 1941 under the headline "Where Germans Rule: Death Dance before Polish Mass Execution," portrayed victims digging their own graves or facing the death squad. The journal told its readers that "behind these pictures is a story of cold-blooded horror reminiscent of the Middle Ages" (quoted in Zelizer, 1998: 43).

49. This is the radical and corrosive theme of Bauman's provocative *Modernity and the Holocaust* (1989). While Bauman himself professes to eschew any broader universalizing aims, the ethical message of such a perspective seems clear all the same. I am convinced that the distrust of abstract normative theories of justice, as expressed in such postmodern efforts as Bauman's *Postmodern Ethics* (1993), can be understood as a response to the Holocaust, as well, of course, as a response to Stalinism and elements of the capitalist West. In contrast to some other prominent postmodern positions, Bauman's ethics is just as strongly opposed to communitarian as to modernist positions, an orientation that can be understood by the centrality of the Holocaust in his critical understanding of modernity. Bauman's wife, Janina, is a survivor and author of a moving Holocaust memoir, *Winter in the Morning* (1986). The dedication of *Modernity and the Holocaust* reads: "To Janina, and all the others who survived to tell the truth."

50. "Lachrymose" was the characterization given to the historical perspective on Jewish history developed by Salo Baron. The most important early academic chronicler of Jewish history in the United States (Liberles, 1995), Baron held the first Chair of Jewish History at Harvard. Baron was deeply affected by what seemed, at the time, to be the reversal of Jewish assimilation in the fin-de-siècle period. In response to this growth of modern anti- Semitism, he began to suggest that the medieval period of Jewish-Gentile relations—the long period that preceded Jewish "emancipation" in the Enlightenment and nineteenth century—actually may have been better for the Jewish people, culturally, politically, economically, and even demographically, than the post-emancipation period. Postwar Jewish historiography, not only in the United States but also in Israel, often criticized Baron's perspective, but as the progressive narrative of the Holocaust gave way to the tragic frame, his

lachrymose view became if not widely accepted then at least much more positively evaluated as part of the whole reconsideration of the effects of the Enlightenment on modern history. See Liberles (1995). For a broader analysis of the contradictory processes of Jewish 'incorporation' into the civil spheres of Europe and the United States, see Alexander, 2006b: 459–548.

51. This has, of course, been the complaint of some intellectuals, from the very beginning of the entrance of the Holocaust into popular culture, from *The Diary of Anne Frank* to Spielberg's later dramas. As I will suggest below, however, the real issue is not dramatization per se but the nature of the dramatic form. If the comic frame replaces the tragic or melodramatic one, then the "lessons" of the Holocaust are, indeed, being trivialized.

52. She adds that "The appeal to pity is...also an appeal to fellow feeling."

53. As observed by Jonathan Lear, "Tragedy...provides us with the appropriate objects towards which to feel pity and fear. Tragedy, one might say, trains us or habituates us in feeling pity and fear in response to events that are worthy of those emotions. Since our emotions are being evoked in the proper circumstances, they are also being educated, refined, or clarified.... Since virtue partially consists in having the appropriate emotional responses to circumstances, tragedy can be considered part of an ethical education" (1992: 318). Is it necessary to add the caveat that to be "capable" of exercising such an ethical judgment is not the same thing as actually exercising it? This cultural shift I am referring here is about capability, which, while clearly a prerequisite of action, does not determine it.

54. Such a notion of further universalization is not, of course, consistent with postmodern social theory or philosophy, and the intent here is not to suggest that it is.

55. My aim in this section should not be misunderstood as an effort to aestheticize and demoralize the inhuman mass murders that the Nazis carried out. I am trying to denaturalize, and therefore sociologize, our contemporary understanding of these awful events. Despite their heinous quality, they could be interpreted in various ways. Their nature did not dictate their interpretation. As Robert Braun (1994) suggests: "Historical narratives do not necessarily emplot past events in the form of tragedy and this form of emplotment is not the only node of narration for tragic events" (182).

What I am suggesting here is a transparent and eerie homology between the tragic genre—whose emotional, moral, and aesthetic qualities have been studied since Aristotle—and how we and others have come to understand what the Holocaust "really was." Cultural sociology carries out the same kind of "bracketing" that Husserl suggested for his new science of phenomenology: the ontological reality of perceived objects is temporarily suspended in order to search for those subjective elements in the actor's intentionality that establish the *sense* of verisimilitude. What the Holocaust "really was" is not the issue for this sociological investigation. My subject is the social processes that allowed the events now identified by this name to be seen as different things at different times. For the lay actor, by contrast, the reality of the Holocaust must be taken as an objective and absolute. Moral responsibility and moral action can be established and institutionalized only on this basis.

In historical and literary studies, there has developed over the last two decades an intense controversy over the relevance of the kinds of cultural methods I employ here. Scholars associated with the moral lessons of the Holocaust—for example, Saul Friedlander—have lambasted the deconstructive methods of narrativists like Hayden White for eliminating the hard-and-fast line between "representation" (fiction) and "reality" (fact). Friedlander organized the tempestuous scholarly conference that gave birth to the collective volume *Probing the Limits of Representation* (1992). In the conference and the books he drew an analogy between cultural historians' questioning of reality and the politically motivated efforts by contemporary Italian fascists, and all the so-called revisionists since then, to deny the mass murder of the Jews. While I would strongly disagree with Friedlander's line of criticism, there is no doubt that it has been stimulated by the way the aestheticizing, debunking quality of deconstructive criticism has, from Nietzsche on, sought to present itself as a replacement for, rather than a qualification of, the traditional political and moral criticism of the rationalist tradition. By contrast, I am trying here to demonstrate that the aesthetic and the critical approach must be combined.

56. Each national case is, of course, different, and the stories of France, the United Kingdom, Italy, the Netherlands and the Scandinavian countries (e.g., Eyerman, 2008) would depart from this account in significant ways. Nonetheless, as Diner (2000) remarks, insofar as "the Holocaust has increasingly become a universal moral icon in the realm of political and historical discourse," the "impact of the catastrophe can be felt in various European cultures, with their disparate legacies [and] even within the realm of collective ... identities" (218). Nonwestern countries, even the democratic ones, have entirely different traumas to contend with, as I have pointed out in my introduction (cf. Alexander and Gao, 2007; Alexander, forthcoming).

57. In fact, I believe that it is because of the symbolic centrality of Jews in the progressive narrative that so relatively little attention has been paid to the Nazis' equally immoral and unconscionable extermination policies directed against other groups—for example, Poles, homosexuals, gypsies, and the disabled. Some frustrated representatives of these aggrieved groups—sometimes for good reasons, other times for anti-Semitic ones—have attributed this lack of attention to Jewish economic and political power in the United States. The present analysis suggests, however, that cultural logic is the immediate and efficient cause for such a focus. This logic is also propelled, of course, by geopolitical and economic forces, but such considerations would apply more to the power and position of the United States in the world system of the postwar world than to the position of Jews in the United States.

As I have shown, it was not the actual power of Jews in the United States but the centrality of "Jews" in the progressive American imagination that defined the

crimes of Nazis in a manner that focused on anti-Semitism. In terms of later developments, moreover, it was only because of the imaginative reconfiguring of the Jews
that political and economic restrictions were eliminated in a manner that eventually
allowed Jews to gain influence in mainstream American institutions. As I will show
below, moreover, as American power declined, so did the exclusive focus on Jews as
a unique class of Holocaust victims. This suggests, as I will elaborate later, that the
contemporary omnipresence of the Holocaust symbol has more to do with "enlarging the circle of victims" than with focusing exclusively on Jewish suffering.

The most significant scholarly example of this tendentious focus on "Jewish
power" as the key for explaining the telling of the Holocaust story is Peter Novick's
book *The Holocaust in American Life* (1999). To employ the categories of classical
sociological theory, Novick might be described as offering an instrumentally oriented "status group" explanation à la Weber, in contrast to the more culturally oriented late-Durkheimian approach taken here. Novick suggests that the Holocaust
became central to contemporary history because it became central to America, that
it became central to America because it became central to America's Jewish community, and that it became central to Jews because it became central to the ambitions
of Jewish organizations that were central to the mass media in all its forms (207).
Jewish organizations first began to emphasize the Holocaust because they wanted
to "shore up Jewish identity, particularly among the assimilating and intermarry-
ing younger generations" (186) and to maintain the Jews' "victim status" in what
Novick sees as the identity-politics shell game of the 1980s—"Jews were intent
on permanent possession of the gold medal in the Victimization Olympics" (185).
Despite acknowledging that it is "impossible to disentangle the spontaneous from
the controlled" (152), he emphasizes the "strategic calculations" (152) of Jewish organizations, which are said to have motivated them to emphasize the Holocaust in
responsive to "market forces" (187).

The analysis here fundamentally departs from Novick's. Whereas Novick
describes a particularization of the Holocaust—its being captured by Jewish identity
politics—I describe its universalization. Where Novick describes a nationalization,
I trace internationalization. Where Novick expresses skepticism about the metaphorical transferability of the "Holocaust," I describe such metaphorical bridging as
essential to the social process of moral engagement. In terms of sociological theory,
the point is not to deny that status groups are significant. As Weber clarified in his
sociology of religion, however, such groups must be seen not as creators of interest
per se but as "carrier groups." All broad cultural currents are carried by—articulated
by, lodged within—particular material and ideal interests. Even ideal interests, in
other words, are represented by groups—in this case status groups rather than classes.
But, as Weber emphasized, ideal and material interests can be pursued only along the
"tracks" that have been laid out by larger cultural ideas.

The sense of the articulation between these elements in the Holocaust construction is much more accurately represented in Edward T. Linenthal's book *Preserving*

Memory: The Struggle to Create the Holocaust Museum (1995). Linenthal carefully and powerfully documents the role of status group interests in the fifteen-year process involved in the creation of the Holocaust Museum in Washington, D.C. He demonstrates, at the same time, that the particular parties were deeply affected by the broader cultural context of Holocaust symbolization. President Carter, for example, initially proposed the idea of such a museum partly on political grounds—in order to mollify a key democratic constituency, the Jews, as he was making unprecedented gestures to Palestinians in the diplomatic conflicts of the Middle East (17–28). Yet, when a Carter adviser, Stuart Eizenstat, first made the written proposal to the president, in April 1978, he pointed to the great popularity of the recently broadcast *Holocaust* miniseries on NBC. It was in terms of this broader context—in which the Holocaust was already being universalized—that Eizenstat also warned the president that other American cities, and other nations, were already engaged in constructing what could be competing Holocaust commemorative sites. Even Linenthal, however, sometimes loses sight of the broader context. Describing the contentious struggles over representation of non-Jewish victims, for example, he speaks of "those committed to Jewish ownership of Holocaust memory" (39), a provocative phrasing that invites the kind of reductionist, status-group interpretation of strategic motivation that Novick employs. As I have shown in this essay, the Holocaust as a universalizing symbol of human suffering was, in a fundamental sense, inextricably related to the Jews, for the symbol was constructed directly in relationship to the Jewish mass murder. This was not a matter of ownership but a matter of narrative construction and intensely experienced social drama, which had been crystallized long before the struggles over representation in the museum took place. As a result of the early, progressive narrative of the Nazis' mass murder, non-Jewish Americans had given to Jews a central pride of place and had greatly altered their attitudes and social relation to Jews as a result. The conflicts that Linenthal documents came long after this crystallization of Jewish centrality. They were about positioning vis-à-vis an already firmly crystallized symbol, which had by then become renarrated in a tragic manner. Engorged with evil and universalized in its meaning, the Holocaust could not possibly be "owned" by any one particular social group or by any particular nation. The Holocaust museum was able to gain consensual support precisely because the symbol of evil had already become highly generalized such that other, non-Jewish groups could, and did, associate and reframe their own subjugation in ways that strengthened the justice of their causes. See my discussion of metonymy, analogy, and legality later in this essay.

Norman G. Finkelstein's book *The Holocaust Industry: Reflections on the Exploitation of Jewish Suffering* (2000) constitutes an even more tendentious and decidedly more egregious treatment of Holocaust centrality than Novick's, in a sense representing a long and highly polemical asterisk to that earlier, more scholarly book. Finkelstein bothers not at all with the ambiguity of motives, flatly saying that the Jewish concentration on the Holocaust, beginning in the late 1960s, was "a ploy to delegitimize all criticism of Jews" (37). The growing crystallization of the Holocaust as a metaphor for evil invites from Finkelstein only ridicule and ideology-critique: "The abnormality of the Nazi holocaust springs not from the event itself but from the exploitive industry that has grown up around it...'The Holocaust' is an ideological representation of the Nazi holocaust. Like most ideologies, it bears a connection, if tenuous, with reality...Its central dogmas sustain significant political and class interests. Indeed, The Holocaust has proven to be an indispensable ideological weapon" (150–51).

58. Higham (1984) rightly notes that a range of factors involving what might be called the "modernization" of America's Jewish population—increasingly high rates of urbanization and education, growing professionalization—also facilitated the identification with them of non-Jews. Other, more specifically cultural processes, however, were also fundamentally involved.

59. According to a 1990 survey, when Americans were presented with a list of well-known catastrophic events, a clear majority said that the Holocaust "was *the* worst tragedy in history" (quoted in Novick, 1999: 232, italics in original).

60. The tragic and personal qualities of the *Diary*, which set it against the "progressive narrative" structure of the early postwar period, initially had made it difficult to find a publisher.

Queriod, the literary publishing house in Amsterdam, rejected the manuscript of *Het Achterhuis*, giving as its reasons the fact that "in 1947 it was certain that war and everything to do with it was stone dead....Immediately as the terror was over and the anxieties of that pitch-black night were banished, people did not want to venture again into the darkness. They wished to give all their attention to the new day that was dawning" (Strenghold, 1988: 337).

61. Doneson's helpful historical reconstruction of the dramatization of the *Diary* also emphasizes the personal focus. Like many other commentators (e.g., Rosenfeld, 1995), however, she suggests that this focus undermines the tragic message of the Holocaust rather than generalizing it. In this, she joins the ranks of those who decry the "Americanization" of the Holocaust, an interpretation with which my approach strongly disagrees.

62. This clash of genres was demonstrated by the storm of controversy inside Germany that greeted the 1995 decision by a new German cable company to broadcast old episodes of *Hogan's Heroes*.

63. See the extensive social scientific discussion in Zielinski (1986), from which this discussion is derived.

64. It was after this crystallizing event that some of the intellectuals who had been most associated with focusing public discussion on the Holocaust began to criticize its transformation into a mass collective representation. Elie Wiesel made his famous declaration (quoted earlier) that the ontological nature of Holocaust evil made it impossible to dramatize. Complaining, in effect, that such dramatization stole the Holocaust from those who had actually suffered from it, Wiesel described the television series as "an insult to those who perished, and those who survived"

(quoted in Morrow, 1978). Such criticism only intensified in response to the subsequent flood of movie and television dramatizations. In *One, by One, by One: Facing the Holocaust*, for example, Judith Miller issued a fervent critique of the appropriation of the original event by the mass media culture of the "Holocaust industry" (1990: 232). Rather than seeing the widespread distribution of the mass-mediated experience as allowing universalization, she complained about its particularization via "Americanization," presumably because it was in the United States that most of these mass media items were produced: "Europe's most terrible genocide is transformed into an American version of kitsch" (232).

Aside from knee-jerk anti-Americanism, which has continued to inform critiques of the "Holocaust industry" in the years since, such a perspective also reflects the anti–popular culture, hermeneutic tone-deafness of the Frankfurt School's "culture industry" approach to meaning. (See Docker [1994] for a vigorous postmodern criticism in this regard.) Such attacks stand outside the interpretive processes of mass culture. In place of interpretations of meaning, they issue moral condemnations: "This vulgarization is a new form of historical titillation...In societies like America's, where the public attention span is measured in seconds and minutes rather than years or decades, where sentimentality replaces insight and empathy, it represents a considerable threat to dignified remembrance" (Miller, 1990: 232). Such complaints fundamentally misapprehend cultural processes in general and cultural trauma in particular. (See my later discussion of the "dilemma of uniqueness.")

While such typically leftist complaints are well intended, it is revealing that their "anticommodification" arguments overlap quite neatly with the conservative, sometimes anti-Semitic language that German conservatives employed in their effort to prevent the *Holocaust* miniseries from being shown in their country. Franz Joseph Strauss, the right-wing, nationalist leader of the Bavarian Christian Democrats, called the series "a fast-buck operation." The German television executives opposed to airing the series condemned it as "a cultural commodity...not in keeping with the memory of the victims." *Der Spiegel* railed against "the destruction of the Jews as soap opera...a commercial horror show...an imported cheap commodity...genocide shrunken to the level of *Bonanza* with music appropriate to *Love Story*." After the series was televised and its great impact revealed, one German journalist ascribed its effect to its personal dramatization: "No other film has ever made the Jews' road of suffering leading to the gas chambers so vivid....Only since and as a result of 'Holocaust' does a majority of the nation know what lay behind the horrible and vacuous formula 'Final Solution of the Jewish Question.' They know it because a U.S. film maker had the courage to break with the paralyzing dogma...that mass murder must not be represented in art" (quoted in Herf, 1986: 214, 217).

65. See the Arendt-Jaspers correspondence on these issues and the astute analysis by Richard J. Bernstein in *Hannah Arendt and the Jewish Question* (1996).

66. "The capture and trial of Eichmann and, in the following years, the controversies surrounding Hannah Arendt's *Eichmann in Jerusalem* were something of a

curtain raiser to the era of transition. For the mass public this was the first time the Holocaust was framed as a distinct and separate process, separate from Nazi criminality in general" (Novick, 1994: 161). It was only as a result of this separation that the poet A. Alvarez could have made his much-noted remark in the *Atlantic Monthly*, to the effect that "while all miseries of World War II have faded, the image of the concentration camp persists" (quoted in Zelizer, 1998: 155).

67. Novick (161) goes on to observe that "it was in large part as a result of the acceptance of Arendt's portrait of Eichmann (with an assist from Milgram) that 'just following orders' changed, in the American lexicon, from a plea in extenuation to a damning indictment."

68. See, in more depth, Browning, "Ordinary Germans or Ordinary Men? A Reply to the Critics," in Berenbaum and Peck (1998: 252–65), and Goldhagen, "Ordinary Men or Ordinary Germans?" in Berenbaum and Peck (1998: 301–308).

69. "Spielberg does not show what 'Germans' did but what *individual* Germans did, offering hope that one of them—Schindler—would become one of many. Unlike *Holocaust*...Spielberg can tell a 'true tale' that must seem doubly strange. While the events in *Schindler's List* may contradict the idea of the Nazi state as the perfect machine, the State's and Schindler's deficiencies provide a paradox of choice—'the other Nazi,' the German who did good" (Wiessberg, 1997: 178, italics in original).

70. By "force of arms" I refer to the ability of the North Vietnamese to successfully resist the United States and South Vietnamese on the ground. David Kaiser's *American Tragedy* (1999) demonstrates that, in purely military terms, the Americans and South Vietnamese forces were never really in the game and that, in fact, the kind of interventionist war the United States benightedly launched could not have been won short of using nuclear arms. If the United States had not intervened militarily in Vietnam, America might not have lost control over the means of symbolic production, and the Holocaust might not have been universalized in the same way.

71. The power of this symbolic reversal is attested to by the fact that, two decades later, an American psychologist, Herbert C. Kelman, and a sociologist, V. Lee Hamilton, published *Crimes of Obedience: Toward a Social Psychology of Authority and Responsibility* (1989), which in developing a theory of "sanctioned massacre" drew explicit connections between American military behavior at My Lai and German Nazi behavior during the Holocaust.

72. A relatively recent demonstration of this polluting association was provided by the *New York Times* review of a much-trumpeted televised television show called *Nuremberg*. "Here's the defining problem with *Nuremberg*, TNT's ambitious, well-meaning two-part miniseries about the trial of Nazi war criminals: the 'best' character in the movie is Hermann Göring. Through Brian Cox's complex performance, Göring (founder of the Gestapo, Hitler's no. 2) becomes his finest self. He is urbane, loyal, and courageous—and he gets the best lines. The victors will always be the judges, the vanquished always the accused," he says with world-weary knowingness (Julie Salamon, "Humanized, but Not Whitewashed, at Nuremberg," July 14, 2000: B 22).

73. In 1995, the Smithsonian Museum in Washington, D.C., had planned to mount an exhibition commemorating the Allies' defeat of Japan and the successful conclusion of World War II. The plans included highlighting the plane that had dropped the atomic bomb on Hiroshima. The public uproar that greeted these plans eventually had the effect of preventing the exhibition from ever going forward. See Linenthal (1995).

74. These suggestions were made, for example, in both Laqueur (1980) and Dawidowicz (1982). The scholarly arguments along these lines culminated with the publication of David S. Wyman's book *The Abandonment of the Jews: America and the Holocaust, 1941–1945* (1984).

75. Linenthal's otherwise helpful discussion implies that this disjunction between historical fact qua the historical discipline and historical fact qua memorialization casts doubt on the latter's validity. I would suggest (Alexander, 2003), to the contrary, that these are different arenas for the mediation of cultural trauma, and each arena has its own framework of justification.

76. See, for example, the brilliant but mythologizing biography of Jean Lacouture, *De Gaulle: The Rebel 1890–1944* (1990). After the Allied armies, primarily British and American, had allowed the relatively small remnant of the French army under De Gaulle to enter first into Paris, as a symbolic gesture, De Gaulle dramatically announced to an evening rally that Paris "has risen to free itself" and that it had "succeeded in doing so with its own hands."

77. Max Ophuls's film *The Sorrow and the Pity* exercised a profound expressive effect in this regard, as did the American historian Robert O. Paxton book *La France de Vichy*. For an overview of these developments, see Hartman, "The Voice of Vichy" (Hartman, 1996: 72–81).

78. How many Austrians themselves—or Swiss, or Dutch for that matter (Eyerman, 2008)—have come to accept this new position in the Holocaust story is not the issue, and there certainly is a new right movement in Continental Europe that often takes on anti-Semitic tones and minimizes Nazi atrocities against Jews. That said, there have definitely been deep and significant cultural processes inside various European nations that have transformed former victims into quasi-perpetrators. This process of symbolic inversion is well illustrated by the emergence of an association in Austria, the Gedenkdienst, or Commemorative Service Program. This government-sponsored but privately organized program allows young men to perform alternative service by volunteering in a Holocaust-related institution somewhere in the world: "The interns are challenging their country's traditional notion of its wartime victimization—that Austria simply fell prey to Nazi aggression. In fact, thousands of Austrians acted as Nazi collaborators and likely committed war crimes against Jews....'I want to tell [people] that I acknowledge it,' Zotti [a Gedenkdienst volunteer] says, 'It's important for me. It's my country. It's my roots. I want to put it in the light of what it is'" (*Los Angeles Times*, July 30, 2000: E3).

79. The phrase has been evoked innumerable times over the last three decades in both theological and secular contexts—for example, Vigen Guroian's "Post-Holocaust Political Morality" (1988).

80. According to a poll taken during the 1990s, between 80 and 90 percent of Americans agreed that the need to protect the rights of minorities, and not "going along with everybody else," were lessons to be drawn from the Holocaust. The same proportion also agreed that "it is important that people keep hearing about the Holocaust so that it will not happen again" (quoted in Novick, 1999: 232).

81. On May 20, 1999, the *San Francisco Chronicle* ran the following story from the *Los Angeles Times* wire service:

> The Justice Department renewed its long legal battle yesterday against alleged Nazi death camp guard John Demjanjuk, seeking to strip the retired Cleveland autoworker of his U.S. citizenship. For Demjanjuk, 79, the action marks the latest in a 22-year-old case with many twists and turns.... The Justice Department first accused Demjanjuk of being Ivan the Terrible in 1977, and four years later a federal judge concurred. Demjanjuk was stripped of his U.S. citizenship and extradited in 1986 to Israel, where he was convicted of crimes against humanity by an Israeli trial court and sentenced to death. But Israel's Supreme Court found that reasonable doubt existed on whether Demjanjuk was Ivan the Terrible, a guard [in Treblinka] who hacked and tortured his victims before running the engines that pumped lethal gas into the chambers where more than 800,000 men, women and children were executed.... Returning to a quiet existence in Cleveland, Demjanjuk won a second court victory last year when [a] U.S. District Judge—citing criticism of government lawyers by an appellate court panel—declared that government lawyers acted "with reckless disregard for their duty to the court" by withholding evidence in 1981 that could have helped Demjanjuk's attorneys.... The Justice Department [will] reinstitute denaturalization proceedings based on other evidence. ("U.S. Reopens 22-Year Case against Retiree Accused of Being Nazi Guard": A4)

82. The first issue of the journal *Holocaust and Genocide Studies* carried an article by Seena B. Kohl entitled "Ethnocide and Ethnogenesis: A Case Study of the Mississippi Band of Choctaw, a Genocide Avoided" (1986: 91–100). After the publication of his *American Holocaust: The Conquest of the New World* (1991) David E. Stannard wrote:

> Compared with Jews in the Holocaust...some groups have suffered greater *numerical* loss of life from genocide. The victims of the Spanish slaughter of the indigenous people of Mesoamerica in the sixteenth century numbered in the tens of millions.... Other groups also have suffered greater proportional

loss of life from genocide than did the Jews under Hitler. The Nazis killed 60 to 65 per cent of Europe's Jews, compared with the destruction by the Spanish, British, and Americans of 95 per cent or more of numerous ethnically and culturally distinct peoples in North and South America from the sixteenth through the nineteenth centuries....Among other instances of clear genocidal intent, the first governor of the State of California openly urged his legislature in 1851 to wage war against the Indians of the region "until the Indian race becomes extinct." (2, italics in original)

Stannard is ostensibly here denying the uniqueness of the Holocaust, even while he makes of it a pivotal reference for moral determinations of evil.

83. Delanty (2001) makes an apposite observation, suggesting that "the discourse of war around the Kosovo episode was one of uncertainty about the cognitive status of war and how it should be viewed in relation to other historical events of large-scale violence" (43). Delanty directly links this discursive conflict, which he locates in what he calls the "global public sphere," to the ethical questions of what kind of interventionist action, if any, outsiders were morally obligated to take: "The implications of this debate in fact went beyond the ethical level in highlighting cultural questions concerning the nature of war and legitimate violence...about what exactly constitutes violence [and] who was the victim and who was perpetrator [and] the constitution of the 'we' who are responsible" (43). Yet because Delanty views this discursive conflict as primarily cognitive, between more or less similarly valued "cognitive models," he fails sufficiently to appreciate the moral force that the Holocaust's engorged evilness lent to the metaphors of ethnic cleansing and genocide. This leads Delanty to make the perplexing observation that "as the war progressed, the nature of the subject of responsibility, the object of politics and whether moral obligations must lead to political obligation became more and more uncertain," with the result that the "obligation to intervene was severely limited" (43). Yet, if the analysis in the present essay is correct, it would seem to suggest precisely the opposite: Given the uneven weighting of the polluted symbols of violence, as the Yugoslavian wars progressed, during the decade of the 1990s, the Holocaust symbol gained increasing authority with the result that the immanent moral obligations became increasingly certain and the political obligation to intervene increasingly available.

84. The very same day, Germany's deputy foreign minister for U.S. relations, a Social Democrat, "suggested why Germany was able to participate in the NATO assault on Yugoslavia: The '68ers,' veterans of the student movement, used to tell their elders, 'We will not stand by, as you did while minority rights are trampled and massacres take place.' Slobodan Milosevic gave them a chance to prove it" (*San Francisco Chronicle*, May 14: A1).

85. For a detailed discussion of the fundamental analogizing role played during media construction of the Balkan crisis by recycled Holocaust photos, see Zelizer (1998: 210–30).

86. The date was December 11, 1946.

87. On the fiftieth anniversary of that proclamation, Michael Ignatieff recalled that "the Holocaust made the Declaration possible," that it was composed in "the shadow of the Holocaust," and that "the Declaration may still be a child of the Enlightenment, but it was written when faith in the Enlightenment faced its deepest crisis of confidence" (1999: 58).

88. As Martha Minow writes (1998),

> The World War II trials [should] receive credit for helping to launch an international movement for human rights and for the legal institutions needed to implement such rights. Domestic trials, inspired in part by the Nuremberg trials, include Israel's prosecution of Adolph Eichmann for this conduct during World War II; Argentina's prosecution of 5,000 members of the military junta involved in state terrorism and the murder of 10,000 to 30,000 people; Germany's prosecution of border guards and their supervisors involved in shooting escapees from East Germany; and Poland's trial of General Jaruzelski for his imposition of martial law.... Nuremberg launched a remarkable international movement for human rights founded in the rule of law; inspired the development of the United Nations and of nongovernmental organizations around the world; encouraged national trials for human rights violations; and etched a set of ground rules about human entitlement that circulate in local, national, and international settings. Ideas and, notably, ideas about basic human rights spread through formal and informal institutions. Especially when framed in terms of universality, the language of rights and the vision of trials following their violation equip people to call for accountability even where it is not achievable. (27, 47–8)

89. The scholar was Yehuda Bauer. See note 40.

90. Despite his misleading polemics against what he pejoratively terms the "Holocaust industry," it is revealing that even such a critic of popularization as Finkelstein realizes that the uniqueness of Holocaust evility does not preclude, and should not preclude, the event's generalization and universalization:

> For those committed to human betterment, a touchstone of evil does not preclude but rather invites comparisons. Slavery occupied roughly the same place in the moral universe of the late nineteenth century as the Nazi holocaust does today. Accordingly, it was often invoked to illuminate evils not fully appreciated. John Stuart Mill compared the condition of women in that most hallowed Victorian institution, the family, to slavery. He even ventured that in crucial respects it was worse. (Finkelstein, 2000: 148)

Citing a specific example of this wider moral effect, Finkelstein observes that, "seen through the lens of Auschwitz, what previously was taken for granted—for example, bigotry—no longer can be. In fact, it was the Nazi holocaust that discredited the scientific racism that was so pervasive a feature of American intellectual life before World War II" (2000: 148).

91. This instrumentalizing, desacralizing, demagicalizing approach to routinization is captured in the quotation with which Max Weber famously concluded *The Protestant Ethic and the Spirit of Capitalism* (1958 [1904]: 182). Observing that modernity brought with it the very distinct possibility of "mechanized petrification, embellished with a sort of convulsive self-importance," Weber added this apposite passage: "Specialists without spirit, sensualists without heart; this nullity imagines that it has attained a level of civilization never before achieved." This understanding has been applied to the memorialization process—as kind of inevitable, "developmental" sequence—by a number of commentators, and, most critically, in Ian Buruma, *The Wages of Guilt* (1994), and Peter Novick, *The Holocaust in American Life* (1999).

92. I am grateful to the author for sharing his findings with me.

93. Internal memo from Alice Greenwald, one of the museum's consultants, and Susan Morgenstein, the former curator and subsequently director of temporary exhibits, February 23, 1989.

94. Interview with Ralph Applebaum, chief designer of the Holocaust Museum.

95. Internal memo from Cindy Miller, project director, March 1, 1989.

96. This is Linenthal's own observation.

97. A *Los Angeles Times* description of that city's museum brings together its tragic dramatization, its participatory experiential emphasis, and its universalizing ambition:

> The 7-year-old West Los Angeles museum is internationally acclaimed for its high-tech exhibits, for pushing ideas instead of artifacts. You know right away that this is not the kind of museum where you parade past exhibits on the walls. The place is dark and windowless with a concrete bunker kind of feel, lit by flashes from a 16-screen video wall featuring images of civil rights struggles and blinking list of words: *Retard. Spic. Queen.* (July 30, 2000: E1, italics in original)

The exhibition at the Los Angeles museum begins by asking visitors to pass through one of two doors marked "unprejudiced" and "prejudiced."

REFERENCES

Abzug, Robert H. 1985. *Inside the Vicious Heart: Americans and the Liberation of Nazi Concentration Camps.* New York: Oxford University Press.

Alexander, Jeffrey C. 1983. *Max Weber: The Classical Attempt at Synthesis.* Vol. 3 of *Theoretical Logic in Sociology.* Berkeley: University of California Press.

Alexander, Jeffrey C. 1998. "Bush, Hussein, and the Cultural Preparation for War: Toward a More Symbolic Theory of Political Legitimation." *Epoche* 21(1): 1–14.

———. 2003. *The Meanings of Social Life: A Cultural Sociology*. New York: Oxford University Press.

———. 2006a. "Cultural Pragmatics: Social Performance between Ritual and Strategy" in *Social Performance: Symbolic Action, Cultural Pragmatics, and Ritual*, eds. J. Alexander, B. Giesen, and J. Mast (pp. 29–90). Cambridge: Cambridge University Press.

———. 2006b. *The Civil Sphere*. New York: Oxford.

———. Forthcoming. "Postcolonialism, Trauma, and Civil Society: A New Understanding," in *Conflict, Citizenship and Civil Society*, eds. S. Koniordos et al. London: Routledge.

Alexander, J. C., and Philip Smith, 2003. "The Strong Program in Cultural Sociology: Elements of a Structural Hermeneutics," pp. 11–26 in Alexander, *The Meanings of Social Life*.

Alexander, J. C., Ron Eyerman, B. Giesen, N. J. Smelser and P. Sztompka, 2004. *Cultural Trauma and Collective Identity*. Berkeley: University of California Press.

Alexander, J. C., Bernhard Giesen, and J. Mast, eds. 2006. *Social Performance: Symbolic Action, Cultural Pragmatics, and Ritual*. Cambridge: Cambridge University Press.

Alexander, J. C. (with Rui Gao), 2007. "Remembrance of Things Past: Cultural Trauma, the 'Nanking Massacre' and Chinese Identity," in *Tradition and Modernity: Comparative Perspectives*, eds. Yan Shaodang, et al. (pp. 266–94). Beijing: Peking University Press, 2007.

Amishai-Maisels, Ziva. 1988. "Christological Symbolism of the Holocaust." *Holocaust and Genocide Studies* 3(4): 457–81.

Arendt, Hannah. 1951. *The Origins of Totalitarianism*. New York: Harcourt Brace Jovanowich.

Aristotle. *Poetics* I. 1987. Richard Janko, trans. Indianapolis: Hackett.

Aron, Raymond. 1990. *Memoirs: Fifty Years of Political Reflection*. New York: Holmes and Meier.

Baer, Alejandro. 1999. "Visual Testimonies and High-Tech Museums: The Changing Embodiment of Holocaust History and Memorialization." Unpublished manuscript, Department of Sociology, University of Madrid.

Bauer, Yehuda. 1986. Editor's introduction. *Holocaust and Genocide Studies* 1(1): 1–2.

Bauman, Janina. 1986. *Winter in the Morning*. London: Virago.

Bauman, Zygmunt. 1989. *Modernity and the Holocaust*. Cambridge, UK: Polity Press.

———. 1993. *Postmodern Ethics*. Oxford: Blackwell.

———, ed. 1968. *State and Society*. Berkeley: University of California Press.

Benn, David Wedgewood. 1995, June 5. "Perceptions of the Holocaust: Then and Now." *World Today*, 102–103.

Berenbaum, Michael. 1998. Preface to *The Holocaust and History: The Known, the Unknown, the Disputed, and the Reexamined*, eds. M. Berenbaum and Abraham J. Peck (pp. xi–xii). Bloomington: Indiana University Press.

Berenbaum, Michael, and Abraham J. Peck, eds. 1998. *The Holocaust and History: The Known, the Unknown, the Disputed, and the Reexamined.* Bloomington: Indiana University Press.

Bernstein, Richard J. 1996. *Hannah Arendt and the Jewish Question.* Cambridge, UK: Polity Press.

———. 2001. "Radical Evil: Kant at War with Himself." In *Rethinking Evil,* ed. Maria Pia Lara (pp. 55–85). Berkeley: University of California Press.

Bier, Jean-Paul. 1986. "The Holocaust, West Germany, and Strategies of Oblivion, 1947–1979." In *Germans and Jews since the Holocaust: The Changing Situation in West Germany,* eds. Anson Rabinbach and Jack Zipes (pp. 185–207). New York: Holmes and Meier.

Braun, R. 1994. "The Holocaust and Problems of Historical Representation." *History and Theory* 33(2): 172–97.

Brooks, Peter. 1995. *The Melodramatic Imagination.* New York: Columbia University Press.

Browning, Christopher. 1992. *Ordinary Men: Reserve Police Battalion 101 and the Final Solution in Poland.* New York: HarperCollins.

———. 1996, October 18. "Human Nature, Culture, and the Holocaust." *The Chronicle of Higher Education,* A72.

Buck, Pearl S. 1947, February. "Do You Want Your Children to Be Tolerant?" *Better Homes and Gardens,* 33.

Buruma, Ian. 1994. *The Wages of Guilt: Memories of War in Germany and Japan.* New York: Farrar Straus Giroux.

Carter, Hodding. 1947, November. "How to Stop the Hate Mongers in Your Home Town." *Better Homes and Gardens,* 45.

Caruth, Cathy. 1996. *Unclaimed Experience: Trauma, Narrative, and History.* Baltimore: Johns Hopkins University Press.

———, ed. 1995. *Trauma: Explorations in Memory.* Baltimore: Johns Hopkins University Press.

Chang, Iris. 1997. *The Rape of Nanking: The Forgotten Holocaust of World War II.* New York: Basic Books.

Clendinnen, Inga. 1999. *Reading the Holocaust.* Cambridge: Cambridge University Press.

Cohen, Roger. 1999, June 26. "Berlin Holocaust Memorial Approved." *New York Times,* A3.

Dawidowicz, Lucy. 1982. *On Equal Terms: Jews in America, 1881–1981.* New York: Holt, Rinehart, and Winston.

Delanty, Gerard. 2001. "Cosmopolitanism and Violence." *European Journal of Social Theory* 4(1): 41–52.

Deutscher, Isaac. 1968. "The Jewish Tragedy and the Historian." In *The Non-Jewish Jew and Other Essays,* ed. Tamara Deutscher (pp. 163–64). London: Oxford University Press.

Diamond, Sander A. 1969. "The Kristallnacht and the Reaction in America." *Yivo Annual of Jewish Social Science* 14: 196–208.

Dilthey, Wilhelm. 1976. "The Construction of the Historical World in the Human Sciences." In *Dilthey: Selected Writings*, ed. and trans. H. P. Rickman (pp. 168–245). Cambridge: Cambridge University Press.

———. 1962. *Pattern and Meaning in History.* New York: Harper and Row.

Diner, Dan. 2000. *Beyond the Conceivable: Studies on Germany, Nazism, and the Holocaust.* Berkeley: University of California Press.

Dinnerstein, Leonard. 1981–82, September–June. "Anti-Semitism Exposed and Attacked, 1945–1950." *American Jewish History* 71: 134–49.

Dodson, Dan W. 1946, July. "College Quotas and American Democracy." *American Scholar* 15(3): 267–76.

Doneson, Judith E. 1987. "The American History of Anne Frank's Diary." *Holocaust and Genocide Studies* 2(1): 149–60.

Drinan, Robert F. 1987. "Review of Ann Tusa and John Tusa, *The Nuremberg Trial.*" *Holocaust and Genocide Studies* 3(2): 333–34.

Eisenstadt, S. N. 1982. "The Axial Age: The Emergence of Transcendental Visions and the Rise of Clerics." *European Journal of Sociology* 23(2): 294–314.

Erlanger, Steven. 2001, April 2. "After the Arrest: Wider Debate about the Role of Milosevic, and of Serbia." *New York Times*, A8.

Eyerman, Ron. 2001. *Cultural Trauma: Slavery and the Formation of African American Identity.* New York: Cambridge University Press.

———. 2008. *The Assassination of Theo van Gogh: From Social Drama to Cultural Trauma.* Durham, NC: Duke University Press.

Feingold, Henry L. 1974. *Zion in America: the Jewish Experience from Colonial Times to the Present.* Boston: Twayne.

Finkelstein, Norman G. 2000. *The Holocaust Industry: Reflections on the Exploitation of Jewish Suffering.* London: Verso.

Friedlander, Saul. 1978. *History and Psychoanalysis.* New York: Holmes and Meier.

———. 1992. *Probing the Limits of Representation.* Berkeley: University of California Press.

Frye, Northrop. 1971 [1957]. *Anatomy of Criticism.* Princeton: Princeton University Press.

Fussell, P. 1975. *The Great War and Modern Memory.* Oxford: Oxford University Press.

Garber, Zev, and Bruce Zuckerman. 1989. "Why Do We Call the Holocaust 'The Holocaust'? An Inquiry into the Psychology of Labels." *Modern Judaism* 9(2): 197–211.

Geertz, Clifford. 1973. *The Interpretation of Cultures.* New York: Basic Books.

———. 1984. "Distinguished Lecture: Anti Anti-Relativism." *American Anthropologist* 86: 263–78.

Gleason, Philip. 1981. "Americans All: World War II and the Shaping of American Identity." *Review of Politics* 43(4): 483–518.

Goldhagen, Daniel. 1996. *Hitler's Willing Executioners: Ordinary Germans and the Holocaust.* New York: Knopf.

Goodman, Tanya. 2009. *Staging Solidarity: Truth and Reconciliation in a New South Africa.* Boulder, CO: Paradigm.

Greene, Joshua M., and Shiva Kumar. 2000. Editors' introduction to *Witness: Voices from the Holocaust,* eds. Joshua M. Greene and Shiva Kumar (pp. xxi–xxviii). New York: Free Press.

Guroian, Vigen. 1988. "Post-Holocaust Political Morality: The Litmus of Bitburg and the Armenian Genocide Resolution." *Holocaust and Genocide Studies* 3(3): 305–22.

Harris, Robert. 1992. *Fatherland.* London: Hutchinson.

Hart, Walter R. 1947. July. "Anti-Semitism in N.Y. Medical Schools." *American Mercury* 65: 53–63.

Hartman, Geoffrey H. 1996. *The Longest Shadow: In the Aftermath of the Holocaust.* Bloomington: Indiana University Press.

———. 2000. "Memory.com: Tel-Suffering and Testimony in the Dot Com Era." *Raritan* 19: 1–18.

Hayes, Peter, ed. 1999. *Lessons and Legacies,* Vol 3: *Memory, Memorialization and Denial.* Evanston, IL: Northwestern University Press.

Herf, Jeffrey. 1984. *Reactionary Modernism.* New York: Cambridge University Press.

———. 1986. "The 'Holocaust' Reception in West Germany." In *Germans and Jews since the Holocaust: The Changing Situation in West Germany,* eds. Anson Rabinbach and Jack Zipes (pp. 208–233). New York: Holmes and Meier.

Higham, John. 1984. *Send These to Me.* Baltimore: Johns Hopkins University Press.

Hollinger, David. 1996. *Science, Jews, and Secular Culture: Studies in Mid-Twentieth-Century American Intellectual History.* Princeton, NJ: Princeton University Press.

Ignatieff, Michael. 1999. "Human Rights: The Midlife Crisis." *New York Review of Books* 46(9): 58–62.

Kaiser, David. 1999. *American Tragedy.* Cambridge, MA: Harvard University Press.

Kampe, Norbert. 1987. "Normalizing the Holocaust? The Recent Historians' Debate in the Federal Republic of Germany." *Holocaust and Genocide Studies* 2(1): 61–80.

Kane, Anne. 1992, Spring. "Cultural Analysis in Historical Sociology: The Analytic and Concrete Forms of the Autonomy of Culture." *Sociological Theory* 9(1): 53–69.

Kant, Immanuel. 1960. *Religion within the Limits of Reason Alone,* trans. Theodore M. Greene and Hoyt H. Hudson. New York: Harper.

Keller, Suzanne. 1963. *Beyond the Ruling Class.* New York: Random House.

Kelman, Herbert C., and V. Lee Hamilton. 1989. *Crimes of Obedience: Toward a Social Psychology of Authority and Responsibility.* New Haven: Yale University Press.

Kohl, Seena B. 1986. "Ethnocide and Ethnogenesis: A Case Study of the Mississippi Band of Choctaw, a Genocide Avoided." *Holocaust and Genocide Studies* 1(1): 91–100.

Korman, Gerd. 1972. "The Holocaust in American Historical Writing," *Societas* 2: 251–70.

Kuper, Leo. 1981. *Genocide: Its Political Use in the Twentieth Century*. New Haven, CT: Yale University Press.

La Capra, Dominick. 1994. *Representing the Holocaust: History, Theory, Trauma*. Ithaca, NY: Cornell University Press.

Lacouture, Jean. 1990. *De Gaulle: The Rebel, 1890–1944*, trans. Patrick O'Brien. New York: HarperCollins.

Langer, Lawrence L. 2000. "Foreword." In *Witness: Voices from the Holocaust*, eds. Joshua M. Greene and Shiva Kumar (pp. xi–xx). New York: Free Press.

Laqueur, Walter. 1980. *The Terrible Secret: Suppression of the Truth about Hitler's "Final Solution."* Boston: Little, Brown.

Lear, Jonathan. 1992. "Katharsis." In *Essays on Aristotle's Poetics*, ed. Amelie Oksenberg Rorty (pp. 315–40). Princeton, NJ: Princeton University Press.

Lemkin, Ralph. 1994. *Axis Rule in Occupied Europe*. Washington, DC: Carnegie Endowment for International Peace.

Liberles, Robert. 1995. *Salo Wittmayer Baron: Architect of Jewish History*. New York: New York University Press.

Linenthal, Edward T. 1995. *Preserving Memory: The Struggle to Create the Holocaust Museum*. New York: Viking Books.

Lipstadt, Deborah E. 1996. "America and the Memory of the Holocaust, 1950–1965." *Modern Judaism* 16: 195–214.

Ma, Sheng Mei. "Contrasting Two Survival Literatures: On the Jewish Holocaust and the Chinese Cultural Revolution." *Holocaust and Genocide Studies* 2(1): 81–93.

Magnuson, E. 2008. *Changing Men, Transforming Culture: Inside the Men's Movement*. Boulder, CO: Paradigm Publishers.

Miller, Judith. 1990. *One, by One, by One: Facing the Holocaust*. New York: Simon and Schuster.

Minow, Martha. 1998. *Between Vengeance and Forgiveness: Facing History after Genocide and Mass Violence*. Boston: Beacon Press.

Morrow, Lance. 1978, May. "Television and the Holocaust." *Time*, 1, 53.

Naimark, Norman. 2001. *Fires of Hatred: Ethnic Cleansing in Twentieth-Century Europe*. Cambridge, MA: Harvard University Press.

Neal, Arthur. 1998. *National Trauma and Collective Memory*. Armonk, NY: Sharpe.

Norich, Anita. 1998–99. "*Harbe sugyes*/Puzzling Questions: Yiddish and English Culture in America during the Holocaust." *Jewish Social Studies* 1–2 (Fall/Winter): 91–110.

Novick, Peter. 1994. "Holocaust and Memory in America." In *The Texture of Memory: Holocaust Memorials and Meaning*, ed. James E. Young (pp. 159–65). New Haven: Yale University Press.

———. 1999. *The Holocaust in American Life*. New York: Houghton Mifflin.

Nussbaum, Martha. 1992. "Tragedy and Self-sufficiency: Plato and Aristotle on Fear and Pity." In *Essays on Aristotle's Poetics*, ed. Amelie Oksenberg Rorty (pp. 261–290). Princeton, NJ: Princeton University Press.

Ofer, Dalia. 1996. "Linguistic Conceptualization of the Holocaust in Palestine and Israel, 1942–53." *Journal of Contemporary History* 31(3): 567–95.

Perlez, Jane. 2001, April 2. "Milosevic Should Face Trial by Hague Tribunal, Bush Says." *New York Times*, A6.

Perry, George Sessions. 1948, November 13. "Your Neighbors: The Golombs." *Saturday Evening Post,* 36.

Rambo, Eric, and Elaine Chan. 1990. "Text, Structure, and Action in Cultural Sociology: A Commentary on 'Positive Objectivity' in Wuthnow and Archer." *Theory and Society* 19: 635–48.

Rohde, David. 1999, June 2. "The Visitor: Wiesel, a Man of Peace, Cites Need to Act." *New York Times,* A1.

Rorty, Amelie Oksenberg. 1992. "The Psychology of Aristotelian Tragedy." In *Essays on Aristotle's Poetics*, ed. A. O. Rorty (pp. 1–22). Princeton, NJ: Princeton University Press.

Rosenfeld, Alvin H. 1995. "The Americanization of the Holocaust." *Commentary* 90(6): 35–40.

Shapiro, Edward S. 1992. A *Time for Healing: American Jewry since World War II.* Baltimore: Johns Hopkins University Press.

Shirer, William L. 1969. *The Collapse of the Third Republic: An Inquiry into the Fall of France in 1940.* New York: Simon and Schuster.

Short, K. R. M. 1981. "Hollywood Fights Anti-Semitism, 1945–47." In *Feature Films as History*, ed. K. R. M. Short (pp. 157–189). Knoxville: University of Tennessee.

Silk, Mark. 1984. "Notes on the Judeo-Christian Tradition in America." *American Quarterly* 36: 65.

Smith, Philip. 1998. "Barbarism and Civility in the Discourses of Fascism, Communism, and Democracy." In *Real Civil Societies*, ed. J. Alexander (pp. 115–37). London: Sage.

———.2006. *Why War? The Cultural Logic of Iraq, the Gulf War, and Suez.* Chicago: University of Chicago Press.

Stannard, David E. 1991. *American Holocaust: The Conquest of the New World.* Oxford: Oxford University Press.

———. 1996, August 2. 'The Dangers of Calling the Holocaust Unique." *Chronicle of Higher Education*, B1–2.

Stember, Charles Herbert. 1966. *Jews in the Mind of America.* New York: Basic Books.

Strenghold, Leendert. 1988. "Review of *Back to the Source." Holocaust and Genocide Studies* 3(3): 337–42.

Thompson, Kenneth. 1997. *Moral Panics.* London: Routledge.

Turner, Victor. 1969. *The Ritual Process.* Chicago: Aldine.

van Gelder, Lawrence. 1999, May 5. "After the Holocaust, If There Can Indeed Be an After." *New York Times*, D1.

Weissberg, Liliane. 1997. "The Tale of a Good German: Reflections on the German Reception of *Schindler's List.*" In *Spielberg's Holocaust: Critical Perspectives on "Schindler's List,"* ed. Yosefa Loshitzky (pp. 171–192). Bloomington: University of Indiana Press.

Welles, Sumner. 1945, May 5. "New Hope for the Jewish People." *Nation* 160: 511–13.

Whitman, Howard. 1949, January 8. "The College Fraternity Crisis." *Collier's,* 34–35.

Wiesel, Elie. 1978, April 16. "Trivializing the Holocaust." *New York Times* 2: 1.

Wines, Michael. 1999, June 13. "Two Views of Inhumanity Split the World, Even in Victory." *New York Times* 4: 1.

Wyman, David S. 1984. *The Abandonment of the Jews: Americans and the Holocaust, 1941–1945.* New York: Pantheon.

Young, James E. 1993. *The Texture of Memory: Holocaust Memorials and Meaning.* New Haven: Yale University Press.

Zelizer, Barbie. 1998. *Remembering to Forget: Holocaust Memory through the Camera's Eye.* Chicago: University of Chicago.

Zielinski, Siegfried. 1986. "History as Entertainment and Provocation: The TV Series 'Holocaust' in West Germany." In *Germans and Jews since the Holocaust: The Changing Situation in West Germany,* eds. Anson Rabinbach and Jack Zipes (pp. 258–286). New York: Holmes and Meier.

PART II

COMMENTARIES

Allegories of Evil: A Response to Jeffrey Alexander

Martin Jay

Allegorization, it has long been, recognized, is an inevitable feature of all history writing. No matter how disinterested and neutral the historian tries to be, the very act of writing a meaningful narrative fashioned out of an infinity of potentially relevant texts and contexts compels him or her to create a gap between what happened in an unrecoverable past and what is represented of that past in the present. As Hans Kellner points out,

> What the allegorist does, and what the historian does as well, is to create a *counter*-discourse which confronts the "evidence" with the real meaning of the latter, a meaning that is different from or presumed to be hidden in the evidence. The counter-discourse is thus dependent upon *both* the evidence *and* the system of understanding that makes a counter-discourse necessary. All forms of historical *explanation* as such thus make use of allegorical devices to mediate between the evidence and the history created from it.[1]

If all history is inevitably allegorical, to some extent or another, it is thus possible only to confront one counter-discourse with another, not to dispense with allegorization entirely in the name of letting the evidence speak for itself or the events be recounted as they actually unfolded.

Some historical events seem, however, more prone to explicit allegorization than others, serving over time as the occasion for competing counter-discourses that claim to find in them a latent meaning that has been hitherto undisclosed. The ones that seem most prone to intense allegorical reconstruction are those that provide putative "lessons" for the present, lessons with strong moral or political implications. Perhaps no candidate for allegorization has been riper for multiple interpretations in modern history, as Jeffrey Alexander clearly shows, than the bewildering mixture of acts, events, and incomprehensible suffering that has come to be called "the Holocaust."

Alexander astutely notes that a cultural grid rather than individual choice determines the allegories that are most persuasive, at least for certain periods and certain communities of interpretation. He points in particular to what he calls the "universalization" of the Holocaust as an instance—indeed, *the* most unequivocal instance—of something called "radical" or "absolute evil" and its function in a meta-historical narrative of "redemption." By the former he means the gradual adoption of the Holocaust as an exemplary trauma whose ramifying effects are not limited to those who were its direct victims and whose responsibility was not confined to those who were its most immediate perpetrators. Even those who did not experience it as victim, victimizer, or even uneasy witness have been compelled to "remember" it as a cautionary tale of the highest significance. By the latter he means the functionalization of the Holocaust as a moment in a grand narrative with a "comic"—that is, positive—even triumphalist ending. For those who read it this way, the Holocaust has been turned into a "prelude and incitement to moral and social progress." Although by and large applauding the former, as a source of constructing moral universals for humankind as a whole, Alexander is far less comfortable with the latter, preferring what he calls the "tragic" alternative he sees as ultimately more efficacious in increasing "moral and social justice." For "comedization," he worries, risks "trivialization and forgetting."

By and large I share Alexander's sweeping historical reconstruction of the ways in which the Holocaust served these ends, but would make several emendations. First, although his argument about universalization begins by claiming that it has reached global proportions, he ends by conceding that it has made only modest inroads in non-Western cultures that were far away from the actual events. "What is unclear," he admits, "is the degree to which the cultural work that constructs these traumas, and responds to them, reaches beyond issues of national identity and sovereignty to the universalizing, supranational ethical imperatives increasingly associated with the 'lessons of post-Holocaust morality' in the West." In fact, as Cambodia, Rwanda, and Darfur show, whatever these "lessons" may have been, they certainly were not able to head off comparable events in those unhappy places, nor even stimulate Western intervention in time to make much of a difference. "Never again" turns out to be empty rhetoric for a good part of the world.

If this is the case, we have to ask hard questions about the transferability of vicarious trauma from one culture to another, from one historical memory to another. As a number of observers have noted, there is something disproportionate in the American fixation on the Holocaust as a universal moral tale. Alexander himself marshals most of his evidence from the American case, where even as early as Roosevelt's response to *Kristallnacht* in 1938, it was used to emphasize "the purity of the American nation." (One might add that the actual deaths in the German pogrom were far fewer than in such notorious American race riots as Tulsa seventeen years earlier).[2] The real work of universalization occurred, as Alexander notes, after the war, when the focus shifted from war crimes and general Nazi atrocities against liberal and democratic values to the specific killing of the Jews, which had hitherto been subsumed under more general categories. Ironically, a stress on the specific nature of Jewish suffering, which sometimes descended into an unseemly competition for the title of most victimized, went along with an attempt to make the Holocaust a universal moral lesson for all of humankind. What perhaps made this attempt so problematic is that it fails to register the contradiction between identifying the Holocaust as utterly unique and incomparable and then analogizing it to other possible genocidal horrors (real or threatening).

Somewhat similar patterns, to be sure, can be discerned in a few other cases besides America. As Samuel Moyn has shown in A *Holocaust Controversy*, his recent study of the reception of Jean-Claude Steiner's 1966 book on Treblinka, the French also vigorously debated whether or not to emphasize the exclusively Jewish dimension of Nazi crimes.[3] Daniel Rousset in particular criticized Steiner's focus on the Jewish genocide in favor of a more wide-ranging analysis of *l'univers concentrationnaire*, a world of totalitarian horror that knew no ethnic limits. But as Alexander correctly notes, it was in the United States that the campaign for universalization based paradoxically on the special role of Jewish victims was most vigorously waged. Battles over the Jewishness of Anne Frank, as Alexander spells out, were more fervently fought here than in Europe.

Alexander perhaps underestimates in his narrative of this American-centric universalization two important counter-examples: (1) the continuing power of an alternative type of universalization in the Soviet bloc, where the specificity of Jewish victimhood was occluded in the name of crimes against humanity, especially its "progressive" exemplars; and (2) the particularist reading of the Holocaust provided by Zionists who learned very different lessons from the trauma than the vicarious ones adopted in America. When he says that at some point "the United States government, and the nation's authoritative interlocutors, lost control over the telling of the Holocaust story," he exaggerates the extent to which it ever had a monopoly over that narrative.

To take the former first, until the fall of the Soviet empire, denying the predominantly Jewish nature of the Holocaust was a salient feature of virtually all the memorials to its victims. Concentration camp sites in Poland, Czechoslovakia, and East Germany played up the role of other groups, defined either politically or nationally rather than ethnically or religiously. Communist universalist ideology combined with residues of earlier nationalist, sometimes anti-Semitic attitudes to reduce stressing the Jewish dimension of the events. Ironically, in the Soviet Union, many Jews doggedly preferred to identify themselves with the socialist project rather than assume their ethnic identity, despite all the accumulating evidence that the latter could be a matter of life and death.[4] Indeed, even after the fall of the Soviet empire, sites like Auschwitz-Birkenau continued to be contested territory, with some Poles placing the losses their people suffered above those of—or at least alongside of—the Jewish victims. In countries like Estonia, Latvia, and Lithuania, resistance to special commemoration of the Jews as victims remains strong to this day, largely because it involves an awkward acknowledgment of the complicity of local populations.[5] Although it might be said that universalization of a sort occurred in Eastern Europe, it was of a very different kind from that highlighted by Alexander on the basis of the American story, whose protagonists, Alexander notes, were often GIs who liberated the camps.[6] The American story was often allegorized in "comic," triumphalist terms, allowing Americans to see their victory in the war as the victory of good over evil. The Eastern European story, in contrast, was told with shades of gray, often turning darker as the stain of perpetrator guilt spread beyond the Germans to local collaborators.[7]

A further dimension of the story, which Alexander never pursues, is the way in which Eastern Europeans who were themselves victims of communism—and often in exile as a result—refused to give special weight to the Holocaust as a crime against Jews because they focused on another candidate for the role of maximum evil, the Gulag and Stalinist crimes. Without opening up the can of worms that is the debate over totalitarianism and the relative extent of the horrors perpetrated by its several exemplars, it can be said that works like the *The Black Book of Communism*, edited by Stéphane Courtois,[8] had a similar relativizing effect on some Western observers when it was published in France in 1997.

In the second case, that of Israelis whose allegorization of the events was understandably central to their own existence as a new state, the lesson that was taken from the Holocaust was very different from both the American and Eastern European versions of universalization.[9] They may have shared the "comic," triumphalist conclusions drawn by some Americans to the extent that the creation of a Jewish state, able to protect itself against the still virulent threat of anti-Semitism, could be understood as the positive outcome of the suffering of European Jewry. But rather than taking the Holocaust as a universal moral example capable of inspiring greater tolerance and understanding among those chastened by its horror, they saw it as a warning against trusting universalist pretensions of any kind. That is, only a specifically Jewish state, relying entirely on its own self-defense abilities, could prevent another Holocaust in the future. The optimistic faith in what Alexander calls "the story of redeeming Nazism's victims by creating a progressive and democratic world order" was not shared by many who saw ethnic purity—the right of the Jewish people to their own home—as more important than democratic inclusion. Here the importance of Jewish rebellion rather than passive victimhood was emphasized, with the Warsaw Ghetto uprising playing a major role (or the Treblinka revolt, which Jean-Claude Steiner had also featured in his account). The ease with which Arabs were assimilated into the role of Nazi perpetrators in the Israeli popular imagination testifies to the power of this allegorization. Here the lesson learned was resolutely particularist, repudiating any assimilationist residues from the liberal past as a recipe for disaster. To this day, as the Israeli historian Tom Segev has recently pointed out, many Zionists are uneasy with the universalization of the Shoah.[10] Alexander perhaps does not sufficiently acknowledge that triumphalist comedization can come in both universal and particularist forms.

Alexander is, however, correct in noting the ubiquity of religious language in virtually all of the allegorizations he discusses. What needs also to be acknowledged is the irony that much of this rhetoric is more Christian than Jewish in origin and implication. Thus, for example, when one commentator says of Anne Frank that "some even see her as kind of saint and pray to her," he is imposing a version of martyrology that is far more at home in certain variants of Christianity than in Judaism, which has no use for saintly mediation. The pervasive use of *redemption*, *apocalyptic*, and *the sacred* (which Alexander, perhaps thinking too much of Durkheim, calls a sociological rather than a religious category) also suggests a more generic version of religion, which is another version of universalization. When Elie Wiesel introduces the portentous category of "ontological evil"[11] or Hannah Arendt ratchets up Kant's modest idea of "radical evil" as a synonym for human frailty into the worst possible evil one can imagine (and therefore not simply an expression of the human condition), it is clear that the normal level of allegorization in any historical account has come to seem insufficient.[12] What seems to be at stake, Alexander notes, is the very existence of the species. I think this is what he is driving at when he introduces the odd notion of the "engorgement" of evil.

What perhaps needs to be emphasized more than Alexander does is that the move from a comic to a tragic emplotment still remains an allegorization, still a kind of counter-discourse no more or less "true" to the facts. In fact, there is a third alternative that he neglects to mention, which has gained considerable popularity, at least among intellectuals in the l980s. I am referring to the way in which Auschwitz became a metonym for the impossibility of allegorization itself, a kind of symbol of historical unintelligibility and radical unrepresentability. Thus, Adorno made it into a challenge to the belief that narration could do justice to events so awful that they defied explanation and Lyotard made it into a synonym for the death of meta-narratives.[13] For them neither a comic nor a tragic emplotment could adequately express the mysterious impossibility of such a thing happening in the modern world. The Holocaust became a kind of rebuff to the very belief in historical meaningfulness or the ability of contextualization to make sense of traumatic events (and perhaps not them alone). As Giorgio Agamben would put it, "The aporia of Auschwitz is, indeed, the very aporia of historical knowledge: non-coincidence between facts and truth, between verification and comprehension."[14]

This, too, can be understood as a kind of universalization of the events, albeit not a directly moral one. Or rather, if it is moral, it is only in the sense of wanting to resist the subsumption of events under general categories or tropic emplotments (like tragic or comic),[15] as well as resisting the religious vocabulary of redemption and the sacred. The latter, its critics argued, did a disservice to the utter meaningless of the annihilation of victims whose deaths could not be redeemed by making them part of larger story, either comic or tragic. As Adorno bitterly put it, in mocking the claim made by Rilke for a proper death, "nowadays people merely snuff out."[16] Unlike the millions of soldiers who died in the war, theirs was not a "sacrifice" or "martyrdom" in the service of a cause, but rather a rebuke to the consolation implied by the very concept of sacrificial violence.

This anti-allegorizing allegorization, too, can be faulted for a kind of ahistorical universalization—what Dominick LaCapra calls the transcendentalization of trauma as perpetual absence rather than historical loss[17]—which makes Auschwitz a metonym for the human condition, or at least modernity, at its most bleak. Here the lesson is not "never again" but rather "always already." We are perhaps back to a slightly sharpened version of Kant's bland notion of radical evil as the human condition rather than Arendt's more historical claim that it was specific to Nazism. In either guise, it was another version of allegorization.

It may well be wise to concede that no matter what emplotment is favored (even attempting to thwart emplotment per se), allegorization will inevitably happen. A similar concession may be necessary when we consider one of the most obvious paradoxes of the universalizing moralization of the Holocaust: its tension with the alleged uniqueness of the Nazi genocide, so often defended with exorbitant fervor. Logically, the two fail to compute. Take, for example, the almost comical impossibility of Joschka Fischer's defense of the NATO intervention in Yugoslavia, which Alexander describes in the following terms: "He, too, insisted that the uniqueness of Serbian evil made it possible to draw analogies with the Holocaust." What this claim adds up to is that analogies can be drawn only if the two parties to the analogy cannot be compared. Alexander acknowledges this paradox by calling the Holocaust a "bridging metaphor," which is "unique and nonunique at the same time." But whether this leads to what he calls a "moral learning process" or produces a moral quagmire in which the Holocaust is instrumentalized for not always moral purposes is a question that cannot be answered by sociological methods alone.

NOTES

1. Hans Kellner, "Triangular Anxieties: The Present State of European Intellectual History," in *Modern European Intellectual History: Reappraisals and New Perspectives*, edited by Dominick LaCapra and Steven L. Kaplan (Ithaca, NY: Cornell University Press, 1982), p. 132.

2. Walter Rucker and James Nathaniel Upton, eds., *Encyclopedia of American Race Riots* (Westport, CT: Greenwood, 2006). It is estimated that 300 blacks died in Tulsa and 91 Jews during *Kristallnacht*.

3. Samuel Moyn, A *Holocaust Controversy: The Treblinka Affair in Postwar France* (Waltham, MA: University Press of New England, 2005).

4. For a provocative account of the continuing acceptance by many Soviet Jews of communism's universalist pretentions, see Yuri Slezkine, *The Jewish Century* (Princeton, NJ: Princeton University Press, 2004), chapter 3.

5. Efraim Zuroff, "Eastern Europe: Anti-Semitism in the Wake of Holocaust-Related Issues," *Jewish Political Studies Review* 17 (Spring 2005):1–2. Before Western observers feel too superior, it should be noted that collaboration there was also often hushed up after the war. In fact, as noted in *The Holocaust Encyclopedia*, edited by Walter Laqueur, "In Britain the administrators and the police in the Channel Islands (the only part of the United Kingdom occupied by the Germans) who had helped with the deportation of Jews continued to work in their old positions, and some of them even received the Order of the British Empire for the bravery they had shown in the war years" (New Haven, CT: Yale University Press, 2001), p. xv.

6. That all of the major annihilation camps—Majdanek, Chelmno, Belzec, Sobibor, Treblinka, and Auschwitz-Birkenau—were in the territory overrun by the Soviet army doesn't seem to have deterred the assignment of the liberator role to the Americans.

7. Alexander, to be sure, does mention some identification of Americans with the perpetrators because they failed to act in time, but this type of guilt is a far cry from that attributable to some of the local populations in occupied Eastern Europe.

8. Stéphane Courtois et al., *The Black Book of Communism: Crimes, Terror, Repression,* translated by J. Murphy and M. Kramer (Cambridge, MA: Harvard University Press, 1999).

9. Alexander does, to be sure, devote a paragraph to the Zionist use of the Holocaust, but he folds it into his larger argument about American universalization, claiming that "this convergence of progressive narratives... led the postwar paths of the United States and the state of Israel to become so fundamentally intertwined." I would agree about the intertwining, but there is still a tension between the ethos of a secular, nondenominational, universalist democracy and the exclusivist, ethnically defined particularism of a distinctly "Jewish state."

10. Tom Segev, interview with Lukasz Gelacki, "Israels säkularar Mythos: Über den Holocaust nach seiner Universalisierung," *Mittelweg 36* 15:5 (October/November 2006): p. 87.

11. One can sympathize with Wiesel's struggle to find an adjective to intensify the evil he is describing, and which he witnessed first hand, but *ontological* is not the right one. No death is more "real" than any other. Genocide is certainly deplorable in moral terms, but its victims are no more or less dead than the victims of, say, a tsunami or earthquake. Alexander claims that for a sociologist, evil is really an epistemological category because of how it is represented or coded. But this attribution is not quite right, either, as not all representations or codes are morally charged. In general, Alexander's treatment of this issue seems to me muddy, as he contrasts ontological with contingent and relative, as if *ontological* were a synonym for *necessary* and *absolute*. What could it mean to call the Holocaust a necessary evil?

12. See Richard Bernstein, "Radical Evil: Kant at War with Himself," in *Rethinking Evil: Contemporary Perspectives,* edited by María Pía Lara (Berkeley: University of California Press, 2001), p. 55–85.

13. Theodor W. Adorno, *Negative Dialectics*, trans. by E. B. Ashton (New York: Routledge, 1973), 361–68; Jean-François Lyotard, *The Differend: Phrases in Dispute,* translated by Georges Van Dan Abeele (Minneapolis, University of Minnesota Press, 1988), 86–106.

14. Giorgio Agamben, *Remnants of Auschwitz: The Witness and the Archive*, translated by Daniel-Heller Roazen (New York: Zone Books, 1999), p. 12.

15. In his typology of historical narratives in *The Contest of the Faculties* (1798), Kant would have called this the position of the Abderites, from an ancient people who foolishly ran around in circles. He opposed it to the prophets of decline, whom he called "moral terrorists" and the believers in progress, whom he called "eudaemonists."

16. Theodor W. Adorno, *Minima Moralia: Reflections from Damaged Life*, translated by E. F. N. Jephcott (London: Berghahn, 1974), p. 233.

17. Dominick LaCapra, *Writing History, Writing Trauma* (Baltimore: Johns Hopkins University Press, 2001).

FROM DENIAL TO CONFESSIONS
OF GUILT: THE GERMAN CASE

Bernhard Giesen

JEFFREY ALEXANDER'S PART I OF THIS VOLUME FOCUSES ON THE U.S. postwar history, but it claims more than to just tell the American story of coping with the Holocaust. Instead the Holocaust is presented as a new transnational paradigm of collective identity. There is, indeed, convincing evidence to support this thesis.

More than the Gulag, the Holocaust has been dealt with as a global icon of evil. Today the use of the term, while originally limited to the Nazi genocide of the European Jews, is extended to cover genocidal events in which no Jewish victims are involved. Thus the circle of victims is continuously widening, and so does the circle of perpetrators. It now includes not just the collaborators in continental Europe and the bystanders who decided not to intervene but also the Allied forces that ignored the plea to bomb the extermination camp in Auschwitz-Birkenau. In Alexander's illuminating phrase, "we are all the victims and all the perpetrators..."

What Alexander calls the "tragic narrative" corresponds strikingly to the notion of "metaphysical guilt" coined by the philosopher Karl Jaspers after the war (Jaspers, 1996). According to Jaspers, there is not only the criminal guilt of the individual who decided to act against the law and who as a person is held responsible for the violation of the law. Even if a dehumanizing action was in accordance with the law and ordered by authorities, the person who committed this action can be morally guilty. While criminal and moral guilt refers to individual persons and their actions, collective or political guilt refers to a community in the name of which the perpetrators committed their crimes. It extends to all members of this community and it transcends historical changes and constitutional turnovers. Collective guilt is a stigma that generates a feeling of shame even for those who, as individuals, were not involved in the evil.

And there is finally the metaphysical guilt of humankind. This metaphysical guilt refers to the general human condition after the Holocaust. After Auschwitz we cannot continue to believe in the triumphant narrative of progress and modernity, but instead we are vexed by the haunting awareness that, in the midst of modernity, there can be an abyss of inconceivable barbarism and that, in fact, this barbarism occurred. The total absurdity, the void of meaning of Auschwitz generated, for all humankind, a trauma that will not pass away. Unlike the voluntary and contingent decision of the criminal perpetrator, the metaphysical guilt of humankind is more the stain of radical evil, a defilement of innocence that can neither be repaired by punishment and repentance nor be overcome by conceding the ignorance and false assumptions of the perpetrators. Thus the Holocaust has generated a negative anthropology that can be linked to the theology of original sin as described by Augustine.

Before we turn to the general intellectual roots of this negative theology I will, in the following remarks, outline the German history of coping with the Holocaust. The case of Germany differs strongly from that of the United States. Germany was unquestionably the prime nation of perpetrators and, at the first glance at least, we should expect a strong reluctance to accept the tragic narrative of the Holocaust as a core element of German national identity. Rarely do nations agree on a negative representation of their collective identity. Should the German postwar history, however, fit into Alexander's conception of a tragic narrative, this would provide strong evidence for his assumption that the Holocaust takes the position of a transnational narrative of collective identity.

The immediate postwar Germany was governed by a coalition of silence with respect to the Holocaust. Rarely was the Holocaust mentioned in public addresses (Giesen, 2004). The older generation remained mute because it had backed the Nazi regime, although it could have known better. The *Hitlerjungen* generation, in contrast, remained silent for the very opposite reason: It could not have known better, its world had collapsed, and many felt betrayed and abused. If the unspeakable issue could not be avoided in informal conversations among Germans, those who had been enthusiastic followers of National Socialism sometimes coped with the trauma of total defeat and the dismantling of the horror by denying the obvious facts. They considered the documentary evidence to be faked by the Allied forces. The vast majority maintained that they had not known anything about the mass murders. *"Wir wussten von nichts..."*

When confronted with the undeniable evidence and the piercing questions, many Germans took refuge in demonizing the origin of evil. Blame was centered on Hitler and his henchmen. They were presented as demons and soul stealers who had seduced and intoxicated the innocent German people. Hitler, once the charismatic redeemer, was converted to a devil, a crazy epileptic, a monster, an "Asian Barbarian" completely alien to German culture. This demonization of Nazism reversed the previous heroification of the *"Führer"* and moved the crimes and their perpetrators into a realm of unreal nightmares beyond conception and description. Similar to the period of latency in the case of individual trauma, here too the traumatizing event—the Holocaust—is removed from the collective consciousness and shifted to the level of haunting dreams.

But many Nazis had survived in postwar Germany. If their identity was disclosed, they would have to be expelled from the community in order to restore its purity. And they were put on trial as individual criminals, sentenced to jail in "the name of the German people," and thus decoupled and expelled from the nation so that the country could view itself as innocent again. In Alexander's view, in a metonymic move the evil of Nazism was coped with by cutting out its main representatives. Till the end of the fifties the German response to the Holocaust was in line with the general expectation that no nation would accept a negative image of its collective identity. Negative evidence is denied, ignored, or related to a few culprits who are treated as exceptions.

The fragile combination of a new political start and the assumption of an enduring identity of decent Germans (who considered themselves to be the true victims of the catastrophe) persisted until the sixties, when a new generation entered the political stage. This generation was born after the war. It did not have personal memories of the Nazi past; its members broke the coalition of silence and faced their parents with inconvenient questions that, until then, had been the mark of outsiders. They wanted to know about the guilt of their parents, and they constructed a boundary between insiders and outsiders in the midst of their own families. The new generation shifted sides and identified with the victims; it became fashionable to give children Jewish names. The trauma was now considered from an outsider's perspective, and it became the stigma of the entire German nation.

The new narrative of the collective guilt of an entire generation changed the notion of guilt itself. It was no longer limited to the voluntary acts of individuals who decided deliberately to violate the basic moral rules of a community. Instead, guilt extended to those members of a political community who, although not actively engaged in crimes, did not prevent those crimes from being committed in the name of this community.

Because the new narrative decoupled the collective guilt of a political community from the active involvement of individual members it also allowed a ritual admittance of guilt by representatives who were innocent as individuals. Most important in this respect was certainly the famous 1970 scene of German Chancellor Willy Brandt's kneeling before the monument to the victims of the Warsaw Ghetto uprising (Schneider, 2006). With this spontaneous gesture, the head of the German government acknowledged the Jewish victims of the uprising against German occupation. The chancellor's representative confession of collective guilt was no longer relativized by reference to the sufferings of Germans or to a fatal blindness and seduction. Brandt took on the burden of collective guilt although he was innocent as a person, thereby enacting a new narrative of German national identity. This action gained him immense respect as an individual and as the German chancellor, and it led to reconciliation between Germany—the nation of the perpetrators—and the nations of its victims. It ended the postwar period.

After this gesture, the trauma could be worked through in different institutional arenas, ranging from historical research to media entertainment, from literature to museums, from monuments to school education. The ordinary German was seen as entangled in tacit consent to Nazism, the hidden traces and remainders of the Nazi past were laid open, individuals who could be metonymically or analogically linked to Nazism were ousted from public office, the Holocaust exhibitions attracted huge numbers of visitors, and ultimately the Holocaust memorial in Berlin became the national symbol of a new, united Germany. Dan Diners (1988) has described the Holocaust as the unwritten constitution of Germany.

This new pattern of constructing a collective identity by public confession of guilt assumed its first and most impressive contour in the German remembrance of the Holocaust, but later the practice was not limited to Germany, although nobody followed the German model precisely. Indeed, in many Western nations, political representatives have solemnly admitted their countries' crimes of the past. The French president has deplored the extensive French collaboration in the deportation of its Jews during the war.

Former Norwegian President Bruntland has noted that—contrary to the national master narrative of resistance—more Norwegians died as members of the Waffen-SS than as victims of the German occupation. The Pope apologized for the Catholic Church's failure to intervene in the persecution of European Jews. In the debate about Jedwabne Poland—itself a nation of victims—there are debates about its own genocidal crimes committed against Polish Jews under the German occupation (Gross, 2001). And even the Italian postfascist leader Fini laid flowers on the graves of victims of the German occupation, even though his own party is considered to be a successor to the country's fascist collaborators.

The new pattern of public confessions of guilt extends well beyond the Holocaust and European Jews. U.S. President Clinton intended to confess the guilt of white Americans for racism and slavery as well as for genocide committed against Native Americans. The Dutch government offered apologies to the victims of that country's colonial exploitation. The Australian government did the same for its past actions against its aborigine population. And French public debate—in spite of the pompous celebrations of its centenary—paid increasing attention to the victims of *la terreur* during the French Revolution. So, the French president apologizes to the descendants of Alfred Dreyfus; the Pope apologizes for the misdeeds of the Inquisition, the crusades, and the persecution of the Jews; the Queen of England apologizes for the wrongs done to the Maori of New Zealand. Sometimes these apologies are reluctantly given in response to public pressure, and sometimes the admission of guilt is lacking, but strong public sentiment is pressing for the apology. The Amritsar massacre in India in 1919 and the Irish famine in the 1840s are cases in point for British public debate, for example.

This "politics of apology" (Cunningham, 1999), or the widespread readiness to see responsibility and redress it, does not presuppose direct and personal involvement in the crimes—that is, it occurs not in spite of a lack of involvement but because of it. Political representatives can admit collective guilt for the very reason that they are not responsible as persons. It is not individual moral or criminal guilt that is at stake. These apologies are ritual confessions of collective guilt, and so differ from the confessions of personal wrongdoing. Again, Willy Brandt is the paradigm. He who was a political refugee from the Nazi terror, and never a citizen of the Third Reich, confessed the guilt of his fellow Germans, whom he represented as a politician. This presupposes that the representative is beyond suspicion, or that he is masking his personal interests or hiding history behind his public office. For the situation to be otherwise the always fragile and precarious claim to represent the nation would be eroded by one of the most critical risks of moral communities: the suspicion of hypocrisy.

Contrary to common assumptions about authenticity, representation of the nation succeeds here, not because the representative is "one of us," sharing the same memories with the other members of the community, but because individual identity and memory, on the one hand, and collective identity and memory, on the other, are no longer tightly coupled. The separation of individual crime from collective guilt shows some striking parallels to the post-axial age distinction between the impersonal conception of the sacred and the embodiment of the sacred in the person of the hero. The charismatic center of society has to be separate from its representation in particular individuals; the triumphant hero who merges the public and the private is bound to meet tragic defeat. In a similar way, but with reversed perspective, the public memory of victims has to be separate from the private guilt of individual perpetrators. All this seems to support Alexander's thesis about the rise of the Holocaust narrative as a transnational paradigm of collective identity.

But as widespread as this shift is from triumphant to tragic master narrative, it is hard to deny that cultures and political communities differ strongly in their acceptance of the rituals of repentance and their mourning for past victims. The readiness of the German public to accept the Holocaust legacy contrasts strikingly with the long-lasting refusal of postwar Japan to admit national responsibility for Japanese war crimes in China or Korea during the Second World War. The Nanking massacres are among the most horrible and brutal episodes of genocide in this century, but they had not been mentioned in official speeches by political representatives of postwar Japan. Only recently, as a result of long negotiations, did the Japanese government concede to war crimes committed by individual Japanese soldiers, and it signed a document containing an official excuse for the war crimes in Korea. Alexander mentions the Japanese and the Russian cases as exceptions to the Holocaust narrative that has spread in the West.

Another striking exception is Turkey, whose government has never admitted the existence of the Armenian genocide of 1915, and which recently declared itself to be offended by an official French statement about it. This refusal to admit guilt for past actions is particularly remarkable, as the contemporary Turkish nation was born after the event, following the Ottoman Empire's dissolution after 1918. The threat of possible Armenian claims on

Turkish territory may support this refusal, but only uncompromising strategic thinking would accept this as a satisfactory explanation. The Turkish government did not deny the death of Armenian victims, but it did refuse to accept collective guilt or responsibility; instead, the deaths of the Armenian victims are attributed to individual perpetrators and considered to be collateral damage from the war.

What are the cultural frames that support this acceptance by Western nations of the tragic narrative of the Holocaust but that impede its acceptance by Japan and Turkey? One of the most deeply rooted cultural frames is the Judeo-Christian mythology of sacrifice, repentance, and redemption by God's grace. In the Old Testament, this is represented by Abraham's sacrifice of his son Isaac, a pattern that is repeated in the New Testament with the self-sacrifice of Christ, who by his death saved people from collective guilt. Western politicians confessing the guilt of their nations are, hence, relying (mostly without being aware of it) on a pattern of Christo-mimesis that is deeply rooted in occidental mythology. Since Augustine of Hippo and the Council of Trent this redemption of a collectivity by the self-sacrifice of an innocent individual is linked to the idea of original sin, referring to Saint Paul's reflection on sin as the basic human condition. Augustine pointed to the universal ethical opposition between good and evil as represented by Adam, who was the first to act against God's will and to sin, and to Christ's self-sacrifice that overcame that original sin and gave way to the possibility of salvation.

This fundamental opposition can be translated into different secularized domains and be explicated on different levels. On the level of the individual, the opposition separates those who, by personal decision, have opted for evil ("personal sin") from those who, by personal commitment and decision, lead a virtuous life ("saved"). On the general level of the human condition, this opposition appears as two eschatological modes of existence: on the one hand, barbarism, absurdity, and decay—in Augustine's phrasing, "the original sin" represented by Adam—and on the other hand, creation, enlightenment, and an ethical life—in Augustine's phrasing, "salvation" represented by Christ. In between the individual level and the universal level, we can position the eschatological fate of collectivities. In the Judeo-Christian tradition there are peoples and nations that are chosen as a collectivity, not by the merits of their members but by God's grace. Israel claimed this privilege and, later on, the Dutch, the British, and the United States (Walzer, 1965; Smith, 2003; Gorski, 2000). Their counterpart are peoples that, by God's disgrace, are condemned as a collectivity; they are not explicitly mentioned in the Old or New Testament, but mythological symmetry hints at their existence and there are no texts from the scriptures that deny their existence. Thus, in the occidental mythology, there is a balance between good and evil, between individual perpetrators and morally upright persons, between chosen people and condemned people, between original sin and original salvation. The negative anthropology after the Holocaust, and the discourse about Germany as a nation of perpetrators, could easily spin off into a reliance on this fundamental opposition between redemption and condemnation.

In contrast to the occidental connection between collective guilt and individual innocence, the Confucian tradition can hardly conceive of one's collectivity in negative terms. From a Confucian perspective, the attribution of guilt to individual and to community is reversed. While war crimes committed by individual Japanese perpetrators can easily be admitted, the nation has to remain without blemish. The collectivity is sacred and the representatives of the state are vested with unconditional authority. This Confucian reversal is even more striking in the case of Japan. Japan is a non-axial age civilization that does not separate political authority from religious authority (Eisenstadt, 1996). The Tenno is not only the emperor but is also sacred, even divine. Under these conditions it is impossible to challenge the ruler in the name of God: the ruler is God. Hence the reluctance, or even refusal, of the Japanese government to admit national responsibility for the Nanking massacres is deeply rooted in Japanese culture and civilization.

In a similar way, although for different reasons, the Turkish government has rejected until now any international pressure to apologize for or even recognize responsibility for the Armenian genocide. While not denying the massacre and the number of victims, the official Turkish response is to blame individual perpetrators. The truth about the motivations of the perpetrators might destroy the official founding myth of modern Turkey: it was not for religious hatred but for reasons of ethnic cleansing in the pursuit of a modern nation-state that the so-called Young Turks, who are now revered as the founding fathers of modern Turkey, expelled the millions of Armenians and let them starve on death marches.

Finally there are, even in the West, a few voices, like Robert Faurisson in France, Wolfgang Fröhlich in Austria, Christian Lindtner in Denmark, and David Irving in Britain, who maintain that the Holocaust is a myth based on faked evidence. This denial of the Holocaust is applauded by small right-wing audiences in the respective countries and is backed by some anti-Israel politicians in the Middle East. Iranian President Mahmoud Ahmadinejad recently held a conference of these people, denying or questioning the Holocaust. The zeal of these people in denying what has been documented by a multitude of historians and testified by survivors cannot, however, change the salience of the Holocaust narrative as one of the core paradigms of collective identity in the Western world. And even those who attack Israel occasionally use the term *holocaust* to describe Israel's policies toward the Palestinians. Could there be another example more convincing to support Alexander's thesis?

REFERENCES

Alexander, Jeffrey C., Ron Eyerman, Bernhard Giesen, & Neil J. Smelser. 2004. *Cultural Trauma and Collective Identity*. Berkeley: University of California Press.

Cunningham, Michael. 1999. "Saying Sorry. The Politics of Apology." *Political Quarterly* 70(3): 285–93.

Diner, Dan. 1988. *Zivilisationsbruch. Denken nach Auschwitz*. Frankfurt am Main: Fischer Taschenbuch.

Eisenstadt, Shmuel N. 1996. *Japanese Civilization: A Comparative View*. Chicago: University of Chicago Press.

Giesen, Bernhard. 2004. *Triumph and Trauma*. Boulder, CO: Paradigm.

Gorski, Philip. 2000. "The Mosaic Moment: An Early Modernist Critique of Modernist Theories of Nationalism." *American Journal of Sociology* 105(5): 1428–68.

Gross, Jan Tomasz. 2001. *Neighbours: The Destruction of the Jewish Community in Jedwabne, Poland*. Princeton, NJ: Princeton University Press.

Jaspers, Karl. 1996. *Die Schuldfrage: Zur politischen Haftung Deutschlands*. Munich: Piper.

Levy, Daniel, & Natan Sznaider. 2001. *Erinnerung im globalen Zeitalter: Der Holocaust*. Frankfurt am Main: Suhrkamp.

Schneider, Christoph. 2006. *Der Warschauer Kniefall. Ritual, Ereignis und Erzählung*. Konstanz: UVK.

Smith, Anthony D. 2003. *Chosen Peoples: Sacred Sources of National Identity*, New York: Oxford University Press.

Walzer, Michael.1965. *The Revolution of the Saints*. Cambridge, MA: Harvard University Press.

Multidirectional Memory and the Universalization of the Holocaust

Michael Rothberg

When I say: "a single thing," I am really saying what it is from a wholly universal point of view, for everything is a single thing.

G. W. F. Hegel, *Phenomenology of Spirit*

ON NOVEMBER 9, 1961, THE NOVELIST MARGUERITE DURAS published an article titled "Les Deux Ghettos" (The Two Ghettos) in the newsweekly *France-Observateur*.[1] Duras was well known at the time for her screenplay for Alain Resnais's 1959 film *Hiroshima, Mon Amour*, a film that uses a love story to juxtapose memories of life under Nazi occupation in France with memories of the bombing of Hiroshima. "Les Deux Ghettos" also employs an aesthetic of juxtaposition: taking the form of two interconnected interviews, it brings together memory of the Holocaust and recent developments in the ongoing struggle between France and the Algerian independence movement, the Front de Libération Nationale (FLN). Announced on *France-Observateur*'s front page, Duras's article is explicitly linked by the editors to the events of October 17, 1961, when Maurice Papon's Paris police massacred dozens of peacefully demonstrating Algerians, dumped some of the bodies into the Seine, and arrested more than 11,000 others, who were then held in makeshift camps set up in sports stadiums at the edges of the city.[2] Duras's article approaches the massacre in roundabout fashion, through a historical analogy between Nazi policy and the context of Fifth Republic France. An editorial note describes Duras's method by comparing it to the magazine's own attempts to get to the bottom of the police massacre: "Marguerite Duras also asked questions, first to two Algerian workers and then to a survivor of the Warsaw ghetto. The questions are identical, the answers are eloquent. The time of the ghettos, which we thought had disappeared, has it returned?" This note is accompanied by a pair of photographs juxtaposing an Algerian man, bundled into a winter coat and rubbing his hands for warmth, and a Jewish ghetto inmate, her face in shadow and a yellow star marking her fate. Alongside Duras's article another photograph shows the deplorable conditions of the Nanterre *bidonville,* or shantytown, where many Algerian migrants lived—a scene that, absent the dark-skinned girl in the right foreground of the picture, could easily enough be mistaken for a Nazi ghetto for Jews. In the article itself, Duras asks brief, pointed questions about the persistence of fear and the possibilities for happiness and love for her Jewish and Algerian subjects, who are victims of two differently repressive racial regimes, one "safely" located in the past, one reaching new paroxysms of violence in the present.

Duras's article might be said to illustrate one of the central arguments of Jeffrey Alexander's important essay "The Social Construction of Moral Universals."[3] Sometime around 1961, the Nazi genocide of European Jews went from being perceived as a terrible wartime atrocity with limited implications to being an event uniquely suited to illuminating historical evil wherever it cropped up. Thus, Alexander would most likely see in "Les Deux Ghettos" an exemplification of moral universality—that is, the way the Holocaust serves in Duras's article as a template of cruelty that can be used to foster understanding of the present and promote ethical and political action. Such a reading would be plausible, but it remains worth asking whether Duras's article is best described as an exemplification of the Holocaust's simultaneous uniqueness and moral universality. While Alexander's model is powerful, I will return to Duras's article later in order to argue that a close look at the context of 1950s and 1960s France suggests a somewhat more complicated, "multidirectional" logic at work—a logic that has significant implications for theorizing collective memory in an age of globalization.

In providing a sociological explanation for the transformation of the collective perception of the Nazi genocide, Alexander's chapter makes a significant contribution to an understanding of the historical development and social implications of Holocaust memory. While his argument is geared primarily to the U.S. context, the framework for understanding Alexander offers certainly has implications that go well beyond that particular setting. Alexander's most important insights concern the meanings that the Holocaust has accrued in retrospect: he brackets the events of the genocide themselves and seeks to change our understanding of the now-accepted narrative of Holocaust memory's emergence and transformation over the past sixty years. How, he asks, did consciousness of the Nazi genocide of European Jews move from the margins to the center of Euro-American culture and in the process become a global symbol of evil? Because a great deal of consensus exists on this general movement, Alexander's question has been addressed frequently in recent years. By rejecting what he terms "naturalist" explanations, however, Alexander offers a new, sociological account of this globally significant transformation. The nature of his account, which draws on theories of narrative, genre, and rhetoric, can only please a literary critic, because it confirms the crucial nature of the tools of cultural analysis that define our discipline. Alexander's discussion of Holocaust memory exemplifies the larger "cultural turn" that he recommends for sociology, and like his particular analysis, this larger theory is welcome for the kinds of interdisciplinary opportunities it opens up for scholars working at the intersection of the humanities and social sciences.

While I appreciate both the methodological moves of Alexander's cultural sociology and the particular arguments he develops about the mutations of the Holocaust's meanings, I will nevertheless, in the spirit of critical exchange, offer some commentary on the underlying presuppositions of his argument about moral universalism. In particular, I will suggest the need to disarticulate notions of universalism from Americanization and bring to view the heterogeneity of exchanges between memory of the Holocaust and memory of other histories of trauma and extreme violence. Alexander's discussion of the construction of universalism focuses almost entirely on a single national context—the United States—and draws its sources from an overwhelmingly English-language archive. My research into Holocaust memory during the Algerian War of Independence convinces me that Holocaust memory is best thought of as transnational—a scale that is located between the national and the global and is potentially in tension with the universal. In addition, I find that the narratives evoked by transnational Holocaust memory do not always fit the binary opposition between progressive and tragic narratives proposed by Alexander.

A shift in terminology helps bring into view the change in perspective I propose. Instead of talking about the *moral universalism* of the Holocaust, I focus on forms of *multidirectional Holocaust memory* that emerge out of transnational encounters. My notion of multidirectional Holocaust memory is meant to capture the interference, overlap, and mutual constitution of the seemingly distinct collective memories that define the postwar era and the workings of memory more generally.[4] In this chapter and elsewhere, I draw particular attention to the forms of discursive exchange that link the legacies of the Holocaust and European colonialism in an age defined both by decolonization and a coming to terms with the Nazi past.

Alexander's answer to the question of how the Holocaust became *the* socially recognized catastrophe of the modern era concerns the shift between two narrative structures: (1) an understanding of the events of the Second World War begins within a framework he describes as the "progressive narrative"; (2) these events later get reframed as part of a "tragic narrative" or "trauma-drama." The progressive narrative identifies the major protagonists of the story as particular groups. In this narrative, Nazis embody a situated and thus containable form of evil; Jews are identified as one of several specific groups of Nazi victims; and, most important, the Allies, especially the United States, carry a redemptive power to defeat and eliminate evil and assimilate the victims into a story of progressive overcoming. As Alexander summarizes, according to the progressive narrative, Nazism was "coded as evil and weighted in the most fundamental, *weltgeschicht[liche]* (world-historical) terms"; yet, "it was narrated inside a framework that offered the promise of salvation and triggered actions that generated confidence and hope." This narrative, within which little place is accorded for recognizing the specificity of the Nazi genocide of Jews, lasts from the period of the war until the early 1960s.

Sometime around the 1961 Eichmann trial in Jerusalem—and here Alexander remains solidly within the consensus on how to periodize Holocaust memory—a transformation takes place driven by a new narrative regime. Now, even as the Holocaust comes to be recognized as a unique, sui generis event, the protagonists of the story begin to take on ever more generalizable traits and the meaning of the events turns into a universal moral code. Within the new tragic narrative, the Holocaust becomes a "sacred-evil" that "block[s]" the progressive narrative and replaces it with a "sense of historical descent...a falling away from the good." The progressive narrative's optimism gives way to tragic catharsis: new forms of identification link the general public to Holocaust victims and survivors, and even to perpetrators. Victims are "personalized" through figures such as Anne Frank, while perpetrators become "everymen" via Hannah Arendt's concept of the "banality of evil." Meanwhile, even the former liberators find themselves contaminated by genocidal potential—the Vietnam War's impact on America's reputation for good is key here—and national myths of innocence are shattered by a new emphasis on collaboration and complicity in France, Austria, Switzerland, and elsewhere. This "less nationally bound, less temporally specific, and more universal drama" "stimulate[s] an unprecedented universalization of political and moral responsibility." Driven by rhetorical tropes such as metonymy and analogy, as well as new forms of legal reasoning and new international institutions predicated on notions of "universal human rights," the Holocaust becomes a "bridging metaphor" that enlarges the scope of the event's implications in a process Alexander calls the "engorgement of evil."

This process of reframing or remaking the meanings of the same events produces the paradoxical result that Alexander sees as defining the Holocaust's actuality: simultaneous with the emergence of a strong sense of the Holocaust's uniqueness comes a broad sense of the Holocaust's applicability as a moral standard to almost any potentially tragic historical (and sometimes even personal) occurrence. This paradox also produces a further irony, one which Alexander acknowledges briefly in conclusion, but which I believe deserves further scrutiny: even as tragedy replaces progress as the guiding genre for processing the events, a new form of progressive narrative emerges built on the universal potential of human rights ideology. The story Alexander tells is largely convincing and helps explain both the fact and the cultural meaning of the Holocaust's radical inflation of significance in the last forty years. But a number of questions remain. Most obviously, it is worth asking whether Alexander's narrative is not too schematic. Clearly, its two moments contain a number of internal contradictions and tensions. Must these forms of heterogeneity be downplayed in order to make sense of larger patterns? While I have addressed this question elsewhere,[5] here I want to focus on a second and more politically weighted issue: the necessity of thinking critically about the limits of the universalization Alexander describes. Alexander's description of universalization as a sociological process differs from the philosophical version alluded to in my epigraph from Hegel, but it may bring with it some of the same problems attendant on progressive visions of intellectual and historical change. In particular, more needs to be said about the relations among universalization, Americanization, and globalization, and about the roles they play in Alexander's new posttragic, moral narrative.

Alexander ends his essay by remarking on the paradox I mentioned a moment ago: that the turn away from the progressive narrative results in a potentially progressive end. Referring to critiques of the modernity of the Holocaust, he writes:

> what was once described as a prelude and incitement to moral and social progress has come to be reconstructed as a decisive demonstration that not even the most "modern" improvements in the condition of humanity can ensure advancement in anything other than a purely technical sense. It is paradoxical that a decided increase in moral and social justice may eventually be the unintended result.

For Alexander, this increase in justice results from the processes of universalization that accompany the "trauma-drama" narrative. In Alexander's account, those universalizing processes are themselves the results of a process that is probably best described as Americanization: he draws attention to the American-produced narratives that subsequently "were distributed worldwide, seen by tens and possibly hundreds of millions of persons, and talked incessantly about by high-, middle-, and lowbrow audiences alike." Alexander is correct that products of the American culture industries, such as the 1978 *Holocaust* miniseries or the theatrical and film adaptations of the Anne Frank story in the 1950s, have played a significant role in the worldwide circulation of the Holocaust as a collective memory and moral symbol. But in what sense does this represent universalization?

Alexander defines universalization of the Holocaust as a process of "detaching the issues surrounding the systematic exercise of violence against ethnic groups from any particular ethnicity, religion, nationality, time, or place," a process that works together with a "deepening [of] emotional identification." An element of detachment is no doubt necessary to the kinds of cross-identity identification that accompany references to the Holocaust beyond its initial historical context (and that would include references by most Jews today as well!). But detachment alone, even in the interests of identification, cannot explain appropriations of the Holocaust: the events must be "reattached" to a new context in order to have any moral purchase. The processes of detachment, reattachment, and identification cannot be explained according to a one-way process analogous to the export of American cultural goods. As I will illustrate with respect to the French-Algerian context, the construction of moral universals entails a more complicated and multidirectional work than Alexander accounts for here; the process is dia-logical and entails the redefinition of both what the Holocaust means and what the events to which it is imaginatively attached mean.

There are at least two additional problems with Alexander's account of universalization via Americanization. First, it occludes the ways that the Nazi genocide became universalized, or, as I would prefer, generalized, in situations where Americanization played no significant role (e.g., in Duras's "Les Deux Ghettos"). And, second, it threatens to leave unquestioned the identification of an American moral mission with a universal mission. Such an identification between a nation or social group and a universal mission would always be problematic—and not only when it concerns the United States—but today, in an era of American neo-imperialism premised on the defense of "freedom," "democracy," and "human rights," it is especially trou-bling. While Alexander might respond that his account of universalization is more descriptive than normative, I would suggest that Alexander con-tributes to the production of a normative notion of Americanization as universalism by failing to put into question the terms of these processes of moral "engorgement." To combat this production it is necessary to specify how self-identified universal moral missions premised on notions of democ-racy or human rights frequently, perhaps inevitably, fail and even produce perverse effects—as the Iraq War has demonstrated all too clearly. Instead of merely lamenting this failure and giving up on the possibility of constructing links between different histories in the interests of moral, ethical, and politi-cal visions, however, I suggest that we need to rethink the basis of historical linkage and comparison from a standpoint less indebted to a universal his-torical narrative than Alexander's ultimately and paradoxically is.

To make these abstract comments more concrete, let me return to my example of France in 1961, late in the Algerian War of Independence. As we've already remarked, this is also the moment of the Eichmann trial, a trial explicitly designed by the Israeli state to promote the uniqueness of the Holocaust. Alexander's well-founded point is that by creating possibili-ties for identification with both victims and perpetrators the trial also gave rise to a vast generalization of the Holocaust's meaning. So much is no doubt true. Notice also that this epochal event leaves behind the frame-work of Americanization. The Eichmann trial was truly transnational: while staged by a nation-state (Israel), it traveled to Europe and North America via radio, television, and print journalism. That is, the trial circulated and accrued meaning in ways that are best described neither as national nor as global. Rather, it circulated according to particular, transnational channels and accrued meanings that were bound to vary according to the sites of its consumption—a consumption that could only become a significant force when "reattached" to local histories and concerns.

In the case of France, news of the capture and trial of Eichmann intersected with a context in which memories of the Nazi past were already in steady circulation. From almost the moment the Second World War and Nazi occupation ended, French intellectuals had been reading their postwar present through the filter of occupation, resistance, collaboration, fascism, and ultimately genocide. As I have sought to show in an ongoing project on Holocaust memory in the age of decolonization, the articulation of the Holocaust's specificity took place in France (and elsewhere) through multidirectional encounters between the history of World War II and the struggles of colonized peoples around the globe to free themselves from European hegemony. This articulation precedes the Eichmann trial, even if the Eichmann trial is then incorporated into the ongoing exchange between Holocaust memory and the discourses of decolonization.[6] In Duras's article, for instance, she asks the Algerian workers, "Do you believe that your condition resembles that of anyone else?" One of them responds: "Me, I think of the Hindus before the arrival of national independence, before even Gandhi. Some comrades say that we are like the Jews under the German occupation. They say: 'This recalls Eichmann's coup [*le coup d'Eichmann*]. All that's lacking is the crematorium and the gas chamber'" (Duras, 1961: 9). Whatever one might make of the empirical historical comparisons at issue, this response perfectly illustrates the permeability of memories at this transitional moment and suggests the mutual determination of the memories of colonialism and genocide.

The conditions of possibility of Duras's article further illustrate the interplay between remembrance of the Nazi past and the decolonization experience of the present. As I have mentioned, the article was conceived as part of a response to the October 17 massacre and round-up of Algerians in Paris. The idea of joining this history to that of the recent genocidal past was not original to Duras; in fact, such a juxtaposition had been a resource of the struggle against colonialism from the moment of World War II's end and it had been a particular rhetorical weapon of *France-Observateur*, the weekly in which the article appeared, and especially of its editor, Claude Bourdet. Already in a December 6, 1951, article protesting arbitrary detentions, closed trials, and obvious evidence of torture on the part of the French police in Algeria, Bourdet had asked, "*Y a-t-il une Gestapo algérienne?*" [Is there an Algerian Gestapo?] (1951: 6–8). A little more than three years later, in an issue headlined "*LA VÉRITE sur les tortures en Algérie...*" [THE TRUTH about the tortures in Algeria...], Bourdet noted the return of torture in Algeria and returned to his earlier rhetoric in the article "Votre Gestapo d'Algérie" [Your Gestapo from Algeria], January 13, 1955: 6–7). At stake in these early examples is primarily memory of the occupation and its brutal repression of the French resistance; there is nothing in these articles by Bourdet to suggest a focus on the specificity of the Nazis' repression of Jews. Such broad antifascist rhetoric, playing on feelings of French national shame and patriotism, continues into the later stages of the war, but is now joined by a new discourse that brings the specificity of the Nazi genocide closer to the surface: antiracism.

The perception of "race" and the experience of racism become more and more prominent in the late stages of the war and, in particular, around the events leading up to and including the October 17, 1961, demonstration—a demonstration protesting a racist curfew and the persistence of racist violence within Paris.[7] The increasing racialization of public space in France during the course of the war drew more and more attention to the victims of various forms of racism and facilitated frequent analogies between Algerians and Jews. "Les Deux Ghettos," for example, draws on a persistent analogy that links Jews and other racialized groups through the figure of the ghetto's segregated social space. As Duras's article demonstrates, together with many other examples, a new sense of the Holocaust's specificity emerged along with a new understanding of the stakes of the war and decolonization. Henri Kréa's "Le racisme est collectif, la solidarité individuelle" [Racism is collective, solidarity individual], an article appearing just two weeks before Duras's in the October 26 issue of *France-Observateur*, also brings together recent events and the two-decade-old past.[8] Like Duras's article, Kréa's short piece is based on interviews—this time with Renault workers who are asked about the attitudes of the working class toward Algerians. The article is accompanied by a photograph of Algerians at the Palais des Sports, one of the sites at which the thousands of demonstrators arrested on October 17 were being held. The caption reads: "*Cela ne vous rappelle rien?*" [Doesn't that remind you of something?]. A clear reference to the roundups of Jews during the occupation—and, in particular, to the infamous *rafle du Vel d'Hiv* in which thousands of "foreign" Jews were arrested by French police and held in a bicycle-racing stadium before being deported—the photograph and caption link the Holocaust and the repression of Algerians through the trope of a gnawing but unspoken memory, a trope that captures the multidirectional intersection of two events that are caught between simultaneous emergence and collective oblivion. The frequent "reminders" of the Holocaust deployed in the fight against colonialism by *France-Observateur* and other anticolonial venues, such as the underground journal *Vérité-Liberté*, testify not so much to the universalization of the Holocaust's meanings but to the emergence of a notion of the Holocaust's specificity through its contact with the ongoing struggle over Algeria.

What we see when we look closely at the French context is that the Holocaust does not simply become a universal moral standard that can then be applied to other histories, but that those *other histories help produce a sense of the Holocaust's particularity.* At the same time, people impacted by those histories, such as the history of colonialism and decolonization, make claims on a *shared but not necessarily universal* moral and political project. In the example of "Les Deux Ghettos," the two juxtaposed histories mutually illuminate each other, and Duras's method of dual interviews ends up revealing both parallels and asymmetries between the lives of Algerians in Paris and Jews in the Warsaw Ghetto. Far from being a floating, universal signifier, the Holocaust emerges in its specificity as part of a multidirectional network of diverse histories of extreme violence, torture, and racist policy.

Reconceptualizing the emergence of the Holocaust's specificity in this way has a series of implications that are simultaneously methodological, theoretical, and ethical. The history of Holocaust memory, in France as elsewhere, is not only a history of the afterlife of the Holocaust; it is also a history of the Nazi genocide's interaction with decolonization, racism, and the legacies of slavery, among other things.[9] Recognizing this interaction means opening up study of Holocaust memory methodologically through multilingual, transnational perspectives that I have been able only to hint at here. Since no one scholar can possibly master the amount of material that becomes relevant through this insight, the project necessarily becomes a collective, collaborative one—hence the importance of this volume! Such methodological concerns need to be matched by theoretical insights, however. The multidirectionality of Holocaust memory can only be glimpsed when we rethink collective memory as an interplay between different pasts and a heterogeneous present, and as obeying a logic other than those of competition and the zero-sum game that so frequently mar discussions of intercultural memory.

Beyond theory and methodology lie the ethical and political stakes of these discussions. If we narrate the history of Holocaust memory only from the perspective of changes in the Holocaust's meanings and occlude the active role that other histories play in this process, we end up with a notion of morality that remains too singular and abstractly universal. A more heterogeneous understanding of moral action that recognizes the importance of comparison and generalization while resisting too-easy universalization may not produce a global moral code, but it may produce the grounds for new transnational visions of justice and solidarity.

NOTES

1. Marguerite Duras, "Les Deux Ghettos," *France-Observateur*, November 9, 1961: 8–10. All translations from the French are my own.

2. Two decades later it would emerge that Papon had also played a role in the deportation of Jews from the Gironde during World War II, a fact that would further intertwine the events of the Holocaust and of the Algerian War of Independence. But at the time of the October 17 massacre, Papon's earlier role was not generally known. For a history of the October massacre and its aftermath, see Jim House and Neil MacMaster, *Paris 1961: Algerians, State Terror, and Memory* (New York: Oxford University Press, 2006).

3. Citations here are from Jeffrey Alexander's essay in part I, this volume.

4. For more on "multidirectional memory," which I contrast to "competitive memory," see Michael Rothberg, "The Work of Testimony in the Age of Decolonization: *Chronicle of a Summer*, Cinéma Verité, and the Emergence of the Holocaust Survivor," *PMLA* 119 (October 2004): 1237–46; and "Between Auschwitz and Algeria: Multidirectional Memory and the Counterpublic Witness," *Critical Inquiry* 33 (Autumn 2006): 158–84. These essays and other related interventions are collected in my book, *Multidirectional Memory: Remembering the Holocaust in the Age of Decolonization* (Stanford: Stanford University Press, 2009).

5. In a chapter of *Multidirectional Memory*, I argue that a vision of the Holocaust as both particular and in contact with other histories was articulated by the African-American scholar and activist W. E. B. Du Bois in the early postwar period at a moment when Alexander's progressive narrative held sway. As an African American and communist fellow-traveler, Du Bois represents a doubly marginalized voice, but this is precisely the point: looking beyond the mainstream can provide counterexamples to the larger dominant narratives usefully tracked by Alexander. My larger

project involves reclaiming such marginal voices in order to find resources for visions of justice alternative to those articulated in the mainstream.

6. In his excellent book *A Holocaust Controversy: The Treblinka Affair in Postwar France* (Waltham, MA: Brandeis University Press, 2005), Samuel Moyn argues that the Eichmann trial had a more delayed and ultimately less epochal significance in France than has heretofore been assumed. Although his argument goes in a much different direction than mine, this contextualization supports my attempt to shift the dominant account of the emergence of widespread Holocaust consciousness.

7. For a historical account that demonstrates convincingly the growing importance of racialization during the Algerian War, see Todd Shepard, *The Invention of Decolonization: The Algerian War and the Remaking of France* (Ithaca: Cornell University Press, 2006). Shepard does not discuss the October 1961 massacre specifically.

8. Henri Kréa, "Le racisme est collectif, la solidarité individuelle," *France-Observateur,* October 26, 1961: 14–15.

9. My difference here with Alexander is primarily one of emphasis. His rich account does, of course, provide insight into how other histories—for example, that of the Vietnam War—intersect with that of the Holocaust and its memory. But the overall trajectory of his narrative tends to downplay the significance of these "intrusions."

ON THE POLITICAL CORRUPTIONS OF A MORAL UNIVERSAL

Robert Manne

IN THIS RESPONSE TO JEFFREY ALEXANDER'S ORIGINAL AND STIMU-lating essay, "The Social Construction of Moral Universals," I will offer a somewhat skeptical critique. To do so, however, it is necessary to outline briefly a political reading of what it is that he has to say.

Alexander begins with the proposition that no event in history, no matter how terrible, interprets itself. Its "meaning" only emerges as a consequence of a great deal of social or cultural work. So it was with the "Holocaust." If the Nazis had been victorious, or even if the Soviet Union had been the sole European liberator of the concentration camps, the Holocaust might never have been "discovered." Although its discovery relied on the role that the American "imperial republic" played in the liberation process in general, and in particular on their arrival in the spring of 1945 at the gates of the German concentration camps and the hetacombs of corpses they then stumbled upon, it is critical to Alexander's argument that, for the Nazi mass murders of the Jews to be transformed into the Holocaust, the fact of the American liberation was not enough.

For the first fifteen years or so after liberation, in his account, the Jewish mass murders were seen as merely the most terrible Nazi wartime atrocity and as the most extreme expression of Nazi racial hatred. Even more important, at this time, the "interpretive grid" through which the murders came to be "coded," "weighted," and "narrated" was what Alexander calls the "progressive frame." Within this frame, America saw its role as the building of a better world. Americans did not identify with the Jewish victims or experience their trauma. The discovery of the Jewish mass murders was seen rather as vindication of the American anti-Nazi struggle, whose political implication was merely the "denazification" of America, achieved by eliminating all residual expressions of anti-Semitism at home; the end of Jewish marginality in America, and the invention of something called "the Judeo-Christian tradition"; and the provision of support for the establishment of the state of Israel, as part of the more general progressive project of creating a democratic, racially tolerant, post-Nazi world.

In was only in the 1960s, Alexander argues, that the Holocaust was discovered. What allowed this to occur was the displacement of the progressive narrative by a "tragic" one. This displacement relied in part on Vietnam, where America became "Amerika," and the postwar progressive narrative collapsed, and where, as a consequence, the United States lost control over the telling of the story of the Nazi mass murder of the Jews, with the trope of American "indifference" in the face of the Holocaust replacing the trope of Americans as the liberators of the concentration camps.

The story of the mass murder of the Jews ceased now to be a mere wartime atrocity. It was experienced for the first time as a "trauma" for its non-Jewish audience, who "identified" psychologically with the victims. The story was now told only in a tone of extraordinary "gravitas." It was seen as an incomprehensible mystery and as a world historical event. It became the "sacred-evil" myth of the age. This story offered its audience catharsis, but no closure, consolation, or easy ground for hope. The Holocaust called into question the idea of progress, "modernity," even the nature of the species. Within the frame of the new tragic narrative, the mass murder of the Jews was departicularized, cut loose from time and place, becoming rather a universal story, available at least in theory to the whole of humankind but embraced in reality only throughout the West.

The myth of the Holocaust became a resource of utmost value to human beings. As a (Western) universal story of tragedy, through by what Alexander calls "symbolic extension," the Holocaust illuminated truly for the first time in human history many other instances of past and future massive crime. It also laid the basis for transformative new legal discourses about universal human rights and the requirement of international intervention to prevent the commission of genocide. It had the capacity in all these ways both to extend the realm of justice and to humanize the world. Alexander's conclusion is paradoxical in the extreme. Released from the postwar progressive frame, the tragic sacred-evil myth of the Holocaust has unintentionally provided grounds for hope about the moral progress of humankind.

I agree with a great deal of Alexander's account. I accept his (and others') basic periodization—that is to say, that the Jewish killings by the Nazis only became the Holocaust sometime in the 1960s, although as will become evident shortly I think his account of why that happened is inconclusive. I agree that since that time the Holocaust has become for the West the most important moral-political myth. I think that his phenomenological account of how the story of the Holocaust is now told is brilliantly and compellingly revealed—its high solemnity and resistance to all consolatory readings; its enclosure in an aura of mystery and incomprehensibility unlike all other even massive crimes of history (where the only mystery ever evoked is the conventional problem of theodicy); its liquidity and lability, or what Alexander calls "the engorgement of evil," and its capacity to pollute in our eyes anything and everything it touches. I also have come to agree with one of his core judgments. Alexander argues that the Holocaust is vulnerable not to "commodification" but only to what he calls the trivialization of "comedization." Although I once shared the kind of high-cultural distaste that Alexander quotes Elie Wiesel expressing about the miniseries *Holocaust* and Claude Lanzmann about the conventional fictive strategy of *Schindler's List*, I am now persuaded by Alexander's contrary reading—that is to say, that if the story of the Holocaust is to become truly universal, serious products of popular culture play a particular role that much finer work, like the books of Primo Levi or Claude Lanzmann's astonishing film *Shoah*, never could. I accept, in short, because of Alexander, that Leavisite or Frankfurt School snobberies with regard to the portrayals of the Holocaust inside the popular culture are both antidemocratic and politically self-defeating.

Yet despite these agreements, in the short space available, I intend to concentrate on some basic misgivings about his case. The first is almost technical. The suggestion that the "sacred-evil," "departicularized," "universal" myth we call the Holocaust emerged only in the 1960s is, as we have seen, at the very center of Alexander's reading of the relevant history. No less so is the suggestion that the Holocaust played a major part in what he calls "an unprecedented universalization of political and moral responsibility" and that it "so enlarged the human imagination that it is capable for the first time in human history of identifying, understanding, and judging the kinds of genocidal mass killings in which national, ethnic, and ideological groupings continue to engage today." One of the major means by which the human imagination became capable of such identification, understanding, and judging was, he argues, the invention via the Holocaust of what is called "a new legal standard for international behavior"—the creation of a body of statutory and customary international law. To underline his point, Alexander quotes with approval Martha Minow's view that what is novel about the twentieth century was not "human torture and slaughter" but "the invention of new and distinctive legal forms of response" and Michael Ignatieff's claim that it was "the Holocaust that made the Universal Declaration of Human Rights possible."

The problem here is that the two halves of this argument seem incompatible. The larger part of the new international customary and statutory law cited by Alexander, Minow, and Ignatieff—the Nuremberg Trials (1945), the United Nations Charter (1945), the Universal Declaration of Human Rights (1948), the Convention on the Prevention and Prosecution of the Crime of Genocide (1948)—all followed hard upon the discovery of the mass killing of the Jews and other associated Nazi crimes but preceded the emergence of what Alexander means by the Holocaust by a decade or more. Moreover, the most important addition to this body of law since this idea of the Holocaust is the creation of the International Criminal Court, whose authority was denied by two of the countries for whom the Holocaust is a core element of collective memory—the United States and Israel. The link between this new postwar body of international law and the crimes of Nazism, including the Jewish mass killings, most of which was written during the period of Alexander's progressive frame, seems clear. The link with Alexander's Holocaust, the universal myth of sacred-evil, is not.

As a consequence of the new legal standards and what is called the "post-Holocaust morality," intervention against any fresh instance of genocide "regardless of personal consequence or cost" could no longer, Alexander argues, be resisted. "[As] a crime against humanity, a "holocaust" is taken to be a threat to the continuing existence of humanity itself. It is impossible . . . to imagine a sacrifice that would be too great when humanity itself is at stake." For Alexander the most telling evidence comes from the Yugoslav civil war of the 1990s. "It was the engorged Holocaust symbol," he argues, "that propelled first American diplomatic and then American-European military intervention against Serbian ethnic violence." In "*A Problem from Hell,*" Samantha Power provides a detailed empirical study with a direct bearing on the question Alexander raises: the relation between the commission of post-Holocaust genocide and the response of the United States and the West. Power shows that during the Bosnian crisis of the early 1990s, images of the Holocaust—especially television film of the cadaverous bodies of

Muslim detainees in the Serbian concentration camps—and interventions by the authoritative symbol of Holocaust consciousness in the contemporary world, Elie Wiesel, played a major role in shaping Western opinion and pushing Western governments into eventual air strikes. But she also shows that, for prudential reasons, Western governments resisted labeling what was taking place as genocide and earlier had essentially stood by while 200,000 people perished. Two years after the end of the Bosnian crisis perhaps 800,000 Tutsis were murdered in Rwanda in the space of one hundred days. Despite the fact that this catastrophe, in its ferocity, pace of killing, and ethnic ambition, more closely resembled the Holocaust than anything that had happened in Bosnia, no Western government was seriously tempted to intervene. The Clinton administration even refused to label what was taking place as genocide, on the ground, as one briefing paper admitted, that a "Genocide finding could commit [the U.S. Government] to actually 'do something.'" Samantha Power concludes: "Despite broad public consensus that genocide should "never again" be allowed, and a good deal of triumphalism about the ascent of liberal democratic values, the last decade of the twentieth century was one of the most deadly in the grimmest century on record." She repeats David Rieff's mordant version of the lesson the Holocaust had actually taught: "Never again would Germans kill Jews in Europe in the 1940s." Power offers a sober but necessary corrective to Alexander's optimism about the impact of "post-Holocaust morality" in the international sphere.

The second problem I have with Alexander's argument is more fundamental. As we have seen, Alexander believes no historical event is self-interpreting. He believes that evil does not exist "naturally" but is "the product of cultural and sociological work." He regards something as central to Western civilization as the division of the world into forces of good and evil as "a contrived binary," at least from the sociological point of view. And in opposition to the two alternative lay theories of trauma—what he calls the Enlightenment version (because of human nature we are capable of seeing atrocities for "what they are") and the psychoanalytic one (the return of the repressed)— he proposes a "theory of cultural trauma" of his own. Alexander regards culture as an independent explanatory variable. In explaining the emergence of the idea of the Holocaust a decade or more after the discovery of the Nazi mass murder of the Jews, all that seems to be required is a description of the work that took place in the cultural sphere. Certainly that is all that we are given. In Alexander's account, the transformation of the mass murder of the Jews into the Holocaust is explained entirely with reference to certain influential cultural products—like the book, play, and film based on the diary of Anne Frank or the extraordinarily successful television miniseries *Holocaust*. Although Alexander admits that he is not able in the space available to provide a "thick description" of the cultural process that produced the Holocaust, he seems to be committed to the idea that the mass murder of the Jews as a wartime atrocity was transformed into the Holocaust simply through the cumulative impact of books and films and television productions. There is, in short, nothing in Alexander's argument to suggest that if he had the time to provide his thick description, it would entail more than a further analysis of large numbers of cultural products, of what he calls the many "bits and pieces."

There are two difficulties with this kind of popular-cultural explanation of the emergence of the Holocaust as the central moral-political myth of the modern Western world. First, if the recognition of evil emerges only as a result of cultural and sociological work, if the idea of evil is epistemological and not ontological, as Alexander claims, and if the common-sense Enlightenment theory of trauma is wrong—that is to say, if humans do not grasp the meaning of how things truly are through the exercise of moral imagination, through the capacity for empathy, and through the use of knowledge, understanding, and reason to compare and judge—it is hard to see why the cumulative impact of cultural products concerning the Nazi mass murder of the Jews, including both popular works like *The Diary of Anne Frank* and the miniseries *Holocaust* and masterpieces like Primo Levi's *If This Is a Man* and Claude Lanzmann's *Shoah,* should have had the power to recalibrate the way in which the events in question were "coded," "weighted," and "narrated," and thereby were transformed from war atrocity into the sacred-evil myth of the Holocaust. If we ask a simple question, "Why has the Holocaust risen above all other instances of massive political evil in our century (the Armenian Genocide, the Stalin Terror, the killing fields of Pol Pot, and so on) to become the sacred-evil myth for our time?" then two answers seem possible. One is scurrilous. It attributes the preeminence of the Holocaust to Jewish cultural power. The second is very close to what Alexander calls the Enlightenment theory of trauma, or our collective capacity to grasp and weigh the meaning of catastrophic events truly. In the Holocaust, several dimensions came together: the victims were identified on the basis of a totalitarian ideology at once paranoid and fantastical;

the victims were entirely innocent of everything that ideology alleged; the ambition to remove this people from the face of the earth was total (neither babies nor one-hundred-year-olds were to be spared; the pace of the killing was furious); some 60 percent of the killings took place within a year; the method of killing—in large part impersonal, bureaucratic, and industrial—reflected aspects of modernity and thus its potential dark side. Without the gradual and general recognition of this uniquely evil constellation, the Holocaust would not, in my view, have become the central sacred-evil myth of our time. The cultural work that Alexander sketches, the "bits and pieces," did not create the myth of the Holocaust, as his analysis tends to suggest. Rather, in its totality, it helped make the true meaning and the mystery of the Holocaust perspicuous.

The second difficulty is more mundane. In an extended footnote, Alexander recognizes that Peter Novick's *The Holocaust in American Life* offers a serious alternative explanation of the emergence of the Holocaust as a central contemporary myth. As is well known, unlike Alexander, Novick deplores the central place the Holocaust has now assumed in American collective memory. And, as is equally well known, he explains its emergence through an analysis of the ideological role it has played in helping Israel escape its growing isolation during the age of decolonization; through an analysis of the role it has played in consolidating the ethnic identity of American Jews at a time when their long-term future was felt to be under threat because of the success of assimilation and the accelerating trend of "marrying out"; and through a reminder of the obvious fact that talented Jews are located throughout the American academy, media, and entertainment industry. Even ignoring for a moment some of the thorny normative issues that divide Alexander and Novick—whether the cultural centrality of the memory of the Holocaust has been, on balance, a humanizing or a harmful force—there is one obvious problem with Novick's historical analysis where Alexander's makes more sense. Alexander is surely right to insist that the Holocaust is a universal (Western) story and not, as Novick's analysis implies, a mainly American one. None the less there are elements of Novick's argument that seem to me almost self-evidently true. It is not plausible to deny that one of the groups that actively disseminated the story of the Holocaust were those who sincerely believed it should and could be used to increase levels of international support for Israel's security concerns. And it seems to me disingenuous and unnecessarily defensive to deny that the profile of American Jews in the universities and schools, and in the world of books and magazines, television, and film, played a part in that process of broad and deep cultural dissemination of the story of the Holocaust on which Alexander's cultural-structural analysis so heavily depends. Alexander dismisses Novick's account too easily, as a tendentious and all too familiar fantasy about "Jewish power." If Novick is tone-deaf to the transformative power of the Holocaust story, Alexander is almost willfully blind to the interests the story serves. His perceptive remark—that Novick's account is Weberian and his own Durkheimian—does not, of course, settle the matter in dispute either way. A more adequate account of the emergence of the Holocaust as a central myth and also of its contemporary role would require, in my view, an assimilation of elements of Novick's skeptical and sardonic Weberian reading with Alexander's more generous and imaginative Durkheimian one.

This leads to my most fundamental misgiving about Alexander's argument: his reading of the place of the Holocaust in contemporary political life. According to Alexander, the Holocaust has given rise to "an unprecedented universalization of political and moral responsibility" and has "enlarged the human imagination" so that for the "first time in history" genocidal killings can be identified, understood, and judged. It has also "deepened contemporary sensitivity to social evil," revealing for the first time (this claim to novelty would surprise traditional adherents of the Abrahamic faiths) that "morality must be universalized beyond any particular time and place." The trench between those societies that have been reshaped by this new "post-Holocaust" consciousness and those that have not is so deep that it has the power to determine the very future of international relations. Because of the arrival of this new consciousness, "a decided increase in moral and social justice may . . . result."

There are very many reasons for doubting Alexander's unambiguously optimistic reading of the impact of the Holocaust on contemporary political life. Take, for example, the case of Israel, the society where the Holocaust is at the very center of collective memory. In essence, as the philosopher Yehuda Elkana once argued, Israel is a society divided between a minority for whom the lesson of the Holocaust is the same as Alexander's—"It will never happen again"—and the majority for whom the lesson is, rather, "It will never happen to us again." As Idith Zertal argues in *Israel's Holocaust and the Politics of Nationhood*, the memory of the Holocaust has frequently been mobilized in ways very far removed indeed from service in the cause of justice. In opposition to the plan for the partition of British-mandated Palestine, Menachem Begin in 1946 likened its Jewish supporters to members of the Judenrate: "wretched Jewish leaders, hated by their people." During negotiations with President Kennedy over an agreement to allow Israel to acquire the atomic bomb, Prime Minister Ben-Gurion made frequent reference to the Holocaust. To legitimize the 1982 Lebanon invasion, Prime Minister Begin described the mission as "above all to root out Arafat/Hitler from his Beirut bunker and avert a new Treblinka." Benjamin Netanyahu, on one occasion, likened the plan for the withdrawal from the West Bank, or "Judea" and "Samaria," to the 1938 cession of the Sudetenlands and, on another, described the United Nations as a "proto-Nazi" organization. And as cultural preparation for the murder of Yitzhak Rabin, members of the Israeli far right produced photographs of the prime minister wearing a swastika armband. The Israeli-Palestinian writer Emile Habibi reflected: "I cannot imagine that, had the Holocaust not happened, the brothers of Heinrich Heine and Maimonides...would have permitted a Jewish government to expel another Semite people out of its home" (quoted in Zertal, p. 127). In Habibi's interpretation, the Holocaust provided not an increase in moral and social justice but a partial explanation of the catastrophe of his people.

Take a different kind of example. No event in twentieth-century history prefigures the Holocaust more closely than the Armenian genocide. Indeed, as the Israeli scholar Yair Auron points out in his *The Banality of Denial*, in 1918 Chaim Weizmann's secretary, Shmuel Tolkowsky, who described the Jewish people as "specialists in martyrdom," asked: "[Among} all those who suffer around us, is there a people whose record of martyrdom is more akin to ours than that of the Armenians?" And yet as Auron shows in great detail, and for reasons that are all to easy to grasp (a combination of Realpolitik and belief about the uniqueness of the Holocaust), of all Western societies there has been none more willing than Israel to collaborate with the Turkish government in its remorseless campaign to deny the Armenians the right to attach the name of Genocide to the murder by the Ottoman Empire of a million or so of their people in 1915–16.

In raising these matters my intention is not to enter into a controversy over Israel's security or foreign policies. The intention is, rather, to begin to problematize Alexander's argument about the unambiguously humanizing impact on contemporary political life of the Holocaust as a universal, tragic, sacred-evil myth.

Another way of problematizing his argument is to examine some of the political consequences of an idea at the heart of the Holocaust myth: the claim of its uniqueness. Alexander avoids a discussion of whether or not the claim is true. It is not his aim, he tells us, to describe the nature of the Holocaust or what it "really was," but rather to locate the form of its representation. For Alexander the Holocaust is simultaneously "unique and not unique." Because it is "unique," it can be a master symbol of human evil. Because it is "not unique," it can act as "a bridging metaphor," shedding light on other evils through analogy.

Alexander seems to underestimate how divisive the claim of uniqueness for the Holocaust has so often proved. He says, for example, that in every Holocaust museum "the fate of the Jews functions as a metaphorical bridge to the treatment of other ethnic, religious, and racial minorities." Alexander has read *Preserving Memory,* Edward Linenthal's fascinating account of the foundation of the Washington Holocaust Museum, the world's most significant institution for such memorialization. Yet his uninflected version of the mission of all Holocaust museums omits mentioning what Linenthal's book documents about the often bitter struggles that were waged over the question of uniqueness: the battle over whether it was 11 million (civilians) or 6 million (Jews) who perished in the Holocaust; the fury at the suggestion that the museum should also memorialize Polish and Ukrainian victims of the Nazis; the grudging admission of the Gypsies; the determined and successful campaign to keep the Armenians out. Alexander argues that Linenthal is wrong to write about "Jewish ownership of the Holocaust." Perhaps so. But Alexander is himself wrong to deny that a claim to ownership is indeed often made.

These battles represented in microcosm the more general cultural conflicts that the sacred-evil myth of the Holocaust in general, and the claims about its uniqueness in particular, have been capable of exciting. Alexander argues that one of the historic crimes for which the Holocaust myth served as metaphorical bridge was the destruction of Native American society. In reality, the claims of some of the more extreme members of the uniqueness school—like Steven Katz in *The Holocaust in Historical Context,* who argues that there is only one case of genocide in the entire course of human history, or Deborah Lipstadt in *Denying the Holocaust,* who argues that to deny the uniqueness of the Holocaust is no different from denying that the mass murder of the Jews took place—have led to polemical rejoinders from scholars of the Native American tragedy, like David Stannard, of an almost anti-Semitic kind. The struggle for what Novick regards as the "gold medal in the victimization games" can be very ferocious indeed. In Australia, to take another example, discussion of the nineteenth-century destruction of Aboriginal society is, on balance, more harmed than illuminated by the myth of the Holocaust and by the claims about its uniqueness. Because the Holocaust is popularly seen as the prototype of genocide, and because the meaning of the Aboriginal tragedy has become part of a general cultural battle known as the "History Wars," any reference to Aboriginal genocide is now routinely dismissed by conservative opinion-makers as straightforward left-wing folly or anti-national treachery.

The power of the Holocaust story, and the claims about its uniqueness, in these cases and others like them operate more as a metaphorical fortress than as a bridge. It is true, as Alexander argues, that the Holocaust has become the measure of evil in our age. But this seems a far more ambiguous matter than Alexander allows. When the sacred-evil myth of the Holocaust becomes entangled in politics, it often becomes depressingly profane.

REFERENCES

Auron, Yair. *The Banality of Denial: Israel and the Armenian Genocide*. New Brunswick & London: Transaction, 2003.

Katz, Steven T. *The Holocaust in Historical Context*, Vol. 1. New York: Oxford University Press, 1994.

Linenthal, Edward T. *Preserving Memory: The Struggle to Create America's Holocaust Museum*. New York: Columbia University Press, 2001.

Lipstadt, Deborah. *Denying the Holocaust: The Growing Assault on Truth and Memory*. New York: Macmillan International, 1993.

Novick, Peter. *The Holocaust in American Life*. Boston: Houghton Mifflin, 1999.

Power, Samantha. *"A Problem from Hell": America and the Age of Genocide*. New York: Basic Books, 2002.

Stannard, David E. "Uniqueness as Denial: The Politics of Genocide Scholarship." In *Is The Holocaust Unique? Perspectives on Comparative Genocide*, ed. Alan S. Rosenbaum. Boulder, CO: Westview, 2001.

Zertal, Idith. *Israel's Holocaust and the Politics of Nationhood*. Cambridge: Cambridge University Press, 2005.

Jeffrey Alexander on the Response to the Holocaust

Nathan Glazer

To begin with there are the events, as horrible and as awful as any in history. Then there are the reports and testimonies of those who lived through those events and survived; those who observed them at first hand as nonvictims; and those who discovered them at the war's end, photographed the sites, the corpses, and the survivors, and reported on them. Then there are the interpretations: why these monstrous things happened, what they meant, how we should respond to them. And then, in Jeffrey Alexander's interesting and important chapter, there is the understanding and interpretation of the responses, and in particular the surprising changes in our responses over the sixty years since the end of the war.

When we consider how we have changed in how we think about the Holocaust, we are three stages past the events themselves. The events become somewhat faded, and we are in that difficult terrain of "representation," which is so prominent in current social science. This is not to depreciate the importance of the task Jeffrey Alexander has undertaken, or the significance of the phenomenon of the striking change in our consciousness and understanding of the Holocaust that he describes. But when one concentrates on "representation," on how we have "constructed" something, and what has led to this distinctive construction, the hard factuality of the events does recede. The events might mean this, or they might mean that, and we inevitably recall those people—they are referred to in Jeffrey Alexander's article, Theodor Adorno and Saul Friedlander most prominently—who warned us that after such events there could be no literary interpretation, perhaps then no social-scientific interpretation: the events themselves put all interpretation in the shade, and perhaps interpretation improperly puts the events in the shade. But before we get to this possibility, let us lay out the problem with which Alexander deals.

At the end of World War II everyone became aware—though the facts were available to those who wanted to know them for years before—of the concentration camps and the death camps, and of the great enterprise of Nazi Germany, conducted with remarkable energy in the midst of a world war that one would have thought required all of Germany's efforts, to exterminate all the Jews. In view of the resources Germany devoted to this effort, it might well have been considered the first Nazi war aim. But that was not how it was seen.

Alexander impressively demonstrates that our initial understanding of these events reduced them to a subordinate element in a great and successful war. This matter of the genocide of the Jews was a minor part or sideshow in the monumental drama of a worldwide war, little noted in histories of the war. When the war was won, the program of extermination was exposed to all, along with many other evils perpetrated by the Nazi enemy. Alexander shows that the Holocaust, then not so named, was incorporated as part of the progressive understanding of our history then prevailing in the euphoria of winning a war against a monstrous enemy, in which problems are confronted, and overcome, in making a better world: History as a progress, in other words, in which we become more enlightened, more understanding, more competent, more tolerant, and in which illusion and bigotry and prejudice and unreason are steadily reduced. As Alexander writes, "The force of the progressive narrative meant that, while the 1945 revelations confirmed the Jewish mass murder, they did not create a trauma for the postwar audience. Victory and the Nuremberg trials would put an end to Nazism and alleviate its evil effects." Alexander favors the somewhat psychologizing and medical term *trauma* to describe the eventual impact of these events on the public mind. I would prefer a more neutral term. But however we describe the impact of the Holocaust, this does not really affect his analysis.

The crucial issue is how matters were represented: According to Alexander, "Neither emotional repression nor good moral sense...created the early response.... It was, rather, a system of collective representations that focused its beam of narrative light on the triumphant expulsion of evil." And then the Holocaust disappears pretty much from the public mind. (Of course when I speak of the "public mind," and "everyone," I am limiting myself to the West—just what these events meant in Japan, or India, or China, or

Latin America, is a different matter, and for most of these countries, except possibly for a few intellectuals, one assumes, not much.) But with the passing decades, the story of the extermination of the Jews begins to reemerge and becomes an ever-larger part of our mental landscape. It is no longer the evil that was successfully overcome in a good war, but part of a new kind of evil, ever-threatening, ever likely to again turn into a horrible reality, and one that casts the human enterprise in a dark perspective: It happened once, it can happen again, and the disappearance of one evil regime, Nazi Germany, is no warrant against its reappearance in many guises, in many different kinds of regimes.

From one genocide, a horror but one decisively overcome by the forces of justice, we begin to see the world as a place where similar events have taken place, and more may. The Holocaust, from being near forgotten, takes up a larger and larger place in our mental consciousness despite its recession in time, joined by many more in reality or possibility. "Rather than seeming to 'typify' Nazism, . . . the mass killings came to be seen as not being typical of anything at all. They came to be understood as a unique, historically unprecedented event, as evil on a scale that had never occurred before."

This is the large picture Alexander sketches, and he asks, then, why this change. We should note that in this process the specific Holocaust, the genocide perpetrated against the Jews by the Germans, does not disappear in the welter of other possible genocides in Rwanda, or Bosnia, or Kosovo, or Darfur, or similar events in the past to which we give ever greater attention, such as the Turkish genocide against the Armenians. We are now much more conscious of genocides of the past and new ones of the present, and those that may yet occur, and thus are aware of genocides as generic possibilities; but the initial genocide that started this process, *the* Holocaust (and the word is generally reserved for the extermination of the Jews), also has reemerged after a long submersion, with its own distinctive particularity as the event it was, and it plays a larger and larger role in our minds.

Holocaust museums and memorials, Alexander reminds us, did not for the most part emerge in the direct aftermath of the war; it was only a few decades after the knowledge of the events was spread across the newspapers that we began to create Holocaust museums, build Holocaust memorials (the largest was opened only recently in Berlin); that our American state educational authorities began to require that the facts of the Holocaust be taught; that the Holocaust emerged as a major theme in novels, poetry, the theater. The Holocaust has become something of a permanent background set, always there—something in the back of our consciousness as we read novels or poetry, see plays and films, view art. It often guides interpretation and understanding and criticism even if there is no direct reference to it in the work under consideration. Not that there is not also a great deal of direct and overt reference: Can one pick up an issue of a serious book review that does not have a few books noted that evoke, directly or tangentially, the Holocaust? Why is it only now, sixty years after the exposure of the death camps and concentration camps, after the news of the 6 million who died became general knowledge, that we are so engaged in cleaning up the aftermath of the Nazi criminal enterprise, with the return of art objects to the descendants of those who collected them and from whom they were stolen, and only now that perhaps some payments on life-insurance policies to descendants of those who died may be made?

There is certainly a mystery here, something to be explained, even if it is not the largest mystery, which is why it happened in the first place. I am particularly conscious of this mystery because I was well aware of what was happening, and its submersion in public consciousness. I was active in the 1940s in a Jewish student Zionist organization, and I edited its newspaper and later became an editor of the *Contemporary Jewish Record*, the journal of the American Jewish Committee, which in every issue printed news of mass murders. I then was an editor of its successor, the new Jewish publication *Commentary*, which also published a monthly chronicle of events of Jewish interest. I was aware of what was being reported and of the scale of what had happened. In retrospect, I am also aware that *Commentary*, on which I served from 1945 to 1952, can be included in this history of early—what shall we call it?—inattention, suppression, repression. In its first years, which coincided with the spread of the news of the mass murders to a world of others, non-Jews, who could not have been expected to have the same interest as Jews in what had happened, *Commentary* did not do very much in either reportage or analysis of the Holocaust. Other issues seemed more important: the fate of the survivors and the rise of the Jewish state, the threat of Communism in the postwar world, the new developments within the American Jewish community. We published at least one powerful memoir: Why not more? I ask myself at this late date. There were certainly others available, even in the early years. Yet there was little effort at interpretation or understanding. I think of one article by Leo Lowenthal, one of the community of Jewish refugee scholars who wrote a great deal for *Commentary* in the early years, trying to explain the Holocaust, and it was not very helpful.

Surviving relatives then began to arrive from the displaced-persons camps in Europe. Some of them lived with us for a while. The Holocaust was not uppermost in our conversations, or in their interests. They did not seem to want to talk about their experiences, and we did not want to press them. That was the past: The issue now was how to live in a new country, to get a job, to find an apartment, to rebuild a life. When I wrote a book on the history of Jews in America (*American Judaism*, University of Chicago Press, 1957), it seemed to me that American Jewish religious life, then engaged in a burst of expansion as Jews moved in great numbers from central cities to suburbs, was remarkably unaffected by the murder of 6 million Jews in Europe. The word *Holocaust* is not in the index. By 1972, when I published a new edition, occasioned by the events of 1967, when Israel seemed on the verge of being overwhelmed by the Arab states and the fear of a new Holocaust swept through the American Jewish community, the change that Alexander describes and analyzes was already well under way; now the word *Holocaust* does appear in the index.

I wrote in that new edition,

> in the mid-fifties, I could see no specific major impact of the Holocaust on the internal life of American Jews. After 1967, this was no longer true. American Jews subtly became more sensitized to the enormity of the extermination of the Jews. The Israeli action in kidnapping, trying, and executing Adolf Eichmann in 1961 had some effect in getting Jews to think about the Holocaust. One can hardly avoid psychoanalytic language. These events had been repressed, not only among many American Jews, but among many of the survivors themselves

I refer to the controversy occasioned by Hannah Arendt's reportage and book on the Eichmann trial, and Elie Wiesel's "direct and unsparing books on the extermination camps" as factors "leading Jews to confront these overwhelming events." But I also note that as late as 1966, "when *Commentary* addressed a series of questions on Jewish belief to a large group of young Jewish religious thinkers and writers ... the Holocaust did not figure among the questions, nor, it must be said, did it figure much among the answers" (*American Judaism*, 1972: 173).

Clearly there was something here to be explained, and without thinking much about it, I simply reverted to what Alexander calls a "commonsensical" explanation, basically popular lay psychoanalysis, and wrote that these events had been "repressed." Alexander does not find this satisfactory:

> What is wrong with this lay trauma theory is that it is "naturalistic," either in the naïvely moral or the naïvely psychological sense. [It] fails to see there is an interpretive grid through which all "facts" about trauma are mediated, emotionally, cognitively, and morally. This grid has a supraindividual cultural status, it is symbolically structured and sociologically determined. No trauma interprets itself.

Facts is in quotes, a signal that we are in the world where facts are not simply themselves but rather have to be interpreted, and where we seek out how things are represented, constructed. The facts do not, cannot, speak for themselves.

It is here that I am given pause, and I wonder where we are being led. Alexander takes us through the stages in which the representation of the Holocaust has changed, from its submersion as part of the progressive narrative, to the international impact of Anne Frank's diary and the subsequent play and movie—but that is still, particularly in the versions given by the play and movie, placeable within the progressive narrative—, to the Eichmann trial, and to the TV miniseries *Holocaust* and its impact in the United States and particularly also Germany. What is creating a new "interpretive grid," he notes, are not merely new and powerful representations but also new realities, and in particular the decline of American political, military, and moral prestige during the Vietnam War.

That is a new reality indeed. America to its most extreme critics becomes "Amerika," linked to Nazi Germany by its actions. The army that had fought the "good" war "came to be identified, by influential intellectuals and a wide swath of the educated Western public, as perpetrating genocide against the helpless and pathetic inhabitants of Vietnam." Alexander describes this development as "losing control over the means of symbolic production." "This process of... symbolic inversion further contributed to the universalization of the Holocaust: It allowed the moral criteria generated by its earlier interpretation to be applied in a less nationally specific and thus less particularistic way."

Alexander does see a problem here—as I do, too—and that is the issue of the relative weight we are to give to "representation" and "fact" or "reality"—which I would prefer not to put in quotes—in affecting opinion, beliefs, and understandings in responses to the Holocaust. Certainly some groups attempt to shape that response for some kind of pragmatic political end—for example, to strengthen understanding of or support for the Jewish state of Israel. I agree with Alexander that such efforts by Jewish organizations, despite the prominence given to them by Peter Novick in *The Holocaust in American Life,* and more tendentiously by Norman G. Finkelstein in *The Holocaust Industry* (see Alexander's extensive note 57, part I, this volume), cannot possibly explain the place the Holocaust has taken in the public mind. There is a larger process of representation, affected by many factors, but what seems central is the decline in the positive assessment of the deployment of American power abroad, both in the minds of many critical Americans and among elite intellectual groups abroad, and this decline cannot be attributed to or controlled by organizational interests. But as Alexander recognizes, "one implication of my discussion . . . is that this perception of [the Holocaust's] moral status is not a natural reflection of the event itself."

I would like, against Alexander, to clam a larger role for "the event itself"; I think we make too much of "representation" in much of contemporary social science, and we allow "events themselves," "facts," and "realities" to fade into a murky background. Admittedly, facts are disputable and realities have to be interpreted, but then some facts are immutable and some realities are indisputable (though there will always be found some to dispute them).

Alexander recognizes the problem and takes it up at length in note 55:

> I hope that my aim . . . will not be misunderstood as an effort to aestheticize and demoralize the inhuman mass murders that the Nazis carried out. I am trying to denaturalize, and therefore sociologize, our contemporary understanding of these awful events. For, despite their heinous quality, they could in fact be interpreted in various ways. Their nature did not dictate their interpretation.

Alexander recognizes the position of Saul Friedlander, who has "lambasted the deconstructive methods of narrativists like Hayden White for eliminating the hard-and-fast line between 'representation' (fiction) and 'reality.'" There is a problem here, and when employed for the Holocaust, as against, say, the battles of Napoleon, there are moral issues involved. Alexander insists he resists full allegiance to the "aestheticizing, debunking

quality of deconstructive criticism. . . . By contrast, I am trying here to demonstrate that the aesthetic and the critical approach must be combined."

In the end, however, I see too much weight in his analysis on the "aesthetic," or "representational," side of the combination as against the weight
of the events themselves. But if one emphasizes the direct effect of fact,
"reality," or the events themselves, how can we understand the lengthy
period of silence about them, and the large change in our understanding that
Alexander describes so well? First, I would not dismiss the idea of repression.
They were terrible events, and without going to technical psychoanalyis or
psychology, there were reasons for survivors to put them aside, and most
did. The organizations of survivors come later, after careers had been made,
families had been created. And the onlookers, even those with the greatest
involvements, such as the Jewish community and its organizations, may well
have been abashed at how little they did. In view of what had happened,
after all, whatever was done was too little, and a sense of guilt had to be pervasive. Jews were perhaps happy to embrace the progressive narrative rather
than confront directly the events themselves and their own responsibility.

But then other facts and events intervened, those referred to by Alexander,
which had to lead to a more direct facing of the events themselves by Jews, as
well as favoring the creation of a new grid of interpretation for genocides in
general. We have to I think differentiate here between a Jewish and a general
response. The Jewish response was shaped by the fear of a new Holocaust
in the events leading up the Israel–Arab wars of 1967 and 1973. The general
response to the Holocaust was shaped by the Vietnam War and the cultural
revolution of the sixties, in which the heroic and noble stature of the United
States as the rescuer of Western civilization was much reduced. Genocide
became a generic phenomenon. Perhaps it was a mistake, from the point of
view of Jewish interests, to coin and popularize the term and to reduce the
Jewish case to only one, if still the most spectacular, example. The general
response and interpretation was adopted by Jews. They could better advance
their interests by hanging on to the coattails of the reinterpretation of the
Holocaust as a generic possibility that any nation or power can perpetrate
and of which any group can become the victim.

I have introduced here the idea of a Jewish interpretation of the Holocaust,
which may differ from a more general response in how and why it under-
goes change. Alexander does not differentiate Jewish responses from other
responses. There is, it is true, much in common in both the specifically
Jewish and more general understanding. But the grids of understanding

and interpretation are not the same. The other genocides that have taken their places alongside the Jewish genocide—those of the past such as the Armenian, those in more recent years following the breakup of Yugoslavia and in Africa, and those possibly to come—have the capacity to reduce the distinctiveness and weight of the Jewish genocide in responses to genocide in general. In his analysis Alexander places the Holocaust in a larger, more general frame: It becomes more than part of the history of the Jews. He notes (in note 57), "little attention has been paid to the Nazis' equally immoral and unconscionable extermination policies directed against other groups...Poles, homosexuals, gypsies, and handicapped." And he writes earlier, in note 28, "That virtually all these non-Jewish victims were filtered out of the emerging collective representation of the Holocaust underlines the arbitrary quality of trauma representations." (Alexander is using a technical meaning of *arbitrary*, but the common meaning will not unduly distort the sense of the passage.) Here Alexander is placing in opposition a "reality"—there were indeed other groups subject to Nazi extermination—against a "representation," which still, but decreasingly, places the Jews in the most prominent position.

But is not this the case of "reality" imposing itself on "representation"? The Jews were, after all, the central target of Nazi hatred. The numbers of Jews who died far exceeded, by various orders of magnitude, those of the other groups subject to extermination policies. The efforts that the Nazis devoted to the extermination of Jews reduced these other efforts to sideshows. The scale of the Holocaust reduces all the comparable genocides to lesser representatives of the genre—indeed, so much lesser as to raise the question of whether the same term should apply to all. The Jews also played a much, much larger role in European and modern society, and in its distinctive scientific and cultural achievements, than the other targets who the Nazis believed consisted of unworthy life. Finally and most markedly, the extermination of the Jews was carried out by the most advanced representatives of Western civilization, using its most advanced technologies. The contrast with other genocides, carried out by societies considered backward or deficient from the point of view of advanced Western civilization—the Ottoman Turks, the Hutus of Rwanda, the Sudanese Arabs—is so marked as to suggest that these other genocides are of a different order of significance altogether. The destruction of the Jews has to raise the most serious and the deepest questions of its meaning, not only for Jews but also for the entire Western world they have so signally influenced.

The Jews, whatever their centrality for the Western culture of the past 150 years, were certainly central for the Nazis—far more so than the others who suffered under Nazi crimes and far more so than the early historians of the war realized. A recent review in the *Times Literary Supplement* (February 2, 2007: 24) brings to our attention this centrality and its increasing recognition by historians: "Until recently few historians took seriously the Nazi elite's identification of world Jewry with the United States. . . . Goering, Goebbels and Hitler interpreted the events of the Second World War through the narrative of a life-and-death struggle against the Jews, who represented the driving force behind the American war effort and the Roosevelt administration" (Anson Rabinbach, reviewing Adam Tooze's *The Wages of Destruction* [Penguin]). A strange representation, but one that led to the most terrible realities. And those realities, I would argue, are still central for our response to the Holocaust.

Life and Death among the Binaries: Notes on Jeffrey Alexander's Constructionism

Elihu Katz and Ruth Katz

Sociologists do not find much interest in events, especially disruptive ones. Among the outpouring of books and papers on the Holocaust, there are very few by sociologists. The same can be said about other historical events and of more recent events such as September 11th, the 2004 tsunami, or Hurricane Katrina. Events are too idiosyncratic; many are one-time affairs, at least ostensibly. Events are seen as parentheses that open and close, nuisances that interfere with the routines that deserve sociological attention. Not much attention is given, somehow, to the possibility that the exception may be the rule, or come to be the rule, or illuminate the rule; or to the idea that deviant cases also need explaining if a theory is to hold.[1]

The Holocaust is more than just deviant, of course. It is a case of such extreme human behavior that it has been declared inexplicable, both by those who would mystify it and by those who prefer to think of it as a barbaric regression in civilization's progress.[2] But mystification of human behavior is a direct challenge to sociology, and to the other social sciences. To remain silent—even for other reasons—is to disgrace sociology, and, in this sense, almost all of us are guilty.

Jeffrey Alexander is an exception. His theoretical interest in "how culture works"[3] has brought him to the gates of Auschwitz. His interest is in the influence of culture—ideas, ideals, myths, narratives—on social structure, rather than the conventional vice versa. His data come from some of the events—not just the Holocaust—that have disrupted and imprinted modern society, and in this respect he is a worthy successor to Victor Turner (1974). He brings theory and method to bear on social trauma and its resolution, daring even to cope with the Holocaust and with the risks of doing so.[4]

But a caveat is also in order. Alexander does not deal with questions of how this horror could have taken place. He is not trying to explain the behavior of the perpetrators, or of their compliant victims, or of the bystanders. His aim, rather, is to tell the story of how the concept, Holocaust, arose from the ashes and may yet change the world. This is no small matter, but in truth it is also an "escape." Alexander implies that the "trauma-drama" that relates the story may yet take a "progressive" turn. Zygmunt Bauman (1989), a rare sociologist who *has* tried to explain why and how, is far less optimistic.

Alexander's "optimism" stems from his assumption that the diffusion of the Holocaust metaphor has made us more wary of the drastic actions of which we are capable. He believes that this "master metaphor" has the power to restrain. But if it has, how are we to understand the genocides and the ethnic cleansings that have taken place during the years since the metaphor has taken charge? Impressed as we were with the way in which Alexander traces the spiraling trajectory of *Holocaust*, we find ourselves—on rereading—hesitant to accept his conclusion that the Good now has a better chance. In fact, we feel unprepared to accept a universalized Holocaust in exchange for the particularized retellings of the Jewish one, or any of the other manmade catastrophes. True, our job is to generalize and explain—based on detailed comparisons—but Evil is not an adequate explanation. And naming is not enough. We are in awe of Alexander's effort to walk along the stations of Holocaust research en route to the dilemma with which he confronts us. With respect, we would like here to attempt to retrace his footsteps, as we imagine them, while adding some observations of our own.

The accounting scheme for studying an event is obvious. We need to know (1) what happened; (2) why it happened, or more forthrightly, how it could have happened; (3) how it came to be known, and remembered; and (4) what were its consequences. As far as the first two items are concerned, we are indebted to the historians and archivists—some of whom display a strong sociological bent—who have done most of the work (with much difference of opinion among them). Only very few sociologists—Bauman for one, Helen Fein (1979) for another—have stood up to this challenge. Alexander builds on these works as well as on the writings of philosophers, journalists, public figures, and creative artists, adding observations of his own and developing points 3 and 4. Without claiming expertise—for lack of which we apologize—we propose here to reconstruct and discuss how Alexander has gone about the task he set himself. The four points above, we believe, will help make plain what Alexander has and has not done, what some others have done, and for better or worse, how it looks to us.[5]

What Happened?

"Did the tree really fall?" We know that it did, in spite of having been so well hidden from view and so quickly covered over. We know because we have lived among the witnesses for over sixty years and because some of our colleagues, the historians, have devoted their lives to uncovering the findings and making them public. The deniers help us remember.

But Alexander says that witnessing is not enough. The tree did not really fall—or, more precisely, it does not matter whether the tree fell—until we are given to understand what the falling *means*, what it stands for. Perhaps somebody set the forest on fire or committed a crime against the environment. Until the event is named, says Alexander, we can't really know its import.

As a cultural sociologist, as a constructionist, this is Alexander's big point. Meaning is negotiable, and there may be—as there certainly was in the present case—an evolution in the naming and in the attributions of meaning. The Nazis had their own words—the euphemistic "Final Solution," for example. The earliest news of the mass killings to reach the outside were classified as acts of war, until the GI liberators called what they saw an "atrocity." The word *genocide* was coined shortly thereafter and figured in later deliberations of the United Nations. Only around the time of the Nuremberg trials did one speak of "crimes against humanity," but it wasn't until the 1960s—twenty years after the war—that the term *Holocaust* began to circulate. It was used, initially, to refer to *this* particular genocide, but eventually it became a yardstick with which to measure others of the world's travesties.

Alexander traces the dynamics of these appellations, substituting present-day *construction* for what we used to call "definition of the situation" and then *framing*. He speaks of *coding, weighting*, and *narrating. Coding* in this case refers to popular discussion of the Holocaust in terms of Good and Evil, which also served to combat the ethic of relativism that prevailed before the war, when it was considered improper to pass judgment on other cultures (just as it is, once again, today). From this coding of ultimate Evil, Alexander turns to the process by which society elevates the issue—"*weights it*"—to the top of its agenda. Novick (1994) shows how this was accomplished in America, after a period of stunned silence.

While Alexander is quite specific about the dynamics of *coding* and *weighting*—even if we are supposed to accept that these processes were largely consensual and not much contested—he is much more vague in his use of *narrative*, his most central concept. He talks about types of narratives—a "progressive" one that tells of the ultimate triumph of Good, and a tragic one. He jumps, abstractly, to a now-universalized "narrative" that refers to "intentional and systematic violence against a stigmatized group," and he is aware of the ever more generalized disasters to which the label is being applied. He is aware also that the universal is at the expense of the particular, but he does not tell us what versions of the original narratives have survived the retellings, if they have. "Auschwitz," we are assured, still means something to most people, but we want to know more about the details of the narrative in which it is embedded. We want to know whether parents are telling their children about the Holocaust of the Jews, or does that no longer matter? We understand that these questions lie beyond the task that Alexander has given himself, but it is from reading Alexander that they arise. Even if we accept that Alexander's task is to follow the succession of codings, weightings, and narratings, it seems to us that the succession of narratives is largely unspoken in the interest of reaching for the generic category that they have become.

Mutatis mutandis, it is worth comparing this case with Alexander's (1988) discussion of the Watergate scandal. The facts of the break-in to Democratic headquarters were reported by police and press at Time One, before the presidential election of 1972. The event was dubbed "Watergate" because that was the locus of the crime, but it did not cause much of a stir. "Dirty politics," or "just politics," was the general reaction. Ironically, Alexander continues, only after Nixon's landslide victory did society take a second look, as the Congress, the courts, and the press reopened the question of what really happened and what it meant. Suspecting Evil, they gave the matter more "weight." It is hard to agree—though it makes a better story—that the facts remained unchanged as the investigations of these agencies of social control shed new light and continually rewrote the narrative. The chain of incriminations led to the office of the president himself, thus "polluting" the moral center of the polity, says Alexander. The forest was now ablaze with malicious "intent," and the situation demanded remedial action far beyond what firefighters could provide.

The narrator of the Watergate event is much more "embedded." Alexander, the sociological observer, walks us through the successive revelations of what happened and the corresponding changes of meaning. At the same time, he tells us the story behind the story, examining the responses of each of the four estates—legislative, judicial, journalistic, and the executive. There is real narrative here—several of them—in succession.

It is worth noting that both these events, the Holocaust and Watergate, were well hidden—in fact, intentionally so—and that narrating them is a hermeneutic matter, based on successive revelations. That they were so carefully concealed implies an awareness of the moral outrage that was being perpetrated. Compare these events with those of September 11th or the Munich Olympics, or other outrageous terror events that are perpetrated unabashedly, in full view of the world, virtually enlisting the media as "co-producers" of their performance. In such cases, the perpetrators agree to show that the tree has been felled—by them!

Why Did It Happen? How Could It Have Happened?

Alexander's job, as he sees it, is not to conduct an independent investigation of what happened, hardly even to review the investigations done by others, but to explore the succession of meanings that have been attached to what happened and to trace the process of their diffusion, their institutionalization, their generalization to other events, and their consequences. The paradox of this process lies in the disconnect between signifier and signified: what happened has forgotten its name and the name has forgotten what happened. One can argue that this is a successful "working through."

It is ironic to note that, logically, given this approach, nothing at all needs to have happened. Stories are not dependent on facts. Consider Michael Walzer's (1985) analysis of the Exodus of the Jews from Egypt. All he (or we) have to go on is the Biblical representation, archaeologists having so far failed to find that the Jews were a major presence in ancient Egypt, whether as slaves or not. Based on the text and on commentaries, Walzer reconstructs how the fate of a group of well-established "guest workers" or "temporary residents" was changed for the worse, lowering them into abusive slavery that led, subsequently, to a revolutionary uprising and escape. But, warns Walzer, true national liberation was not achieved by simply leaving Egypt, or even after the constitution that was forged at Mount Sinai. It took a generation of wandering through the desert, establishment of a division of labor, challenges to the legitimacy of the leader-ship, and much bickering and backsliding. Walzer shows how this paradigmatic narrative diffused throughout the world and served movements of national liberation, both as inspiration and as consolation for failures en route. Walzer explains the disenchantment of the new Pharaohs with the once-welcome immigrants and their paranoid fear that the Jews might rebel or join with their enemies, conspiratorially. He shows the symbolic self-confidence of Moses in slaying a sadistic Egyptian overseer, but yet the initial reluctance of the slaves to follow. Notice how the two stories—the Exodus and the Holocaust—have similar beginnings and opposite endings.

Whether or not there were Jewish slaves in Egypt, we know that the Jews were enslaved in Europe—millions of them. We know that they were slaughtered there for reasons, and in ways, that we must force ourselves to comprehend, not just to name and remember, or universalize. We need a story that will make "sense" of these facts—how it could have happened there and then; and sociologists seem to have shirked this duty, certainly compared to historians.

An outstanding sociological effort to explain this is Zymunt Bauman's *Modernity and the Holocaust* (1989). Rejecting the adequacy of psycholo-gistic explanations such as Goldhagen's (1996), Bauman proposes that the Holocaust is an *enactment* of modernity, not a deviation from it. The very institutions of modernity, says Bauman, made possible the translation of moti-vation into action. In his most-telling assertion, Bauman points his finger at the value-free bureaucracies that have learned to follow orders unquestion-ingly, and to champion means over ends. Such tasks are all the easier when those who are assigned to do the dirty work are at some distance from its consequences, are cognitively alienated, or are psychologically immunized. Along with bureaucracy, technology made this possible, says Bauman, point-ing to another example of modernity. And modern forms of social organiza-tion undermined the victims, too, making them more accessible and more vulnerable, as Hannah Arendt (1963) alleged.

Yehuda Bauer (2001), a distinguished historian of the Holocaust, dis-putes Bauman. He asks why similar conditions elsewhere did not produce the same social and technological abuses. "Why not Italy?" asks Bauer. He shows that there was large variance in the behavior of the Judenräte in spite of the similarities in their organizations. Bauer feels that Bauman underes-timates the extent of anti-Semitism and the extent of "popular demand"—not just at the highest political level—for eliminating Jews and Gypsies and other "pollutants." This is not value neutrality, says Alexander, but an active cultural force that saw the Jews as Evil.

Bauer and the other historians are occupied with the sociological question of the ostensible "cooperation" of the victims, who somehow were also shielded from perceiving the next steps that awaited them in the social and technological machinery of murder. In parallel, Peter Novick (1994) has studied the stunned but mostly passive reactions of bystanders—American Jews—who did not know how to respond to the early postwar revelations, just as they failed to arouse the Allied leadership to act on what they knew during the War (Wyman, 1984; Morse, 1968). Yet another historian, Christopher Browning (1992), has explored the attitudes and behavior of German troops in combat, and with Goldhagen, attests to the likelihood that opportunities to resist commands, or to opt out of inhuman actions, were available to individual soldiers, but they were rarely seized.

As the circle of the guilty grows larger, we all are implicated, Alexander argues. He shares Bauer's conclusion that our very humanity harbors the potential for Evil as well as Good.

How Did It Come to Be Known and Remembered?

The news of what was happening seeped out slowly and was not readily believed; that was the case in the United States, at least. So long as the war continued, there was strong Allied resistance to transporting and resettling refugees, and the pleas for intervention to destroy the death camps were (unforgivably) unheeded. Britain was a major culprit, and the Jewish community of Palestine did not and could not help (Bauer, 2001: 217–19). So long as the war was being fought, we are told by various authors, the fate of the Jews was overshadowed by military priorities. "War" was the attribution of choice, paralleling the "dirty [but routine] politics" of Watergate.

As has already been said, Alexander traces the successive namings of the horrors of Auschwitz as they surfaced, culminating in the term *genocide* in the early forties and then *Holocaust,* with its capital letter, in the sixties. Alexander and Bauer show how *Holocaust* was generalized, devolving from its original focus to other—similar but different—examples of genocide. The loss of uniqueness occupies some Jewish commentators, but there is not much disagreement that universalization of the term benefits mankind, say Bauer and Alexander. Novick and others decry the manipulative use of the term to promote Jewish solidarity, and similar criticism has often been voiced by Israelis.

The diffusion of these names is associated with major landmarks of ritual "action," to use Alexander's term. Yahil (1987/1992) remarks that the Nuremberg focus on crimes against humanity did not single out the Jews as victims, but that the Eichmann trial did. Beyond these remedial forums (cf. the parallel response in Watergate), the continuing weight accorded to the Holocaust is attributed, by all, to the steady flow of literary, artistic, and philosophical attention. *The Diary of Anne Frank*, published in 1944, is the best known of the literary bibliography of the Holocaust; Spielberg's *Schindler's List* and Landsberg's *Shoah* top the cinematic list. Ironically, the TV miniseries *Holocaust* probably had the greatest impact of all, especially in Germany (Knilli & Zielinski, 1982). This corpus of film and television, says Jeffrey Shandler (1999) in his critical overview *While America Watches*, has made a place for the Holocaust in American civil religion, echoing Alexander's statement that the Holocaust has been given sacred status. Friedlander's (1992) *Probing the Limits of Representation* offers a detailed debate on whether certain genres and certain media, but not others, are appropriate for representation of the Holocaust, to which Alexander says yes, ruling out comedy. But LaCapra (1992) disagrees, and Lang (1992) says that since there can be no limit, the facts should be chronicled in their raw state. These questions are echoed in Loshitsky's (1997) *Spielberg's Holocaust*, a symposium on critical views of *Schindler's List*. The genres of television and film—as well as museums—offer "redemptive solace," according to Shandler (1999). They direct viewers' attention away from the narrative, even away from the mystery. In other words, these films have a cathartic function, as Alexander notes in his discussion of tragedy.

These genres seem to be a clear victory for emotion over information. However, their success in evoking empathy and guilt raises the question of whether the Holocaust is not trivialized, and even misinterpreted, thereby. Emotion is easily evoked by story-telling; and it may well be—as Iyengar (1991: 56–57) finds—that viewing a homeless person on the evening news directs blame, and perhaps sympathy, to that one person, but that statistics of the *extent* of homelessness direct attention to the generic problem and the responsibility of society. This opens the question of whether personalization of a victim of genocide can communicate the magnitude of an event in which millions were murdered. Altogether, the conditions under which viewer sympathy is aroused for the mediated suffering of others—and which others?—is only now being explored seriously (see Boltansky, 1993). And when does this provoke action?

Another problem with the cinema of the Holocaust is that it specializes in exceptions. Film representations of Holocaust horrors are not "seeable," nor are films of other genocides—*Hotel Ruanda*, for example—unless they show some humanity, some path of escape. In other words, *Schindler's List* or *The Pianist* may have an altogether different message for those who are ignorant of what happened. To understand these films one has to know what they aren't showing.

There can be no doubt that the Jews—especially American Jews—have "used" the Holocaust to hold on to each other, and to arouse the sympathy of others, in an era of secularism, intermarriage, and prosperity. Holocaust Day serves as a reminder to American Jews that if it weren't for the good fortune or good sense of parents and grandparents, they themselves would have been mowed down or shoved into an incinerator. The same thoughts occupy Israelis who used to feel confident about protecting themselves and saving the rest—and now they are not so sure.

Yes, the Jews have made a concerted effort to keep the memory of the Holocaust alive, and have succeeded in doing that for themselves—and, willy-nilly, for the world. These efforts do not always look pretty, as befits what is sometimes derided as "*shoah* business" or as sheer impudence, as when Jewish settlers wear yellow stars and the letter "J" to protest their own government's decision to withdraw from parts of the occupied territories.

The strategies of collective memory are well developed among the Jews; they have a lot to remember. Yerushalmi (1982) stresses two: incorporation into the liturgy, and establishment of holidays. There are holidays of victory, as are Passover and Purim, but also holidays of defeat, such as the 9th day of the month of Ab, the day of fasting to mourn the destruction of the Temple and the beginning of Exile. Indeed, efforts are made continually to combine events of similar trajectory in the same holiday, like Presidents' Day in the United States. Prime Minister Begin tried to combine Remembrance of the Ninth of Ab (Tish'a B'av) with Holocaust Remembrance Day, but Israeli public opinion refused the analogy, protesting that these called up different memories and, furthermore, that the Holocaust ought not be relegated to the summer months when school is out. And thus, the Israeli calendar positions Holocaust Day in a cycle of holidays that leads from Passover to Holocaust Remembrance, to Memorial Day for fallen soldiers, to Independence Day, all in the space of one month and culminating in the harvest holiday that also celebrates the reaffirmation of peoplehood at the foot of Mount Sinai (Handelman and Katz, 1990).

What Are the Consequences?

Alexander suggests that Watergate brought an end to the "imperial presidency," and that the balance of powers between the executive, legislative, and judiciary branches was restored—at least for a while. Most of the effects of the affair were not long-lasting, except perhaps for the closer policing of presidential power. Gladys and Kurt Lang (1983) have suggested that the Watergate hearings broadcast the idea that presidential impeachment is "thinkable." Michael Schudson (1989) anticipated Alexander's conclusion that the memory of Watergate has waned, and that apart from some legislation, its most enduring effect seems to be inscribed in the pejorative suffix *gate*.

By contrast, Alexander believes that memory of the Holocaust will be long-lasting and that it has already had major cultural and structural influences, not only in the West but also elsewhere in the world. For one thing, the word—with its contemporary connotations—has entered the language (we don't know how many languages) and is serving, named or unnamed, as a yardstick to assess nationally inspired evil against racial and ethnic minorities. Indeed, the language of extreme evil has reinstated the binary Good versus Evil, as has been noted, and has empowered us to call on our inborn morality to refuse illegal dictates, however authoritatively spoken.

Structurally, the diffusion of the concept of the Holocaust has legitimized once-unthinkable international intervention in the conduct of nations that are committing atrocities. International courts now pass judgment on leaders and officials, popular and unpopular, who have been accused of crimes against humanity.

Domestically, Novick (1994) and Alexander both show that the status of Jews in America changed drastically as our enemy's enemy became our "best friends," as American anti-Semitism all but disappeared. But this trend may be reversing, following the European lead. And other minorities in America have recognized the Holocaust that had befallen them, as did Native Americans and Japanese Americans, notes Alexander.

Western guilt over the Holocaust—and how it might have been averted or at least downsized—is certainly key to the establishment of Israel, but the extent of its influence is seriously debated (Bauer, 2001). Holocaust deniers, especially on the Left, are said to be motivated by an anti-Semitic desire to undo the legitimacy of the Jewish state (Yakira, 2007), and the cry of "Never Again" is said to motivate Israeli actions, not all of them worthy.

Alexander deserves great credit for taking us at least part of the way on a path where many fear to tread, afraid of not being able to find the way back. He deserves great credit for his capacity to read and to synthesize and package the whole in a challenging way. He has chosen to theorize reactions to the most horrible event in human history in an effort to teach and to preach "how culture works."

Indeed, Michael Schudson's (1989) seminal article by that name offers a frame in which to recapitulate what Alexander has done—that is, to specify the conditions under which a concept will diffuse and be influential. And it's not so easy, Schudson implies, alluding to the experience of mass-communications research. An idea, or symbol or narrative, is most likely to "work," says Schudson, if, first, it is readily accessible, "retrievable," or salient in Alexander's sense of "weighting." Second, it has to have "rhetorical force," as in Alexander's "coding" of the Holocaust as absolute Evil, to communicate "the intentional, systematic, and organized employment of violence against members of a stigmatized collective group." Third, it has to "resonate" with the values and current concerns of its potential audience, implying that the reciprocal of rhetorical force is reception. Fourth, it has to be anchored in one of the loci for preservation of collective memory—what Schudson calls "institutional reception," as in a library, or a textbook, or a holiday. And, fifth, it has to offer the possibility of "resolution"—that is, to take an action in response to the symbol, such as joining the call for intervention in Kosovo or Darfur, or convening an international tribunal, or stopping for a moment of silence as the siren sounds on Holocaust Remembrance Day.

Where we might have hoped for more Alexander, there is less. In spite of his prodigious scholarship, his interest is too narrowly focused, in our opinion. We do not expect him to offer a sociology of what really happened, as Bauman has tried to do. What we do have a right to expect is his insight into the several *narratives* of what happened and how it could have happened—that is, to hear how Holocaust stories are being told today, not by historians, not by survivors, but by different elements in society. In Alexander's zeal to show how the concept has been universalized, the stories—ours and others'—are all but lost to naming and not explaining. Is this true? Is an empty signifier all that we have left? Has the concept really been disconnected from the Jews? This is not a plea for uniqueness; it is a plea for research on how different groups of people talk about the disappearance of the Jews of Europe, if they do, or about other catastrophes, even while they turn their attention to the coming nuclear, or environmental, holocaust. Are we reduced to having to thank the deniers for reminding us that Auschwitz really happened, and that there is still much to tell and even more to explain?[8]

To conclude, let's assume that Alexander is right: that the concept, the Holocaust, has been unleashed from its moorings, that it has reentered the world as a universal signifier, and that that may be a good thing for mankind, including the Jews. Before applauding, however, it would also be well to note that "universalizing" implies normalizing, meaning that the pattern is perceived as somewhat less disruptive than was thought. It also begs for an answer to the question of what mechanisms might be available to activate this new consciousness of Evil and of fellow-feeling when called for. Catholic confession, or South African reconciliation, or international courts come after the fact, and we are unsure of their efficacy, but what mechanisms are available *before* the fact, so to speak?

From Yehuda Bauer we learn that there is an interdisciplinary group scanning the world for indications of incipient genocides. Should there not be another group trying to understand the process by which genocides have been enacted—the stages that describe the butchery of one group of neighbors by another? Here is where sociologists would help by generalizing from concrete cases, past and present. In the meantime, whatever are our attitudes toward the uniqueness of the Jewish case, let us praise the historians who are still trying to understand how it happened, and how it could have happened, before acknowledging the Holocaust in its new role as universal.

Alexander is disturbed by this ambivalence of the Jews, as enlightened victims, to offer up their experience as a warning to the world, even at the cost (or perhaps benefit) of detaching it from themselves. True, the Jews have always been good exporters, and their inventory of exports certainly includes universal paradigms, such as slaves who rebel, diasporas, remnants who return, capitalists, communists, chosen people, and lately, "Mercurians" (Slezkine, 2004). But when the spotlights are turned off and the applause dies down, it starts to hurt again and thoughts turn to self-pity and worse. Before we condemn, should we not also expect ourselves to understand that victims have to struggle with feelings of revenge, diffuse aggressiveness, paranoia, indemnification, and self-hate, even if we prefer that they turn the other cheek, preach the horror of victimization, and intervene on behalf of fellow victims elsewhere?

1. Of course, there are exceptions. Aspects of Watergate, for example, have been studied by Gladys and Kurt Lang (1988), by Michael Schudson (1992), and by Alexander himself (1988). Craig Calhoun (1984) has written about Tianenmen Square. Vaughan (1996) has analyzed the cultural ingredients of the space shuttle disasters. Eric Klinenberg (200x) studied the Chicago "heat wave" disiaster. Dayan and Katz (1992) deal with a series of "integrative" events, lately amended by Katz and Liebes (2007). We wish to thank Kurt Lang (2007) for pointing out that communications scholars (and anthropologists such as Turner, 1974, and Handelman, 1990,) regularly deal with events, while sociologists apparently do not. For a recent review of early sociological writings on the Holocaust (mostly by refugee scholars), see Gerson and Wolf (2007). For a review of stages in the evolution of Holocaust studies, see Horowitz (2008), who also remarks that "Exact analysis of a singular event can illumine the whole specter of...totalitarian practices and the ideologies that guide them." In their recent analysis of Darfur, Hagen and Rymond-Richmond (2008) agree that "Sociologists empirically and theoretically neglect genocide."

2. This is a superficial reference to the *Historikerstreit* over whether the Holocaust should be incorporated as a historical event—not so different from some others, however horrible—into the writing of modern German history or whether it should be set aside and memorialized as an event that defies explanation.

3. This is a title from Michael Schudson (1989) that would serve Alexander equally well. We return to Schudson's scheme at the conclusion of this chapter.

4. On the "risks" of writing on the Holocaust, see Friedlander (1992).

5. One of us is a sociologist, the other a cultural historian; see the references for our readings and rereadings. We fall far short of Alexander in this respect.

6. One has an uneasy feeling comparing the Holocaust even with other tragedies, all the more so in comparing it with other crimes such as Watergate. Invoking *mutatis mutandis* is the magic that makes such sacrilegious comparisons permissible, as does the Hebrew *lehavdil*.

7. As if to claim the status of "media events"—i.e., consensual celebrations warranting live broadcasts, as affirmed by organizers, producers and audiences. See Dayan and Katz (1992), and Katz and Liebes (2007).

8. Two new candidates for cultural research are *Intifada* and *Naqba*, both of which originated in Palestinian Arabic, crossed the border into Israeli Hebrew, and are now diffusing elsewhere. *Intifada* sounded a rallying cry and the hint of organized effort to the sporadic uprisings of Palestinians in the territories occupied by Israel. *Naqba* is the Palestinian designation for the disastrous outcome of contesting Israel's declaration of independence in 1948. The concept has been included in a recent Israeli textbook for Arabic-speaking schools to give Arab citizens of Israel a "narrative of their own," with which to dissociate themselves from the victory narrative of Israeli Jews. We are told that the concept will also be included in Hebrew textbooks of the

same grade to allow each side a glimpse of the other's reading of the "same" situation. *Apartheid* is another good candidate.

REFERENCES

Alexander, Jeffrey. 2003. *The Meanings of Social Life*. New York: Oxford University Press.

Alexander, Jeffrey. 1988. "Culture and Political Crisis: 'Watergate and Durkheimian Sociology." In *Durkheimian Sociology: Cultural Studies*, ed. Jeffrey C. Alexander (pp. 187–224). New York: Cambridge University Press.

Arendt, Hannah. 1963. *Eichmann in Jerusalem*. New York: Viking.

Aschheim, Steven E. 2001. *Hannah Arendt in Jerusalem*. Berkeley: University of California Press.

Bauer, Yehuda. 2001. *Rethinking the Holocaust*. New Haven, CT: Yale University Press.

Bauman, Zygmunt. 1989. *Modernity and the Holocaust*. Cambridge, UK: Polity.

Bilsky, Leora. 2001. "Between Justice and Politics: The Competition of Storytellers in the Eichmann Trial." In *Hannah Arendt in Jerusalem,* ed. Steven E. Aschheim (pp. 232–52). Berkeley: University of California Press.

Boltansky, Luc. 1993/1999. *Distant Suffering*. New York: Cambridge University Press.

Browning, Christopher. 1992. "German Memory, Judicial Interrogation, and Historical Reconstruction: Writing Perpetrator History from Postwar Testimony." In *Probing the Limits of Representation,* ed. S. Friedlander (pp. 22–36). Cambridge, MA.: Harvard University Press.

Calhoun, Craig. 1984. *Neither Gods nor Emperors: Students and the Struggle for Democracy in China*. Berkeley: University of California Press.

Dayan, Daniel, & Elihu Katz. 1992. *Media Events: The Live Broadcasting of History*. Cambridge, MA: Harvard University Press.

Fein, Helen. 1979. *Accounting for Genocide: National Responses and Jewish Victimization During the Holocaust*. New York: Free Press.

Friedlander, S., ed. 1992. *Probing the Limits of Representation*. Cambridge, MA: Harvard University Press.

Gerson, Judith M., & Diane L. Wolf. 2007. *Confronting the Holocaust: Memories and Identities in Jewish Diasporas*. Durham, NC: Duke University Press.

Goldhagen, Daniel. 1967. *Hitler's Willing Executioners*. New York: Knopf.

Hagen, John, & Wenona Rymond-Richmond. 2008. "The Collective Dynamics of Racial Dehumanization and Genocidal Victimization in Darfur." *American Sociological Review*, 73(6): 875–902.

Handelman, Don. (1990). *Models and Mirrors: Toward an Anthropology of Public Events*. New York: Cambridge University Press.

Handelman, Don, & Elihu Katz. 1990. "State Ceremonies of Israel." In *Models and Mirrors: Toward an Anthropology of Public Events* by Don Handelman (pp. 191–233). New York: Cambridge University Press.

Horowitz, Irving Louis. 2008. "Stages in the Evolution of Holocaust Studies: From the Nuremberg Trials to the Present." *Human Rights Review*, at http://www.citeulike.org/journal/springerlink-103917. Accessed 14 October 2008.

Iyengar, Shanto. 1991. *Is Anyone Responsible: How Television Frames Political Issues.* Chicago: University of Chicago Press.

Katz, Elihu, & Tamar Liebes. 2007. "'No More Peace': How Disaster, Terror and War Have Upstaged Media Events." *International Journal of Communication*, 1: 157–66.

Klinenberg, Eric 2002. *Heat Wave: A Social Autopsy of Disaster in Chicago.* Chicago: University of Chicago Press.

Knilli, Friedrich, & Siegfried Zielinski, eds. 1982. *'Holocaust' zur Unterhaltung: Anatomie eines internationalen Bestsellers.* Berlin: Espresso/Elef. Press.

LaCapra, Dominick. 1992. "Representing the Holocaust: Reflections on the Historians' Debate." In *Probing the Limits of Representation,* ed. S. Friedlander (pp. 108–27). Cambridge, MA: Harvard University Press.

Lang, Berl. 1992. "The Representation of Limits." In *Probing the Limits of Representation,* ed. S. Friedlander (pp. 300–17). Cambridge, MA: Harvard University Press.

Lang, Gladys, & Kurt Lang. 1983. *The Battle for Public Opinion.* New York: Columbia University Press.

Lang, Kurt. Personal correspondence, 2007.

Liebman, Charles, & Eliezer Don-Yehiya. 1983. *Civil Religion in Israel.* Berkeley: University of California Press.

Loshitsky, Yosefa. 1997. *Spielberg's Holocaust: Critical Perspectives on "Schindler's List."* Bloomington: Indiana University Press.

Morse, Arthur D. 1968. *While Six Million Died: A Chronicle of American Apathy.* New York: Random House.

Novick, Peter. 1994. *The Holocaust in American Life.* New York: Houghton Mifflin.

Schudson, Michael. 1989. "How Culture Works," *Theory and Society* 18(2): 153–80.

———. 1992. *Watergate and American Memory.* New York: Basic Books.

Shandler, Jeffrey. 1999. *While America Watches: Televising the Holocaust.* New York: Oxford University Press.

Slezkine, Yuri. 2004. *The Jewish Century.* Princeton, NJ: Princeton University Press.

Turner, Victor. 1974. *Dramas, Fields and Metaphors.* Ithaca, NY: Cornell University Press.

Vaughan, Diana. 1996. *The Challenger Launch Decision.* Chicago: University of Chicago Press.

Walzer, Michael. 1985. *Exodus and Revolution.* New York: Basic Books.

Wyman, David S. 1984. *The Abandonment of the Jews: America and the Holocaust, 1941–1945.* New York: Pantheon Books.

Yahil, Leni. 1987/1992. *The Holocaust.* New York: Oxford University Press.

Yakira, Elhanan. 2007. *Post-Zionism, Post Holocaust: Three Essays on Denial, Repression, and Delegitimation of Israel.* Tel Aviv: Am Oved (Hebrew).

Yerushalmi, Yosef Haim. 1982. *Zakhor.* Seattle: University of Washington Press.

PART III

Response to Commentators

ON THE GLOBAL AND LOCAL REPRESENTATIONS OF THE HOLOCAUST TRAGEDY

Jeffrey C. Alexander

I BEGIN WITH A COMIC STRIP, THE WIDELY READ AND MUCH BELOVED *Non Sequitor*, by Wiley.[1] The first window shows a young and sincerely inquisitive little girl with wide eyes, sitting on a park bench next to a grizzled old timer.

Little girl: "I've gotta tell ya, mister, that's an awfully boring tattoo on your arm. It's just a bunch of numbers."

Old timer: "Well, I was about your age when I got it, and kept it as a reminder."

The second window, a close-up of two heads, presents the girl still wide-eyed and curious, the old man frowning and concerned.

Little girl: "Oh...A reminder of happier days?"

Old timer: "No...Of a time when the world went mad."

The old timer continues, with three short outbursts of explanation:

"Imagine yourself in a land where your countrymen followed the voice of political extremists who didn't like your religion.

"Imagine having everything taken from you, your entire family sent to a concentration camp as slave laborers, then systematically murdered. In this place they even take your name and replace it with a number tattooed on your arm.

"It was called *The Holocaust*. When millions of people perished just because of their faith...."

The strip's third and fourth windows follow without dialogue. The third portrays a situation imagined by the little girl. She stands forlornly inside

173

an Auschwitz-type enclosure, surrounded by barbed wire and beneath a malevolent gun tower, wearing striped prison pajamas and yellow star. The fourth window returns to a transformed contemporary reality. It shows the little girl weeping with her head downcast, the old timer gazing sadly at her with forebearing consolation. In the fifth and final window of the comic, the girl is still crying, as she turns to the old timer to ask a last question, to which she receives a surprising reply.

Little girl: "So you kept it to remind yourself about the dangers of political extremism?"

Old timer: "No, my dear. To remind you."

Universalization

This strip of popular culture indicates that the universalization of the Holocaust is alive and well, even as the collective consciousness continually addresses fears of forgetting. Wiley only mentions the actual name of the historical event once, and the Jewish people not all. He assumes that the particulars of plot and the identities of protagonist and antagonist are background knowledge. Rather than being presented as specifics and particulars, these now proverbial events are abstracted and generalized. The antagonists become political extremists who don't like some particular religion, the protagonists becoming millions of people who perished simply because of their faith. The narrative is categorical in its ethical imperative. The little girl and Wiley's attentive readers both are asked to identify with the protagonists and to experience the recounted event's bathetic denouement. The old timer demands that they imagine themselves inside the Holocaust.

Today, more than ever before, individuals, countries, regions, movements, and religions are regarded as civilized to the degree that they identify genocide as an ultimate evil and promise to do everything in their power to make sure that it will never happen again. To be accepted as "members of the human race," they must give evidence that they possess the imaginative faculty of putting themselves in place of the threatened and polluted other. The Holocaust has become the central myth of our time, the epochal legend that forges the ultimate standard of good and evil for what has become—in large part because of its effect—a world that is decidedly after modernity, the postmodern world in which we live today.

In this new world there are few truths that cannot be denied. Sex and gender are up for grabs. Violence can be heroically embraced. Humanism is disputed. The Big Bang may or may not have jump-started the universe. A fourth dimension of this universe might be composed of strings, but then again it may not.

The truth of the Holocaust, however, cannot be disputed. Its deniers are ridiculed and outlawed, often fined, and sometimes even jailed. Iran's President Ahmadinejad convened an international conference so that "both sides" of the Holocaust could be heard, proposing to establish a scholarly committee to determine "whether the mass killings by Nazis of Jews and others really happened." British Prime Minister Tony Blair declared the very idea of such a conference, and a proposal, to be "shocking beyond belief." They are "such a symbol of sectarianism and hatred towards people of another religion," he said, "I find it just unbelievable." The German Prime Minister Angela Merkel condemned President Ahmadinejad's questioning of the Holocaust "in the strongest terms." The Vatican insisted not only that the Holocaust is a truth but an "appalling tragedy to which one cannot remain indifferent."[2]

Iran's foreign minister justified his nation's investigation on the grounds that the Holocaust was not universal but particular. "The word 'Holocaust,'" he said, "turned into one of the most important propaganda tools used to politically justify the support for the Jewish People in the 20th century."[3] Six weeks later, on the eve of the United Nations' International Day of Commemoration in Memory of Victims of the Holocaust, its General Assembly adopted a resolution condemning such a position out of hand. Approved by consensus and sponsored by 104 countries, this attack on Holocaust denial was opposed by only one member, Iran. Its ambassador to the UN described the resolution not as an assertion of truth but as a "political judgment" supporting the particular interests of the Israel and the United States.[4]

In the principal essay that is the subject of this book, I have tried to explain how the mass murder of the Jews came to be represented in such a universal and, hence, "unassailable" way, as a universal truth that cannot be particularized by being tied to specific interests, of either an Iranian, Israeli, or an American kind. As the UN vote suggests, and as the stunned exclamations of European leaders underscore, this free-floating and generalized status is anything but a demonstration of Americanization.[5] Indeed, the world's most powerful nation—this hyperpower that, despite its great resources and strength, has become a collectivity that so many love to hate—is routinely and severely chastised for its hypocritical failure to recognize the imperative of the Holocaust's ethical demands.

In late November 2007, when reviewing an upcoming public television documentary on Darfur entitled "On Our Watch," an American arts journalist promised that "the program and the experts it interviews do not mince words as they explore why the horrors there went unaddressed for years after the first alarms were raised." His account concluded by returning the discussion of contemporary genocide to the original sin of modern humankind: "One particular phrase often associated with genocide gets a thorough workout here, with several commentators noting how hollow a promise it ended up being." To introduce the phrase, the reporter turned to Samantha Powers, and this liberal American critic immediately attached responsibility for the sin to the United States. "'Never again would we like genocide to happen,'" Powers sarcastically observed, "is very different than 'Never again will we stand idly by and let genocide happen.'" The reporter duly noted that Power's book, "*A Problem from Hell*": *America and the Age of Genocide*, won the Pulitzer Prize.[6]

Rather than losing steam, the coded and narrated symbol "Holocaust" has become ever more heavily weighted. Its engorgement with evil is even more overflowing, its polluting power continuously on the rise. In a recent overview, a German scholar suggested that "the remembrance of the Holocaust is in the midst of a profound change." Observing that this shift has "become particularly visible since the turn of the millennium" and the end of the cold war, he suggested, "these crimes have now arrived at the center of European identity." The generalized symbol of evil has, in fact, become more universal still. From Poland, Hungary, and Romania to South Africa and Cambodia, "the Holocaust has become a *worldwide* point of reference and comparison for crimes against humanity...in the hope of recognition and compensation for other crimes and victims" and as a "benchmark for other problematic pasts."[7] If we consider, for example, the process by which academic, aesthetic, and political discourse on the Indian subcontinent has turned in recent years to the "trauma of Partition," we can observe frequent evocations of the earlier European tragedy. The proclamation by the Nobel Prize winner V. S. Naipaul is emblematic: "The Partition was as great a Holocaust as that caused by Nazi Germany."[8]

One decade after I began work on the historical sociological essay that is the subject of this volume, it seems fair to say that processes of cultural extension and psychological identification continue. This has occurred despite the gnawing fears of forgetting and the hand-wringing frustrations over political impotence that, even more so in the wake of September 11, 2001, have energized the nightmarish efforts of revengeful collectivities to hijack the morally universal slogan "Never Again." It is to these latter efforts that I wish to turn my attention here. Before doing so, however, I would like to provide a historical context for my original essay.

A Shifting Historical Context

I composed and researched the "The Social Construction of Moral Universals" in the late 1990s. In retrospect, that earlier time can be seen as one of cautious optimism. The American and European intervention in Kosovo had just given strong evidence for the universalizing power of the Holocaust effect. Dictatorships were still being turned into democracies, and there was a bubbling effervescence about the emergence of global civil society. It was a time to focus on the emergence of global narratives about the possibility of justice, among which there is no more surprising and inspiring story than the transvaluation of the Holocaust. In Bernhard Giesen's words (this volume), this process has provided "a new transnational paradigm of collective identity," according to which the Holocaust became the "global icon of evil." In my own words, "a specific and situated historical event" has become "transformed into a generalized symbol of human suffering," a "universalized symbol whose very existence has created historically unprecedented opportunities for ethnic, racial, and religious justice, for mutual recognition, and for global conflicts becoming regulated in a more civil way."[9]

We live now in a darker time, more divided, more violent, more tense. We have become less optimistic about the creation of a global civil society, more sensitive to the continuing festering of local wounds. It is a time to explore a relationship between cultural trauma and collective identity that in "Social Construction" I acknowledged empirically and theoretically, but I downplayed for moral effect.[10]

The Holocaust Trauma and Israeli Jews

How can the movement from a progressive to a tragic trauma narration create moral particularism alongside universalism, and fuel social splitting and antagonism at the same time as cooperation and expanded solidarity? To answer this question I will look at Israeli Jews.[11] For, even as the Holocaust became a global symbol demanding more civil ties, it was not constructed in a homologous manner in every locality, and perhaps especially not by those who survived this demonic event and traveled to the promised land.[12]

Going beyond the progressive narrative to a tragic vision compels members of a collectivity to narrate and symbolically re-experience the suffering of a trauma's victims. If, however, these victims are represented narrowly—as simply the story tellers themselves—the tragic trauma-drama may not, in fact, have a cathartic and sympathy-generating effect. In this emplotment, the moral implications of the drama of eternal return are inverted. Not being able to get beyond the originating trauma, and feeling compelled again and again to return to it, here means being unable to transcend the particularistic hatreds that inspired the aggression and murder of that earlier time. Narrowing rather than universalizing in morality and affect, earlier hatreds are reproduced, not changed. Rather than expanded human sympathy for the other, we have Hitler's revenging the defeated German people, Serbia's ethnic cleansing, and Hindu nationalism's bloody-minded struggle against Islamic "intruders" today.[13]

In the middle of 2007, David Remnick, the editor of the *New Yorker* magazine, published a controversial "Letter from Jerusalem." It was a conversation with Avraham Burg, once speaker of the Israel Knesset and former director both of the World Zionist Organization and Israel's Jewish Agency. Remnick's conversation with the now embittered Israeli leader pointed directly to the social processes that are at the heart of this book. "As of this moment," Burg observed, "Israel is a state of trauma in nearly every one of its dimensions." Insisting that this is "not just a theoretical question," he asked, "Would our ability to cope with Iran not be much better if we renewed in Israel the ability to trust the world?" Because Israelis identify the Holocaust with Christian Europe's betrayal, Burg reasoned, they do not possess the necessary reserve of trust that could propel a process of peace. "We say we do not trust the world, they will abandon us," Burg explained. Seeing "Chamberlain returning from Munich with the black umbrella," Israelis drew the conclusion that "we will bomb them alone."[14] It is because of this trauma construction, Burg believed, that Israel feels it must go it alone, a path he found deeply self-defeating. "Would it not be more right," he asked, "if we didn't deal with the problem on our own but, rather, as part of a world alignment beginning with the Christian churches, going on to the governments and finally the armies?"

In its early "optimistic years," Burg told Remnick, Israel was different. Paradoxically, "the farther we got from the camps and the gas chambers, the more pessimistic we became and the more untrusting we became toward the world." As Burg sees it, this narrative shift has produced chauvinism and selfishness. Today, the Holocaust trauma fragments and divides, allowing conservative Israelis to justify the oppression of Palestinians. It is because of their Holocaust consciousness, Burg insisted, that his contemporaries are not "sensitive enough to what happens to others and in many ways are too indifferent to the suffering of others. We confiscated, we monopolized, world suffering. We did not allow anybody else to call whatever suffering they have 'holocaust' or 'genocide,' be it Armenians, be it Kosovo, be it Darfur." The Holocaust trauma is remembered in a manner that makes a significant swath of Israeli society impervious to criticism: "'Occupation? You call this occupation? This is nothing compared to the absolute evil of the Holocaust!' And if it is nothing compared to the Holocaust then you can continue. And since nothing, thank God, is comparable to the ultimate trauma it legitimizes many things."

It might have seemed, from a more naturalistic perspective, that the Holocaust would be written directly on the body of Israel and its Jews, whether via first-hand experience or by "natural" identification. In fact, the opposite is the case. Its meaning and message have been up for grabs, and have been crystallized in strikingly divergent ways. "The memory of the Holocaust and its victims," Yechiam Weitz observed, "was accompanied by unending political strife"; these debates "were always bitter, full of tension and emotional," and occasionally "violent and even deadly."[15] The millennia-long sufferings of the Jewish people certainly did create a historical memory of persecution. These tragic iterations were ritualized in religious ceremonies and constituted a cultural legacy that seemed to demand not progress but eternal return. While the post-Enlightenment European emancipation of ghettoized Jews triggered a more progressive narrative, the backlash against Jewish incorporation that exploded in the last decades of the nineteenth century pushed European Jewry to look backward again. Zionism emerged in response to this stinging disappointment. It fought against not only anti-Semitism but also the fatalism and pessimism that so often had marked the Jewish tradition itself. It promised that, if a homeland were regained, the Jewish people would be landed and citied, and their history rewound. The story of the Jewish people could start over again in a healthy and normal way.[16]

Zionist Struggles and Holocaust Memories

This historic dream came to earth in a land peopled mostly by others. Israel's founding did instantiate the progressive narrative of Zionism, but in a decidedly triumphalist and military way. Throughout the late nineteenth and early twentieth centuries, growing Zionist settlement faced increasingly embittered antagonists, not only indigenous Palestinians but other, better organized Arab Muslim populations.[17] Could the Zionists have understood their potential opponents in anything other than an antagonistic way? In fact, different sorts of relations were possible, and some were tried. Of course, the options narrowed substantially after the murder of 6 million Jews. The heinous event gave an extraordinary urgency to the Jewish exodus from Europe, both inside and outside the Jewish community itself. The British folded up their Mandate and the UN declared a fragile, and almost universally unpopular, two-state solution. Even then, however, there was more than one path to take. Despite their territorial ambitions, the more left-wing, socialist, and democratic Israeli fighters conducted their struggles in less violent and pugnacious, more civilly regulated ways. Right-wing Zionists, epitomized by the notorious Stern Gang, were more aggressively violent, demonstrating much less concern for non-Jewish—British and Palestinian—life.[18]

Amid the chaotic conditions and competing ambitions of this postwar struggle, Israel declared its independence, the Arab states and Palestinians declared and acted upon their opposition, and the historical options narrowed further still. Zionist forces engaged in pitched battles against local Palestinian fighters and invading Arab armies. Jewish soldiers individually, and the emerging nation collectively, experienced this birth struggle as a matter of life or death. "We, the Jewish Israelis," the psychiatrist Dan Bar-on recalled, "saw ourselves as surrounded by enemies and having to struggle, physically and mentally, for our lives and survival."[19] Making an analogy with the Holocaust, the only recently terminated and extraordinarily searing experience of racially motivated mass murder, Israeli individuals and their nation identified themselves as victims. Feelings of compassion for displaced Palestinians—who were equally endangered, and most directly by Israeli's own army—were cast aside.

The Israeli state, established upon the blood sacrifice of its courageous but also ethnically cleansing army, honored its soldier-martyrs and inscribed in historical memory the trauma-inspired lesson that only military strength could prevent Jewish defilement and murder from ever happening again.[20] For the new nation's first two decades, the historical record shows, the school textbooks of Israeli children were filled with deeply polluting descriptions of Arabs as savage, sly, cheaters, thieves, robbers, provocateurs, and terrorists. As one Israeli historian has suggested, during these early decades the national narrative hewed closely to the "tradition of depicting Jewish history as an uninterrupted record of anti-Semitism and persecution."[21] The continuing Arab military campaign against Israel was represented inside this frame. Palestinian violence was analogized with pre-Independence "pogroms" against Jews, and Palestinian and Arab leaders were depicted as only the most recent in "a long line of 'oppressors' of Jews during the course of their history."[22]

Insofar as this trauma construction conceived Israeli's origin as an iteration of the Jewish Holocaust experience, an aggressive and military response to the "Palestinian problem" became the only conceivable "solution" to the subjective fears of Israelis and the objective dangers that a series of Arab attacks posed to their nation. And, indeed, so long as military power seemed a viable method of wiping the historical slate clean, even the progressive narrative of Zionism was deeply compromised, linking "bereavement and triumph" in an inward turning, particularistic way.[23] When Holocaust Day was officially declared in 1951, it was not considered a major event, its tragic narration sitting uncomfortably alongside Zionism's future-oriented founding myth. One effort at metonymic resolution placed Holocaust Day seven days before the Memorial Day and Independence Day sequence, in the period that followed upon the Passover celebration of Jewish enslavement and emancipation.[24] The Holocaust holiday, in other words, pointed backward and forward at the same time, as indicated by its formal naming, Yom Hazikaron La'shoah ve La'Gvura (Day of Remembrance of the Holocaust and Heroism), and in both directions remained resolutely particularistic. In its tragic mode, it mourned "the modern attempt to annihilate the Jewish people"; in its progressive mode, it celebrated the Warsaw Ghetto uprising as "the heroic spark" that had reignited Israel's birth.[25]

At the heart of this early Independence Day ritual was a binary that contrasted "passive Diaspora Jewry" of the pre-Holocaust period—"sheep to the slaughter"—with the "active Zionism" of post-Holocaust Israel, "which had fought successfully for statehood." This binary inspired a progressive narrative according to which "resistance fighters ... and soldiers in the War of Independence became the protagonists of the ceremony." It was via this political-cum-cultural process that youthful Israel, in Bar-On's words, "crossed the fragile distinction from being morally right as a persecuted people"—for whom "persecution became imbedded in our internal representations throughout the ages of the Diaspora"—to being a dominant and aggressive military power, one which did not "attempt to include the relevant other but rather to ignore or disgorge him."[26]

Shifting Constructions and Sympathies

It was only later, as Israel became more embattled, and militarized Zionism stymied and wounded, that this ambiguously progressive and narrowly primordial myth of the founding began to fail. Revealingly, the cultural significance of Holocaust Day increased as the trauma-drama framing it became more insistently pessimistic. The turn toward tragedy deepened after the Yom Kippur War in 1973, when Israel barely escaped a catastrophic military defeat. The newly experienced "feeling of dread," according to a contemporary Israeli observer, meant "diminished importance of the fighter as a Zionist role model" and the corresponding reconstruction of the Holocaust drama in a manner that "placed a bolder emphasis on the suffering of the victims and focused greater attention on daily life in the ghettoes and camps." As a consequence, "a different type of bravery was now given prominence—one that was non-military, but involved survival under oppressive conditions."[27]

This new trauma construction provided a script that, in principle and to some degree in practice, allowed Israelis to connect Jewish with Palestinian suffering. An Israeli peace movement emerged that put land for peace on the table, and a new generation of critical historians righteously exposed Israeli complicity in Palestinian expulsion. Leftist critics decried "cognitive militarism."[28] More neutral observers spoke about the decline of "collective commemoration" and the growth of a more individual centered, rights-based political culture.[29] The "devaluation of the myth of heroism"[30] intensified after the 1982 Lebanon War, whose military frustrations produced feelings of futility and whose massacres at Sabra and Shatila ignited feelings of humiliation.[31] The Israeli feminist critic Ronit Lentin forcefully describes how these developments made an expanded solidarity possible:

> After Lebanon, for the first time, the suffering of others, particularly of Palestinian children, not Jewish suffering, was the principal subject of Israeli literary and poetic discourses. The death of Palestinians was described using Shoah images; their fate was equated with the fate of the Jews as Israeli poets and playwrights reflected and compelled Jewish understanding of the suffering of the Palestinians.[32]

Throughout this period of symbolic trauma reconstruction, the emergent Palestinian national movement played a significant role, creating a new dramatic field of performative possibilities. Its energetic and aggressive ideology, and often murderous tactics, presented undeniable evidence of a previously "invisible" nation and people, in this manner providing material that could block the progressive narrative on the Israeli side. Yet, the PLO's terrorism severely restricted its dramatic appeal. In the late 1970s, the world's best-known Palestinian intellectual, Edward Said, declared that, while "we have gained the support of all the peoples of the Third World," the "remarkable national resurgence" of the "Palestinian *idea*" had not yet succeeded, for "we have been unable to interest the West very much in the justice of our cause."[33] While acknowledging how much he resented "the ways in which the whole grisly matter is stripped of all its resonances and its often morally confusing detail, and compressed simply, comfortably, inevitably under the rubric of 'Palestinian terror,'" Said declared himself to be "horrified at the hijacking of planes, the suicidal missions, the assassinations, the bombing of schools and hotels." To redress this performative failure—to attract a Western audience—the trauma-drama of Palestinian suffering would have to be differently told. In order to provide "some sense of the larger Palestinian story from which all these things came," Said explained, there needed to be a new and more compelling focus on "the reality of a collective national trauma contained for every Palestinian in the question of Palestine."[34] A new progressive counter-trauma narrative was projected, describing Palestinian suffering, Western/Israeli domination, and a heroic anti-colonial movement for liberation. It provided a new symbolic protagonist with whom a widening circle of Western citizens, and self-critical Israelis, could identify, or at least ambivalently support. This possibility deepened among many Israelis in the wake of the first Intifada, the relatively nonviolent Palestinian uprising that began in 1987. The expanding solidarity became powerfully institutionalized in the treaties and ceremonies marking the Oslo peace process in 1993.

What has been described as the emergence of "post-Zionism" was cut short by the assassination of Prime Minister Yitzhak Rabin in 1995.[35] Rabin's cruelly calculated murder managed to short-circuit this process of civil repair—one that had in no small part been fueled by the manner in which the Holocaust trauma was being symbolically and morally recast. As this short-circuiting demonstrated, while the earlier, more particularistic trauma-drama had been challenged, its narrowly primordial power had remained powerful. Indeed, even as the Yom Kippur War and the difficulties that unfolded in its aftermath allowed the creation of a more universal-izing tragic narrative, they also energized a much more particularistic kind of tragic story—one that was distinctively more anticivil than the Israeli nation's progressive founding myth. And the emerging Palestinian move-ment that provided opportunities for cross-national solidarity also had an equal and the opposite effect, providing the growing backlash movement—not a protagonist with whom to identify, but a more sharply defined, pol-luted antagonist against whom to carry on its primordial fight. In 1977, the right-wing Likud Party took power on a platform demanding continued occupation and usurpation of the "holy lands," its leaders and supporters fervently opposed to any Palestinian settlement. As part of this same back-lash movement there emerged the Gush Emunim—literally "Block of the Faithful"—a passionate, religiously-inspired, right-wing social force. Its sup-porters began a decades-long, highly successful campaign to take Jewish pos-session of occupied Palestinian land.[36]

In the years that followed, *settler* became as ubiquitous a trope in Israeli society as *survivor*. In fact, the former collective representation drew its sym-bolic strength from the latter. For the Israeli right, Jews needed desperately to annex every inch of Palestinian land that surrounded them, for every non-Jewish person was a potential enemy. They had learned this deeply anticivil lesson from their tragic, and primordial, reconstruction of the Holocaust trauma. Because they experienced the Jewish victimhood of those terrible days as never having gone away, they could glean no bridging metaphors from their re-experience of trauma. Instead, they felt compelled to frame every conflict with outsiders in a boundary-making way.

When the Likud minister of education delivered her Holocaust Day speech in 2001, she proclaimed complete identification with the protagonists in the original trauma. "We shouldn't suppose," she insisted, "that we differ from our grandfathers and grandparents who went to the gas chambers." Rejecting a progressive narrative that would dramatize the distance between the situation of Jews then and now, she insisted "what separates us from them is not that we are some sort of new Jew." What has changed is not the oppo-sition between Jew and Gentile, but its asymmetry. The Jewish side can now be armed. The minister explained: "The main difference is external: we have a state, a flag and army." During the historical Holocaust, by contrast, the Jews had been "caught in their tragedy, [for] they lacked all three."[37] The trauma-drama points toward an ineluctable solution: It is only power and violence that can save contemporary Jews from suffering their ancestors' fate.

Caught up inside this narrowly constructed trauma-drama, the Israeli Right has identified the peace process with Jewish annihilation. In the months before Yitzhak Rabin's assassination, ultra-orthodox magazines attacked the general-turned-peacemaker as a "traitor" and "madman," suggesting he was "anti-religious" and even "non-Jewish." He and his foreign minister, Shimon Peres, were depicted as members of the Judenrat and Kapos, the infamous Nazi-appointed Jewish leaders who had collaborated in the administration of the death camps. At the antigovernment demonstrations that grew increasingly aggressive in the months and weeks before his murder, Rabin was portrayed in posters wearing an SS uniform and cap.[38]

According to this rightist scenario, to recognize the rights of Palestinians is to become an enemy of the Jewish people. Solidarity cannot extend beyond the boundaries of one's own group: it must be primordial, not civil. So reconstructed, the trauma-drama of the Holocaust is a recipe for conflict without end. If this view should prevail, it would not only be severely destabilizing in geopolitical terms; it would also assault the universalizing moral principles that the memory of the Holocaust calls upon all of us to sustain.

NOTES

I thank Roger Friedland, Steven Seidman, Elihu and Ruth Katz, Gershon Shafir, Jose Brunner, and Shai Dromi for their comments on earlier versions of this chapter.

1. This strip is dated June 11, 2002. It can be found on wileyinc@earthlnk.net.

2. Nazila Fathi, "Israel Fading, Iran's Leader Tells Deniers of Holocaust," *New York Times*, December 13, 2006, p. A10. "Both sides" is quoted from Iranian conference documents; "whether the mass killings..." is Ms. Fathi's phrasing; other quotations are from the sources themselves. In this paragraph, when I speak about the truth and facts of the Holocaust not being able to be denied, I do not, of course, attribute this to their empirical facticity, in the scientific sense, but to their moral imperativeness, to the fact that that they have become not a scientific but a "social" fact. In his rather wistful hope that the facts about the monstrous history of the Holocaust could speak for themselves, Nathan Glazer acknowledges that "admittedly, facts are disputable and realities have to be interpreted." When he immediately adds, "but then some facts are immutable and some realities are indisputable," he must be referring to their moral status and historical inscription in the Zeitgeist of a time.

3. Nazila Fathi, "Iran Invites Scholars to Assess Holocaust as History or Fiction," *New York Times*, December 6, 2006, p. A5.

4. "U.N. Condemns Holocaust Denial" (Associated Press Wire), *Los Angeles Times*, January 27, 2007, p. A7.

5. Martin Jay, Michael Rothberg, and Robert Manne contend that quite the opposite is true, that my account of the reconstruction of the Holocaust trauma-drama is American-centric, devoted to describing the Holocaust's "Americanization." While it is true that most of my sources are English and American based, the fulcrum of my argument for universalization of the Holocaust drama is that, in the 1960s, there began a decisive and fundamental *de*-Americanization of the story. This was true in several ways. After having been by far the most influential shaper of the global story, American elites lost control of its narration. This occurred because of the drastic deflation of American social, political, and cultural power during the sixties. As American elites lost hegemonic control over the story, they themselves became subject to its searing criticism, first from the new social movements and later from other nations. As the Holocaust drama became more free-floating, it could be appropriated by groups opposed to American ideology and interests. It could also provide a benchmark for other nations to judge themselves, according the same universalistic yardstick as the one applied to the United States. Bernhard Giesen's chapter in this volume provides the clearest demonstration that the universalization process I have described was not America-centric, but occurred throughout Europe as well and, perhaps paradoxically, most decisively in Germany.

6. Neil Genzlinger, "Where 'Never Again' Is Happening Now," *New York Times*, November 20, 2007, p. E8. As this paragraph suggests, I believe that Robert Manne (this volume) errs in suggesting that the failure actually to prevent genocide falsifies the argument I present. My contention is that a new, distinctively different, and more universalizing normative *standard* has become institutionalized, not that this new standard has consistently been brought to bear, in a regulative manner, on conflicts between and within states. I would insist, however, that the existence of this cultur-ally powerful standard does indeed induce social pressure for such regulative action, hence that its emergence, qua norm, has great social importance. When Manne cites Power as condemning the Clinton administration for refusing to label what was taking place in Rwanda as genocide, on the grounds, admitted in one briefing paper, that a "genocide finding could commit [the U.S. Government] to actually 'do something,'" he is making precisely my point.

7. Dirk Rupnow, "Transforming the Holocaust: Scholarship, Culture, and Politics in a Transnational European and Global Perspective," Grant Proposal to DAAD, Spring, 2007, italics added, quoted with permission of author.

8. Quoted in Jonathan D. Greenberg, "Generations of Memory: Remembering Partition in India/Pakistan and Israel/Palestine," *Comparative Studies of South Asia, Africa and the Middle East* 25(1) (2005), 100 n. 65.

9. Alexander, part I, this volume.

10. The following discussion is responsive to the call of Elihu and Ruth Katz (this volume) to provide an account of "the several narratives of what happened" in order "to hear how Holocaust stories are being told today... by different ele-ments in society." It also answers the forceful criticisms of Martin Jay and Michael

Rothberg (this volume), and Manne (this volume) as well, that my emphasis on the universalizing dimension of the Holocaust must perforce oppose the possibility that the trauma-drama has been employed in particularistic and negative ways. For my exploration of the earlier period of global civil society discussion, which offers a framework to understand the exaggerated, optimistic pronouncements and prophecies of such social theorists as Anthony Giddens and Ulrich Beck, see my "Globalization as Collective Representation: The New Dream of a Cosmopolitan Civil Sphere," pp. 371–82, in *Frontiers of Globalization Research: Theoretical and Methodological Approaches*, edited by Ino Rossi (New York: Springer, 2007). In *The Holocaust and Memory in the Global Age* (Philadelphia: Temple University Press, 2006), Daniel Levy and Natan Sznaider fail sufficiently to separate their assessment of the effects of Holocaust symbolism—in the United States, Germany, and Israel—from the optimism of globalization theory, developing a much more linear and less contradictory perspective than the one I present here. Suggesting that "the particular and the universal are not opposing forces" (p. 8), they assert that Holocaust memories "produce new forms of rooted cosmopolitanism, and...new forms of localism that are open to the world" (p. 3).

11. Nathan Glazer and the Elihu and Ruth Katz (this volume) regret that my orientation to the possibilities for extra-group universalism has turned the attention of my essay away from what the story of the Holocaust has meant for the Jews. Nathan Glazer's striking first-person reconstruction of several decades of American Jewish feelings about the Holocaust partly rectifies this gap, and it generally parallels the account of non-Jewish American consciousness of the Holocaust that I offered in part I (this volume). In this postscript, I do not address the meaning of the Holocaust for the Jews outside Israel, but there are, I think, some very significant overlapping reactions and understandings between Diasporic Jews and those inside Israel. While some American Jews clearly do share the Israeli Right's nationalistic and restrictive understandings, however, I do not agree with Manne's suggestion (this volume), following the implications of Peter Novick's indictment of the Holocaust industry and Jewish roles in it, that my account is "almost willfully blind to the interests the [Holocaust] story serves." It is quite impossible to tell whether a particular kind of narrative—universal or particular—serves a group's interest or does not. The identity in relation to which an interest is defined is formed *through* narrative, not formed before it. A narrative, therefore, cannot be understood to be the result of some putatively transparent interest that responds to an already established, structural identity. This kind of functionalist understanding, which ties the effects of a norm or institution to its social causes, has been more or less thoroughly refuted in contemporary social science. If, nonetheless, we say, for the sake of argument, that the universalizing Holocaust story did, in some manner or other, function to "serve the interests of the Jews," it would not mean, at all, that Jews would have contributed to the construction of this narrative *because* it eventually would serve their religious or status-group interests. The point of my approach to cultural trauma and collective

identity is to show that the nature of trauma interpretation is an open-ended process, that it does not have, or serve, a determinate result.

12. In clarifying the global status of the trauma process I trace in "Social Construction" (part I, this volume), I respond to concerns raised by both Rothberg and Jay (this volume) about the various historically specific pathways by which traumatic constructions of mass murder, and specifically the Holocaust, have developed in such particular regions as the former Soviet Union and its satellites, in France, and in postcolonial contexts. Vis-à-vis these concerns I would continue to argue that there is a globalizing and distinctively universal Holocaust narrative that has gained relative autonomy from local context, an argument I have elaborated further here. In terms of remembering and memorializing the Stalinist mass murders, for example, it seems significant that symbolization of the Holocaust has not yet been successfully inserted into the mainstream Russian retelling of its communist past. Precisely how this global narrative becomes specified in a particular context is a complex sociological process. I view Rothberg's discussion of "re-attachment," not as a challenge to my analysis of this process but, rather, as a perceptive investigation into just how the connection between the local and the global gets carried out—a connection that I myself briefly traced in regard to the "retelling" of the Holocaust trauma by Native, Asian, and African Americans. I would note, however, that the anticolonial discourses Rothberg cites are connected less to the "Holocaust" as a supranational narrative than to specifically Jewish experiences of oppression and resistance—e.g., in the Warsaw Ghetto or to specifically French experiences of anti-Jewish and/or Nazi oppression in Paris. These narrative references, moreover, were woven into the mythology of the French resistance myth. As I suggest in part I, this postwar national narrative was one among the many particularistic and often self-serving victorious national memories that would be severely challenged during the process that allowed the role of perpetrator to be generalized and more widely shared. Finally, as I explore in the discussion that follows, this globalizing narrative does not preclude much more particular kinds of trauma narratives from being constructed vis-à-vis the Holocaust inside regions or on behalf of any particular contemporary group.

13. In a series of influential studies, the psychiatrist Vomik Volkan has explored such narrowing and particularistic responses to trauma and the manner in which they fuel violence and revenge—e.g., "Transgenerational Transmissions and Chosen Traumas: An Aspect of Large-Group Identity," *Group Analysis* 32(1) (2001): 79–97. From a historical and cultural sociological perspective, however, Volkan's work is limited by the individualistic and naturalizing assumptions that seem endemic to the psychoanalytic perspective on collective life. These problems also affect, but in a less restrictive manner, the wide-ranging, politically engaged studies by Dan Bar-On and his colleagues—e.g., Sharon Shamir, Tali Yitzhaki-Verner, and Dan Bar-On, "'The Recruited Identity': The Influence of the Intifada on the Perception of the Peace Process from the Standpoint of the Individual" *Journal of Narrative and Life History*

6(3) (1996): 193–233; and Dan Bar-On, "Israeli Society between the Culture of Death and the Culture of Life," *Israeli Studies* 2(2) (1997): 88–112.

14. David Remnick, "The Apostate: A Zionist Politician Loses Faith in the Future," *The New Yorker*, July 30, 2007, pp. 32–37.

15. Yechiam Weitz, "Political Dimensions of Holocaust Memory in Israel," pp. 129–45, in *The Shaping of Israeli Identity: Myth, Memory and Trauma*, edited by Robert Wistrich and David Ohana (London: Frank Cass, 1995), p. 130. It is paradoxical that in her searching and original investigation *Israel's Holocaust and the Politics of Nationhood* (Cambridge: Cambridge University Press, 2005), Idith Zertal insists on contrasting what she views as the truly "historical dimension of the events" with their "out-of-context use" in the new nation's collective memory, which she condemns for having "transmuted" the facts (pp. 4–5). The position that informs my own approach is that history is never accessible as such. Although making it seem so may provide resources for the kind of ideology critique in which Zertal is so effectively engaged.

16. For an account of this emancipation, its fateful disappointments, and the rise of Zionism as one among several Jewish responses, see Jeffrey C. Alexander, *The Civil Sphere* (New York: Oxford University Press, 2006), chapter 18. The idea of returning to Jerusalem had, of course, long been an essential idiom of Diasporic Judaism.

17. For a particularly rich account of this situation, see Rashid Khalidi, *Palestinian Identity: The Construction of Modern Consciousness* (New York: Columbia University Press, 1997).

18. For a synthetic account of this striking, if still limited contrast between the mentalities and fighting strategies of the left and right-wing forces, see Ian J. Bickerton and Carl L. Klausner, *A Concise History of the Arab-Israeli Conflict,* 4th edition (Upper Saddle River, NJ: Prentice-Hall, 2002), especially pp. 100–115.

19. Bar-On, "Israeli Society," p. 90.

20. For some readers this characterization will appear harsh. It seems to me, however, the ineluctable conclusion from two decades of revisionist Israeli historiography. As such writers as Benny Morris (*The Birth of the Palestinian Refugee Problem, 1947–1949* [Cambridge: Cambridge University Press, 1987]) and Ilan Pappe (*The Making of the Arab-Israeli Conflict, 1947–51* [London: I.B. Tauris, 1992]) have documented in painstaking and painful empirical detail, the Independence conflict involved not just "voluntary" flight but also massive and carefully instigated population transfers, pushing hundreds of thousands of Palestinians off their land and wiping out the Palestinian identities of hundreds of once-Arab villages. None of this is to say that the historical events triggered by the U.N.'s two-state resolution were inevitable or to absolve the Palestinian and Arab parties of their own fateful responsibilities. For a collection of archival-based essays by Arab and Jewish scholars exploring this complex and deeply contradictory period, see Eugene L. Rogan and Avi Shlaim, eds., *The War for Palestine: Rewriting the History of 1948* (Cambridge: Cambridge University Press, 2001). The collection is also notable for Edward Said's "Afterward: The Consequences of 1948" (pp. 206–19). In one of

the radical Palestinian critic's last published essays, he lashes out at the repressive, anti-Semitic, and militaristic conditions that, in his view, had marked so much of Arab and Palestinian political and cultural life in the post-Independence period. For an insightful overview of the polarizing, if delayed, effects of Israeli's "history wars" over its collective identity—and an argument that it is psychologically over-determined—see Jose Brunner, "Contentious Origins: Psychoanalytic Comments on the Debate over Israel's Creation," in *Psychoanalysis, Identity, and Ideology: Critical Essays on the Israel/Palestine Case*, edited by John Bunzl and Benjamin Beit-Hallahmi (Boston: Kluwer Academic Publishers, 2002), pp. 107–35.

21. Elie Podeh, "History and Memory in the Israeli Educational System: The Portrayal of the Arab-Israeli Conflict in History Textbooks (1948–2000)," *History and Memory* 12(1) (2000): 65–100, quoting pp. 75–76.

22. Ibid. This specifically Israeli-Jewish frame complemented the more broadly polluting binary of Western orientalism. Though sweeping and polemical, Said was not wrong when he suggested, thirty years ago, that "between Zionism and the West there was and still is a community of language and of ideology [that] depends heavily on a remarkable tradition in the West of enmity toward Islam in particular and the Orient in general." Asserting that Arabs were "practically the *only* ethnic about whom in the West racial slurs are tolerated, even encouraged," Said suggested that "the Arabs and Islam represent viciousness, veniality, degenerate vice, lechery, and stupidity in popular and scholarly discourse" (Edward Said, *The Question of Palestine* [New York: Times Books, 1979], p. 26, original italics).

23. Avner Ben-Amos and Illana Bet-El, "Holocaust Day and Memorial Day in Israeli Schools: Ceremonies, Education and History, *Israeli Studies* 4(1) (1999): 258–84, quoting p. 267. See also Yoram Bilu and Eliezer Witztum, "War-Related Loss and Suffering in Israeli Society: An Historical Perspective," *Israeli Studies* 5(2) (2000): 1–31; and Doron Bar, "Holocaust Commemoration in Israel during the 1950s: The Holocaust Cellar on Mount Zion," *Jewish Social Studies: History, Culture, Society*, n.s. 12(1) (2005): 16–38; and Dalia Ofer, "The Strength of Remembrance: Commemorating the Holocaust During the First Decade of Israel," *Jewish Social Studies* 6(2) (2000): 29–38.

24. Cf., Zertal, *Israel's Holocaust,"* p. 39, and Don Handelman and Elihu Katz, "State Ceremonies of Israel-Remembrance Day and Independence Day," in *Models and Mirrors: Towards an Anthropology of Public Events*, by D. Handelman (Cambridge: Cambridge University Press, 1990), pp. 191–233. Handelman and Katz interpret this juxtaposition as having suggested that, for the Israelis, Holocaust Day signified an exit from the suffering of Diasporic Jewry, framing the tragedy, in a progressive manner, as adumbrating the emergence of the Jewish state.

25. Ben-Amos and Bet-El, "Holocaust Day," p. 272.

26. Shamir et al., "Recruited Identity," p. 195.

27. Ibid., p. 270. Bilu and Witztum ("War-Related Loss") note, for example, that the psychiatric diagnosis of posttraumatic stress disorder could only emerge in

the wake of the Yom Kippur War, for it implied a weakening of the indomitable Israeli protagonist's military strength: "The myth of heroism, and with it the layers of disregard and denial that had hidden combat stress reactions from the public eye in the preceding wars, were extensively eroded in the 1973 War. Following the utter surprise and confusion at the onset of the war, the military defeats in the first days of fighting, and the heavy toll of casualties—more than 2500 soldiers killed and about 7000 wounded—the war was inscribed in the national consciousness as a massive trauma" (p. 20).

28. Victor Azarya and Baruch Kimmerling "Cognitive Permeability of Civil-Military Boundaries: Expectations from Military Service in Israel," *Studies in Comparative International Development* 20(4) (1985–86): 42–63; Baruch Kimmerling, "Patterns of Militarism in Israel," *European Journal of Sociology* 2 (1993): 1–28; and "Political Subcultures and Civilian Militarism in A Settler-Immigrant Society," in *Security Concerns: Insights from the Israeli Experience*, edited by D. Bar-Tal, D. Jacobson, and A. Kliemann (Greenwich, CT: JAI Press, 1998), pp. 395–416.

29. Bilu and Witztum, "War-Related Loss," p. 25.

30. Ibid., p. 23.

31. While it was Lebanese Phalangists who carried out the massacre against Palestinians, Israel's Kahan Commission stated that the Jewish government had "indirect personal responsibility," and it accused Ariel Sharon, then minister of defense, of "direct personal responsibility"; Kahan Commission, *Israeli's Lebanon War* (New York: Simon and Schuster, 1984), pp. 283–84.

32. Ronit Lentin, *Israel and the Daughters of the Shoah: Reoccupying the Territories of Silence* (New York: Berghahn Books, 2000), p. 145. In its initial response to the massacres at Shabra and Shatila, conservative Likud government officials lashed out against accusations of Israeli complicity, describing them as "a blood libel against the Jewish state and its Government"—i.e., framing them in terms of historical anti-Semitism against the Jewish people. In response, some 300,000 Israelis organized a massive protest in Tel Aviv. The Commission of Inquiry, formed soon after and headed by former Supreme Court Justice Yitzhak Kahan, produced a series of critical findings and recommendations. According to Michel Wieviorka, the global reception of the massacres allowed the normative symbolization of the Holocaust "to be turned against those to whom it hitherto protected" and "from then on, large swathes of international public opinion distanced themselves from the policy of Israel"; Michel Wieviorka, *The Lure of Anti-Semitism: Hatred of Jews in Present-Day France* (Leiden/Boston: Brill, 2007), p. 59. The empathy-creating possibilities of Holocaust memory—the sense for Palestinian suffering that emerged in significant elements of the Israeli public as historical circumstances put roadblocks in the way of the more progressive myth—is ignored by Idith Zertal's reconstruction; her cultural history has no place for the peace movement.

33. Said, *The Question of Palestine*, pp. xi–x, original italics.

34. Ibid., p. xii.

35. See, e.g., Erik Cohen, "Israel as a Post-Zionist Society," in *The Shaping of Israeli Identity: Myth, Memory and Trauma*, edited by Robert Wistrich and David Ohana (London: Frank Cass, 1995), pp. 203–13.

36. As this last reference suggests, the polarizing effects of the Israeli trauma-drama's shifting retellings were deepened by the manner in which these new understandings became nested inside more "fundamentalist," and often more escha-tological, versions of Jewish religion. The followers of Rabbi Zvi Hacohen Kook, out of whom Gush Emunim evolved, believed that by settling in Judea and Samaria they were literally bringing closer the coming of the Messiah. They saw themselves as the avant-gard of both Zionism and Judaism. In fact, the Palestinians were not, initially, Gush Emunim's primary concern. It was only later in the 1970s that they adopted a more militaristic stance.

The same process affected the Palestinian movement, whose more radical and rejectionist elements, publicly dedicated to the annihilation of Israel, increasingly experienced the sources of their trauma, and their possible resolution, through a more "Islamicist" faith. For the intertwining of these religious extremes, see Roger Friedland and Richard Hecht, *To Rule Jerusalem* (New York: Cambridge University Press, 1996), e.g., pp. 168–70 and 355ff.

37. Limor Livnat, "Of Holocaust and Heroism," *Ha'aretz*, April 19, 2001, quoted in Jackie Feldman, "Marking the Boundaries of the Enclave: Defining the Israeli Collective through the Poland Experience," *Israeli Studies* 7(2) (2002): 1–31, p. 1.

38. Lentin, *Israel and the Daughters*, p. 148.

INDEX

Adorno, Theodore, 82 n. 46, 110–111, 146–147

African Americans, 78 n. 34, 188 n. 12
    Tulsa race riots, 107, 112 n. 2

Agamben, Giorgio, 110

Algerian War of Independence, 123–124, 128, 130–132, 134 n. 7. *See also* France; Papon, Maurice

allegorization, 105–111
    and anti-allegorization, 110–111
    of Israeli state, 109
    use of religious language in, 109–110

Allied Forces, WW II
    anti-Semitism within, 46–48, 72–73 n. 9
    perceptions of concentration camp survivors, 5–6
    as perpetrators, 46–48, 91 nn. 76–78, 114, 162

analogy, 52–56, 92–93 n. 82. *See also* Algerian War of Independence; Holocaust analogies; memory, multidirectional

anti-Semitism, 11–13, 36, 76 nn. 21–22, 179
    and art, 81–82 n. 45
    vs. class-based justifications of mass murder of Jews, 75 n. 15
    and Dartmouth College, 22–23
    and French anti-Republicanism, 76 n. 21
    as historical, 83–84 n. 50, 179, 181
    and Israeli state, 109, 189–190 n. 20, 191 n. 32
    and "Jewish power," 85–88 n. 57
    and *Kristallnacht,* 11–14
    as "ordinary," 43–44
    and postwar United States, 7, 21–27, 74 n. 12, 76 n. 24, 136, 144, 162, 165
    as "real," 162
    in (former) Soviet bloc, 108
    as symbol of Nazism, 12
    and symbolic inversion, 91 n. 78
    of U.S. soldiers upon liberation, 72–73 n. 9

anti-anti-Semitism, 14, 21–23, 36–37, 78 nn. 33–34
    as anti-Nazi, 14, 36, 76 n. 24, 85–86 n. 57, 135–136, 165
    as denazification, 20, 136
    Gentleman's Agreement (film), 25, 78 nn. 33–34
    and Jewish immigration/quotas, 25–26
    and popular culture, 23–25
    and progressive narrative, 25–27
    and tolerance of Jews, 25–27